AF705583

Stablecoins Explained

Stablecoins Explained

The Bridge Between Crypto and Cash

Emre Valikar

Mindful Pages

Published in 2026

ISBN: 9789374593653 (PB)
ISBN: 9789374591659 (eBook)

Published by

Mindful Pages
Imprint of Alpha Editions LLC
312 W. 2nd St #1834
Casper, WY 82601, USA

All rights reserved.
No part of this publication may be reproduced, distributed, or transmitted in any form or by any means — including photocopying, recording, or other electronic or mechanical methods — without the prior written permission of the publisher, except in the case of brief quotations used in reviews or permitted by applicable copyright law.
This book was developed using advanced writing tools to support the drafting and ideation process. All content has been thoughtfully curated, refined, and reviewed to ensure quality and relevance.

Content

Introduction

A curious scene has unfolded in modern finance. On one side stands a digital token whose creators insist it should never budge from a single, unremarkable price. On the other side roars a market celebrated for its excesses, swinging with a kind of theatrical volatility that once relegated crypto to the status of a speculative sideshow. The contrast is almost comic: a coin designed not to move, placed in an ecosystem that rarely sits still. Yet out of this tension emerged one of the most consequential ideas of the digital age. Stability—so plain, so apparently dull—has proved to be crypto's most radical ambition. It transforms tokens from curiosities into instruments that can settle bills, cross borders, anchor savings, and weave themselves into the plumbing of everyday economic life.

Consider the quiet routine of modern living: rent that must be paid in sterling, salaries calibrated to monthly budgets, invoices reconciled with precision and predictability. No household or business can thrive in a world where its unit of account behaves like a weather system. Yet millions of people have now used stablecoins for precisely these grounded, practical reasons. What was once dismissed as an arcane financial oddity has become a bridge—sometimes fragile, sometimes elegant—between volatile digital markets and the steady demands of real-world commerce. This book begins with that paradox: the most radical innovation in crypto is not speculation, engineering wizardry, or decentralised governance. It is the promise of staying still.

The rise of stablecoins marks a turning point in monetary imagination. They invite us to ask what "money" truly is: a claim, a record, a trust agreement, a legal construct, a technological artefact, or, more likely, some fusion of them all. Their popularity has not arisen from grand ideological campaigns but from something more mundane and therefore more powerful—a desire for cheaper transfers, faster settlements, and smoother interactions between the old world of banks and the new world of blockchains. When the price of a token does not quake under one's feet, the entire terrain of digital finance becomes more habitable.

Yet stability is never an accident. Behind the calm facade of a stablecoin lies an intricate architecture of pegs, collateral, redemption rights, governance arrangements, oracles, market incentives, and legal structures. Some of these designs are robust; others survive only in tranquil conditions; a few have collapsed spectacularly, leaving investors and policymakers scrambling to make sense of what went wrong. The central claim of this book is simple: you cannot understand stablecoins without understanding how their promises are engineered, maintained, tested, and occasionally broken.

To appreciate the stakes, it helps to look backwards. Monetary history is punctuated by attempts to secure stability through clever mechanisms: gold standards, currency boards, fixed exchange regimes, and managed floats. Each was a blend of politics and economics, power and persuasion. When a peg held, a society gained coherence and calm. When it snapped, the consequences rippled through livelihoods, institutions, and national confidence. Stablecoins sit squarely in this lineage, even as they dress themselves in the language of cryptography and code.

Despite superficial novelty, their challenge is ancient: how does one convince strangers to trust a promise about value? In this sense, stablecoins are part technology and part theatre. Their issuers rely on audits, branding, transparency rituals, and carefully choreographed disclosures to earn credibility. Users lean not only on mathematics or programmatic rules but also on the reputations of institutions, the assurances of regulators, and the behaviour of markets that can turn orderly or chaotic with barely a whisper. All money rests upon stories; stablecoins merely make those stories more explicit.

A common misconception is that the arrival of central bank digital currencies (CBDCs) will render private stablecoins obsolete. It is a tidy hypothesis but one unsupported by experience. Public and private monies have coexisted for centuries: bank deposits circulate alongside central bank notes; money market funds live beside Treasury bills; international payments routinely mix public assets and private claims. Technology does not dissolve this duality; it merely reshapes it. If CBDCs become widespread, they will raise standards, alter expectations, and perhaps nudge the industry towards deeper transparency. But they will not, by themselves, extinguish the demand for tailored features, programmable behaviours, settlement flexibility, or the simple convenience of existing stablecoin rails. Regulation enters this story as both referee and wildcard. It can confer legitimacy, enabling institutional adoption and public confidence. It can also choke innovation under the weight of requirements designed for very different systems. The regulatory debates now unfolding—across the United Kingdom, the United States, the European Union, and beyond—are not merely about consumer protection or market integrity. They are debates about the future expression of sovereignty, the shape of global payments, and the acceptable boundaries of private monetary creation. The wrong decisions could freeze a promising field into irrelevance; the right ones could support a safer, more competitive digital economy. This book aims to serve as a reliable guide through this maze. Its purpose is not to evangelise for or against stablecoins but to offer a clear, rigorous framework to evaluate them. Whether you are a policymaker, developer, investor, executive, or simply a curious reader seeking clarity amid the clamour, the goal is the same: to equip you with the tools to judge claims, spot fragility, and recognise the difference between genuine innovation and clever marketing. Stablecoins deserve neither uncritical praise nor reflexive scepticism. They deserve understanding.

To build that understanding, the book proceeds by examining the four foundational elements of any stablecoin: the issuer, the reserve, the mechanism, and the governance. This deceptively simple map cuts through the noise, allowing us to compare designs that, on the surface, seem incomparable. A regulated issuer holding Treasury bills in custody operates under one logic; a permissionless protocol collateralised by volatile crypto assets operates under another; and an algorithmic scheme with partial reserves lives on yet more precarious ground. The vocabulary may differ, but the underlying questions remain consistent: Who is making the promise? What backs it? How does the price stay aligned with the target? Who decides when adjustments are needed?

From these questions arises a central motif that recurs throughout the chapters to come: trust is not a single object but a stack. At the base lies code and cryptography—useful, elegant, and unforgiving. Above it sits economic design: incentives, collateral, redemption mechanics, market-making arrangements. Layered on top are legal forms, institutional structures, regulatory regimes, and human judgment. The most successful systems are not the most complicated; they are the ones in which each layer reinforces rather than undermines the others. When any layer weakens, the entire stack becomes unstable. Readers will soon see how this motif explains both the triumphs and the failures of the field. The stakes extend far beyond the inner circles of cryptocurrency enthusiasts. Stablecoins touch global remittances, humanitarian aid, corporate treasury operations, emerging market finance, online commerce, and the unglamorous but vital plumbing of settlement networks. For millions of workers sending money home, stablecoins are not philosophical experiments; they are a cheaper, quicker means of supporting family. For fintech firms running cross-border flows, they are operational tools. For decentralised finance platforms, they are foundations upon which everything else is built. And for regulators and central banks, they represent a test: can societies incorporate private digital money without inviting systemic risk? History offers both reassurance and warning. Financial systems adapt, but they rarely do so smoothly. Innovations tend to emerge on the periphery before forcing their way into the mainstream. The first banknotes were viewed with suspicion; the early days of electronic payments were marked by outages and fears of fraud; even the concept of deposit insurance was once controversial. Stablecoins, too, are moving from fringe to infrastructure. Their path will not be linear. It will involve crises, course corrections, improvements in transparency, and, in time, the quiet normalisation that marks all successful monetary technologies.

As with any profound shift, the real danger lies at the extremes. Blind enthusiasm breeds fragility and hubris; rigid rejection forgoes potential benefits. The prudent path lies between the two: a clear-eyed appreciation of risks, a grounded view of use-cases, and a commitment to designing systems that can withstand not only ordinary conditions but also the inevitable shocks. Stablecoins will succeed not because they deliver perfect stability—no system can—but because they can maintain enough stability to be trusted across varied contexts.

As you move through this book, you will encounter stories of tokens that held their pegs through turbulent markets, and others that collapsed in a matter of hours. You will see the power of collateral done well, and the ruinous effects of collateral done poorly. You will follow redemption flows, explore market microstructure, examine governance dilemmas, and watch how regulation interacts with innovation. Throughout, the guiding question remains the same: what makes stability credible?

The answers are not merely technical. They touch on psychology, institutions, incentives, and geopolitics. The choice between a private stablecoin and a public CBDC is, at heart, a debate about the relationship between citizens and the state. The design of a reserve is a question about risk tolerance and transparency. The configuration of an oracle is a matter of trust in data and assumptions about market behaviour. These themes will surface repeatedly, sometimes subtly, sometimes with dramatic force. We stand at an inflection point. Stablecoins have already reshaped parts of the financial landscape, yet their full implications remain unsettled. Will they become the connective tissue between traditional finance and decentralised systems? Will they evolve into programmable cash for consumers and businesses? Will they remain niche tools used primarily for trading and remittances? Or will regulatory decisions draw boundaries that could either support their maturation or confine them to the margins?

This book does not claim omniscience; no text could. But it does make a commitment: to offer readers the clarity and framework needed to navigate whatever comes next. Stability may seem prosaic, but the consequences of getting it wrong—or getting it right—are anything but. The coming years will determine whether stablecoins become a footnote in monetary history or one of its defining chapters.

For now, hold on to the central paradox that opened these pages. In a marketplace known for extremes, the quiet ambition to hold a steady price has become a revolution of its own. The chapters ahead will show how that ambition is built, defended, challenged, and reimagined. They will also reveal why stability, far from being a constraint, is the very feature that unleashes a new design space for money itself. The story is only beginning, and its outcome is still unwritten.

Chapter 1
Money, But Programmable

The first time a software engineer tried to pay their landlord in crypto, the awkward silence said everything. On payday, their wallet showed a handsome balance, flush with tokens that had surged overnight. Two days later, just as the rent transfer was due, the same balance had slumped by a margin that would make a currency trader blanch. The landlord—unmoved by talk of innovative digital assets—wanted the amount listed on the lease, not a number that oscillated with the mood of markets. The engineer ended up converting the tokens, absorbing the loss, and resolving never again to anchor a household obligation to something that behaved more like a tech stock than a unit of account. It was a mundane moment, but it captured a truth that the industry had spent years ignoring: volatility is a barrier to participation, and no amount of rhetoric can compensate for a coin that cannot reliably pay for tomorrow's necessities.

This is where stablecoins enter, unglamorous in their ambition yet transformative in their implications. A token designed not to soar but to remain steady opens doors that no speculative asset can. It can move across borders without friction; it can settle trades without the drag of traditional intermediaries; it can support remittances, payroll, savings, and the everyday choreography of financial life. Stability, paradoxically, is the radical idea—because it unlocks use. Strip away that stability, and crypto reverts to a casino with excellent branding. Introduce it, and blockchains become platforms where ordinary economic activity can actually occur.

But stability is not merely a feature; it is a promise—and promises demand structure. To make sense of any stablecoin, one must understand the machinery behind its claim to hold a steady value. Too often the public conversation collapses into simplistic binaries: "backed" versus "unbacked," "fiat" versus "crypto," "centralised" versus "decentralised." These categories are not unhelpful, but they lack the analytical precision needed to separate robust designs from fragile ones. A better map is required, something grounded enough to cut through marketing gloss yet flexible enough to capture the diversity of real-world models.

This chapter introduces a four-part schema that runs through the entire book: issuer, reserve, mechanism, governance. These four questions—who promises redemption, what backs the promise, how the peg is maintained, and who adapts the system as conditions change—provide the clearest lens for evaluating stability. They transform a messy landscape into a set of comparable structures. A major fiat-backed token may appear simple, even dull, but mapping each part of this schema reveals an intricate choreography of custody chains, treasury operations, authorised participants, market incentives, disclosure regimes, and decision-making processes. The model is not elegant because it is clean; it is elegant because it is complete.

In many ways, the challenge of understanding stablecoins is the challenge of understanding modern money itself. Narratives circulate comfortably—talk of "democratising finance" or "banking the unbanked"—but narratives alone do not build systems. Use-cases do. The stablecoins that have found traction are not the ones with the most stirring origin stories; they are the ones that solved a genuine problem for someone with something practical to do. Exchanges use them to settle trades in minutes rather than days. Card companies use them to provide instant top-ups. Payment startups use them to compress cross-border flows. These are not ideological victories; they are operational ones. Value accrues not to the best storytellers but to the designs that can be trusted in the background while people get on with their lives.

This distinction between narrative and use-case matters because it exposes a recurrent pattern in digital finance. The industry is prone to grand declarations about reshaping society, yet the most significant gains arrive through mundane improvements in plumbing. Stablecoins that thrive do so by shaving basis points off settlement costs, by reducing reconciliation errors, by allowing corporates to sweep funds across geographies without waiting for correspondent banks to wake up. These flows are not glamorous, but they are the bedrock of scale. In the chapters ahead, we will return to this theme repeatedly: systems grow when they solve concrete problems for actors who move real money.

Behind every use-case, however, lies something subtler and far more powerful: trust. Not trust in a single entity or a single line of code, but trust layered across multiple components—technical, institutional, legal, and human. *Trust is a stack.* At the base sits the software: the smart contracts that mint, burn, freeze, or track assets. Above that lies the economic layer: the reserve assets, the incentives for arbitrage, the redemption rights that give a token meaning. Above that sits the legal layer: the corporate forms, the regulatory licences, the contractual commitments. And above that, almost intangible yet decisive, sits the reputational layer: the brand, the transparency practices, the quality of communication, the willingness of the issuer to answer questions when something goes wrong. One wallet provider learnt this the hard way. In its early days, the product did exactly what the documentation promised—no more, no less. It was efficient but faceless, secure but cold. Then came a period of turbulence in the market, and users craved reassurance. The team responded with a disclosure portal, a support desk staffed by humans rather than chatbots, and a cadence of updates that explained not only what was happening but why. Growth followed—not because the code changed, but because the perception of reliability did. The wallet had not suddenly become more advanced; it had become more trusted. Trust, once layered, compounds.

This chapter unpacks these themes because they sit at the heart of programmable money. The phrase "money, but programmable" has been repeated with such enthusiasm that it risks becoming meaningless, yet it captures a profound shift. Money has always been programmable in a loose sense—banks encode rules about overdrafts, payment networks encode fraud checks, accounting systems encode requirements for matching funds. What changes with stablecoins is not the existence of programmability but its granularity, its transparency, and its accessibility. Rules that once lived in proprietary systems now live on public ledgers. Conditions that once required legal agreements can now be embedded in smart contracts. The boundary between "transfer" and "logic" becomes permeable.

The significance of this shift becomes apparent when we return to our opening image: the engineer paying rent. The problem was not that crypto lacked features; it was that it lacked a stable denominator. Once a stable unit exists, everything else becomes programmable: conditional payments, automated payroll, time-bound allowances, escrow flows, settlement races, fee minimisation strategies, even cross-border corporate treasuries that run 24/7 rather than 9–5 across three jurisdictions. Stability liberates programmability. At the same time, programmability amplifies the importance of design. A poorly engineered redemption mechanism can cripple a token even if its reserves are pristine. A flawed governance structure can paralyse decision-making during periods of stress. A narrow oracle setup can expose the system to manipulation. A weak issuer model can cause operational failures that ripple far beyond the protocol itself. Programmable money magnifies the consequences of both good and bad architecture.

And so this chapter serves as both invitation and caution. It introduces the ideas that will be dissected in more depth later—the four-part map, the distinction between slogan and substance, the layered construction of trust—but it also sets the tone for what follows. We are not here to celebrate technology for its own sake, nor to denounce it reflexively. We are here to examine how designs hold up when exposed to human needs, market pressures, adversarial behaviour, and the dull but essential demands of real-world finance.

By the time this chapter closes, you will see why the question is not merely whether programmable money is possible. It already exists. The question is whether it can be stable, comprehensible, and worthy of carrying value through the world. Whether it can earn trust not only from engineers but from landlords, from migrants sending wages home, from treasurers reconciling balances, from regulators assessing systemic risk, and from users who simply want their money to work.

The journey through this chapter will not resolve every question, but it will frame them with the clarity required for the pages ahead. Stability is the quiet force that makes programmability meaningful. Programmability is the force that gives stability purpose. The interplay between them defines the landscape we are about to explore.
Turn the page, then. The mechanics of programmable money await, and with them the deeper question beneath all monetary innovation:

not how to move value, but how to make that movement trustworthy.

Why stability matters

On a humid afternoon in July 2021, in Quezon City on the outskirts of Manila, the remittance queues outside the Western Union branch stretched along the pavement. A nurse, Maria Santos, who had been working a night shift in Abu Dhabi, sent her usual monthly payment home—1,200 dirhams—to cover her parents' utilities and her nephew's school fees. The transfer cost her 17 per cent in fees and unfavourable spread, according to the Bangko Sentral ng Pilipinas' published corridor estimates for that month. She waited. Her parents waited. The queue in Manila waited. For Maria, the cost and the delay had become part of the ritual. When a younger cousin showed her, over a video call, a dollar-denominated stablecoin transfer arriving in under a minute, she laughed. "If my salary moved like your coins," she said, "how would I pay the bills?" Five words followed, quietly, almost as an afterthought: *Stability lets money work.*

That remark captures the centre of gravity in programmable finance. A medium of exchange must hold steady long enough for obligations to be met. If a worker is paid in a token whose value veers unpredictably between a Tuesday and a Friday, the household budget becomes a guessing game. The rhythm of earning and paying—rent on the first of the month, groceries on the seventh, school fees on the fifteenth—depends on a unit that refuses to drift. Stability is not decorative. It is the condition for usefulness. Consider a simple domestic example that played out repeatedly during the crypto bull run of early 2021. Software contractors in Berlin were paid in volatile tokens, a practice fashionable among start-ups experimenting with alternative compensation. One contractor earned the equivalent of €4,000 one month, only to discover that by the time her rent was due a week later, the value had fallen by nearly 30 per cent. Her landlord, tied to the rules of Germany's Mietendeckel long before the law was struck down in April 2021, insisted on euros. She faced a choice: convert immediately upon receipt—surrendering any upside—or ride the fluctuation and risk coming up short. Behaviour reveals the truth: she began converting instantly, treating the token as a temporary instrument rather than as money. *The peg is the promise.* Without it, every transaction becomes a wager.

The contrast is stark when the denomination is stable. When the unit behaves, the payment system opens for ordinary life. This is visible in remittance data from the Central Bank of Nigeria, which noted in its 2020 reporting that settlement costs for certain digital dollar transfers fell to low single digits, compared with traditional corridors that ranged far higher. The difference was not technological brilliance alone: it was the mundane fact that the receiving family knew what the transferred amount would buy once it arrived. The mother purchasing rice in Kano or the student paying exam fees in Ibadan did not need to interpret candlestick charts. They needed a figure that held its shape.

The motif that threads through these stories is the same one that threads through monetary history: *the calm surface.* A currency that behaves like a still pool invites planning; a currency that behaves like a storm invites anxiety. Stablecoins aim to engineer that calm—sometimes convincingly, sometimes only in fair weather—yet the ambition underpins every practical use-case. Payments settle because both sides trust the denomination. Remittances flow because families can rely on the amount. Treasury teams reconcile balances because they can record a number without hedging a moving target. Stability sits beneath every other claim.

That stability is not automatic. It is designed. To understand why, one has to move beneath the surface and examine the architecture that keeps a price pinned. A widely used fiat-backed stablecoin, such as those issued by Circle Internet Financial from 2018 onward, offers a clear example. The issuer—a legally incorporated entity subject to oversight—holds reserves in cash and short-dated government obligations. The reserve composition is disclosed through monthly attestations by Grant Thornton LLP. The mechanism allows authorised market participants to create or redeem tokens at par through primary market flows. And governance decisions—from adjusting banking partners to defining redemption windows—are made by an identifiable leadership team answerable to both regulators and users. These elements—issuer, reserve, mechanism, governance—form a map. Each part answers a specific question: who promises redemption; what stands behind the promise; how price alignment is maintained; and who adapts the system when conditions shift.

Take the mechanism itself. It is not simply a technical device; it shapes behaviour. When arbitrage opportunities emerge—say, the token trades at a small discount in secondary markets—authorised participants step in, redeem at par, and narrow the spread. This behaviour is observable in trading data from exchanges such as Coinbase (San Francisco, 2012) and Bitstamp (Ljubljana, 2011; later Luxembourg), which saw consistent patterns during brief dislocations in 2019 and 2020. The peg held because a structure existed around which rational actors could cluster. The implication is clear: stability is less about optics and more about architecture.

Yet the map also exposes limitations. A counter-example sits in the events of May 2022, when the TerraUSD system—originating in Seoul in 2018—collapsed after its algorithmic peg failed to withstand selling pressure. Its mechanism relied on mint-burn dynamics without sufficient reserves; its governance struggled to respond swiftly; its issuer was embedded in a complex, lightly regulated network. This does not negate the promise of stable value; it demonstrates that without a resilient reserve and credible redemption path, price stability is a façade. The counter-example sharpens the insight: the four-part map is not merely descriptive. It is diagnostic.

Concrete flows reveal where the value of stability is actually realised. Exchange operators, for instance, make settlement decisions minute by minute. When acting as principals, they absorb counterparty risk; when acting as agents, they pass it along. A stable unit reduces that risk by clarifying the economic exposure of each leg of a trade. In 2020, Binance introduced stablecoin-settled futures, enabling traders to keep margins denominated in a unit that did not fluctuate with collateral volatility. Behaviour changed: margin calls became more predictable; liquidation events became less reflexive. The peg influenced not just payments but market microstructure. Card-linked programmes also demonstrate the quiet power of a steady denomination. In Singapore in 2022, the fintech firm StraitsX reported that users topping up cards via stablecoins benefited from near-instant settlement without reconciling scattered FX rates. The stable unit served as a predictable intermediary. What matters here is not the public narrative about "building the future of payments," but the concrete decision of a commuter who relies on a card reader flashing *Approved*. The behaviour is the proof that stability has crossed from concept to practice.

This cuts against the grain of much of the sector's self-presentation. Narratives attract early adopters; use-cases attract everyone else. Grand claims about financial liberation rarely explain why a corporate treasury team in Johannesburg would choose a stablecoin to sweep end-of-day balances. But show them a reconciliation pipeline that reduces settlement breaks from hours to minutes, and the decision becomes straightforward. Price stability is the enabler. Without it, every integration must hedge volatility. With it, the integration becomes operational rather than speculative. Of course, stability also faces limits. Even well-collateralised tokens have traded one or two per cent off par during periods of market stress. During the banking turmoil of March 2023, one major fiat-backed stablecoin briefly slipped to around $0.88 after uncertainty about its exposure to a failing institution in California. The episode demonstrated that even with high-quality reserves, perception can move price. Markets tested the peg, and the issuer's later disclosures restored confidence. The lesson is not that stability is illusory, but that it is contingent on transparency, redemption access, and the credibility of communication. A still pool remains calm only when the walls around it hold.

Threaded through all of this is the quiet motif of the calendar. Bills come due on fixed dates. Payroll lands on fixed dates. School fees, loan repayments, rent—each marks a position in time. A unit of value that refuses to hold steady between those dates undermines the very activities that payments systems are meant to support. Maria's remittance in Manila, the contractor's rent in Berlin, the commuter's tap-in in Singapore: each instance shows how the calendar exposes volatility. Stability is the answer to time's demands. The deeper implication of these examples is that stable value is not merely a technical parameter; it is a social commitment. When two parties agree to settle in a given unit, they are engaging in a compact about the future. They are asserting that the number printed on the invoice will mean roughly the same thing when the transfer arrives. Every payment system—whether hawala networks active since the eighth century, sterling banknotes following the Bank Charter Act of 1844, or stablecoins running on public blockchains—must grapple with this commitment. Trust is never abstract. It manifests in the choice to send money now rather than wait, to accept a token rather than demand cash, to record a figure in a ledger rather than convert immediately.

Visible behaviours confirm this. Migrant workers who choose stablecoins for remittances often convert immediately into local currency; what matters is the predictable transit. Traders who hold stablecoins on exchanges do so because settlement requires a constant unit. Households that store a portion of savings in dollar-denominated digital tokens do so because local inflation erodes alternatives; they compare the cost of conversion with the reliability of the peg. These decisions are observable, measurable, and rooted in daily life.

If stability makes programmable money usable, the question that lingers is how far this usability can stretch. What happens when regulatory regimes tighten redemption rules, when central banks introduce wholesale CBDCs, when liquidity in secondary markets thins, or when reserve compositions shift under pressure? The tension between engineered stability and market reality remains, unresolved and compelling. The next sections test that tension and ask what it takes for a steady unit to survive contact with the world.

The four-part map: issuer, reserve, mechanism, governance

In February 2023, when the New York Department of Financial Services announced that Paxos Trust Company must halt new issuance of Binance USD, a $16-billion stablecoin then circulating widely on global exchanges, traders in Singapore, London, and São Paulo watched the token drift to $0.98 before pulling back towards par. The price wobble lasted hours, not days. The peg did not fail. But the moment exposed a deeper truth visible to anyone scrutinising the order books: markets were not reacting to blockchain data; they were reacting to an issuer, to reserve arrangements, to a redemption mechanism, and to the decisions of a governing body responding to a regulator. The token's behaviour mirrored its architecture. It showed its seams. That brief slip revealed the map.

The episode crystallised a recurring motif in digital finance, a motif as old as banking itself: structure surfaces under stress. A stablecoin's elegance, or its fragility, is revealed not when conditions remain calm but when an unexpected constraint—regulatory, operational, or liquidity-driven—presses against its promises. The price movement of BUSD in New York and abroad reminded observers that a token's stability is only as credible as the entity that stands behind it, the assets that anchor it, the mechanism that translates redemption rights into behaviour, and the governance processes that shape every response. Five words can summarise the moment: design choices become public.

The need for a schema becomes obvious when the market begins to test boundaries. In the case of BUSD, the *issuer* was Paxos, a regulated trust company chartered in New York. The *reserves* were held in cash and short-dated US Treasury bills. The *mechanism* allowed authorised participants to mint and redeem at par, using systems audited by WithumSmith+Brown. And the *governance* structure placed both strategic and operational decisions in the hands of identifiable executives answerable to state supervisors. When the regulatory order arrived, each part of this structure influenced price behaviour: traders evaluated issuer strength, reserve credibility, redemption access, and the capacity of governance to respond coherently. The peg bent but did not break. The architecture held.

The four-part map—issuer, reserve, mechanism, governance—has emerged as the most reliable way to evaluate stablecoin designs because it captures the components that shape real-world behaviour. In a field crowded with rhetoric, this map cuts through noise by forcing a simple question: *Who promises what, and how is that promise kept?* The motif of visible seams returns here; each part of the map reveals a seam, a potential stress point or stabiliser. Understanding where these seams lie is essential for anyone assessing how a token will behave when pressure mounts.

The first dimension, the issuer, is not an abstraction; it is a legal entity embedded in a specific jurisdiction, subject to identifiable constraints. Circle Internet Financial, incorporated in Boston in 2013, publishes monthly reserve reports for USDC and maintains accounts at regulated custodians. That choice influences market behaviour. The issuer's domicile determines which regulator may intervene, which disclosures are mandated, and how disputes are resolved. When Circle's USDC briefly traded at $0.88 in March 2023 following uncertainty around Silicon Valley Bank's receivership, it was Circle's rapid disclosure of exposure amounts—$3.3 billion, confirmed in an SEC filing—that steadied secondary markets. The behaviour was visible: redemptions surged, redemptions cleared, and the price climbed back towards par. The issuer acted. The market responded. Structure surfaced.

The reserve dimension is equally concrete. A reserve is not merely a balance sheet line; it is a portfolio of assets with observable maturities, liquidity profiles, and credit risks. The composition matters. When Tether Holdings Ltd., founded in Hong Kong in 2014, began publishing quarterly attestation reports in 2021 showing increasing allocations to US Treasury bills and declining allocations to commercial paper, traders noticed. Secondary market discounts narrowed from peaks seen during the May 2022 turmoil, when questions around reserve quality widened spreads on several Asian exchanges. The shift in reserve composition—measurable, dated, and reported—changed behaviour. Holders converted less aggressively. Arbitrageurs priced risk differently. The peg reflected reserve structure, not narrative.

The mechanism sits at the centre of peg maintenance. It is not an idea; it is a sequence of actions linking redemption rights to market prices. A mechanism shows itself in order books. During the March 2020 COVID-driven liquidity crunch, when market volatility spiked across regions, USDC's reliance on authorised market participants for primary market flows shaped how quickly price deviations closed. Traders on Bitstamp in Luxembourg, observing a temporary premium above $1.01, redeemed at par and sold into the order book, compressing spreads within hours. Mechanisms commit actors to behaviours; behaviours maintain stability. The motif of visible seams appears again: mechanisms reveal their strength when pressure tests them.

Governance completes the map. Governance determines who can adjust parameters, alter reserve guidelines, approve new banking partners, modify oracle configurations, or freeze compromised addresses. Its influence became clear during Ethereum's transition to proof-of-stake in September 2022. Circle stated, publicly and unequivocally, that USDC would support the canonical chain as determined by the Ethereum Foundation. The clarity of this governance stance removed uncertainty for exchanges in Chicago, London, and Singapore, which queued settlement plans around "The Merge." The peg remained orderly because governance acted decisively.

Yet even this neat schema faces limitations, and those limitations strengthen the case for using the map rather than weaken it. The credible counter-example comes from TerraUSD (UST), the algorithmic token launched in Seoul in 2018. UST had an issuer of sorts in Terraform Labs, though the project presented itself as decentralised. Its reserves were partial and volatile. Its mechanism—minting and burning against LUNA—depended on continuous market confidence. Its governance allowed parameter changes but lacked effective circuit-breakers. In May 2022, when UST slipped below $1 on Binance and Huobi, the mechanism's reflexivity accelerated the decline. The four-part map did not fail; it predicted the collapse by exposing the weak seams long before the disorder arrived.

The key implication is that the map does not judge; it clarifies. It does not ask whether a stablecoin is "centralised enough" or "decentralised enough." It asks whether the issuer can defend redemption, whether the reserve can survive liquidity shocks, whether the mechanism can align incentives, and whether governance can adapt without panic. This clarity transforms analysis from speculation to structure.

Consider how the map informs practical decisions. A trader deciding whether to hold stablecoins over a weekend examines redemption windows—the mechanism—and checks attestation dates—the reserve. A remittance firm evaluating settlement exposures in Nairobi or Accra examines issuer licensing and governance playbooks. A corporate treasury team implementing intraday sweeps in Johannesburg checks reserve maturities and redemption processing speeds. These decisions are concrete and measurable. They reveal behaviour that underpins the stability narratives.

This concreteness becomes sharper when applying the full map to a major fiat-backed stablecoin. Take USDC as it stood in September 2023, supported by public filings. The issuer, Circle, operated as a regulated money transmitter in multiple US states and held additional permissions in the European Union. The reserves, reported monthly and audited annually, consisted almost entirely of cash and US Treasuries maturing within 90 days. The mechanism relied on a network of authorised participants for minting and burning, with redemption executed through bank rails during business hours. Governance included a risk committee, public policy disclosures, and explicit commitments to manage contract upgrades transparently. Mapping these components reveals the system's strengths: transparency, liquidity, and predictability. It also exposes seams: dependence on US banking hours, concentration in US Treasuries, and reliance on identifiable institutions that may face jurisdictional tension.

The motif of seams returns again. Each seam represents both a potential fault line and a locus of strength. The issuer seam ties the token to a legal environment that can protect users but can also impose abrupt constraints, as Paxos learnt in 2023. The reserve seam can reassure holders through daily liquidity but can also create exposure to sovereign risk if maturities concentrate too narrowly. The mechanism seam shapes arbitrage behaviour but can slow under extreme congestion, as seen during the March 2020 volatility. The governance seam secures adaptability but can raise questions about concentration of power.

Two contrasting examples illuminate the range. First, MakerDAO's DAI—a decentralised stablecoin originating in Copenhagen in

2017—uses overcollateralised crypto assets in its reserves and liquidates positions on-chain via automated auctions. Its mechanism responds instantly to oracle price feeds. Its governance relies on token-holder votes that can alter parameters such as collateral types and stability fees. When DAI traded above peg in March 2020 due to collateral scarcity, governance voted to broaden eligible assets. The price restored. Structure surfaced; actors responded.

Second, JPMorgan's JPM Coin, deployed internally in 2019 for wholesale settlement, relies on a single issuer with centralised governance and reserves fully backed by demand deposits at JPMorgan Chase. It is not publicly traded, and its mechanism operates entirely within institutional rails. The peg is never tested in the wild because the token never meets wild conditions. It is stable by design, but its stability cannot be generalised beyond its context. These examples extend the map without distorting it. They demonstrate that forms vary, but the schema endures.

The counter-example that most challenges the schema's universality is the emergence of hybrid tokens that use partial reserves combined with algorithmic elements. They stretch the map but do not break it. Their issuers may be decentralised autonomous organisations; their reserves may include volatile assets; their mechanisms may rely on dynamic supply adjustments; their governance may be distributed across token holders. Analysing them through the map reveals risks faster than any narrative: reserves may decay, governance may fragment, and mechanisms may falter. The limitation becomes a diagnostic strength.

Threaded through these examples is a quiet image: seams under stress. Viewed together, the map is not a classification exercise; it is a way of seeing. It allows professionals across industries to compare architectures, researchers to test hypotheses, students to connect design decisions to market behaviour, and policymakers to evaluate systemic implications. It replaces handwaving with structure, and structure improves judgment.

Yet the map leaves a question hanging. If stability is a function of issuer credibility, reserve quality, mechanism design, and governance capability, what happens when these components pull against each other? What if the issuer's legal duties constrain the mechanism? What if reserve assets create geopolitical exposure? What if governance actions destabilise expectations? The unresolved tension endures: can a stablecoin be engineered so that its seams remain strong even when the world pulls in directions no schema can fully predict?

Use-cases vs narratives

Shortly after 9 a.m. on 3 August 2022, in a glass-walled office overlooking Raffles Place in Singapore, an operations manager at Crypto.com watched a blinking dashboard of settlement queues. A large Asian exchange had just pushed through a batch of stablecoin-settled trades—hundreds of positions that needed reconciling before the next funding window. The flow cleared in under four minutes. Thirty minutes earlier, a comparable batch in Thai baht had taken over an hour, slowed by correspondent banks in Bangkok and a mismatch in cut-off times. No press release celebrated the stablecoin-run batch. There was no heroic messaging. But the operators saw the difference on their screens: the quiet efficiency of a unit that held its value and moved without waiting for wire-room hours. Five words passed between two staff members: *The flow tells the truth.*

The episode captures a pattern visible across venues from Zürich to São Paulo. Narratives travel quickly; operational value reveals itself slowly, through concrete flows. The slogan of "borderless finance" rarely convinces an exchange treasurer. A cleared ledger and a reconciled balance do. The motif visible in that Singapore meeting—the blinking dashboard—returns throughout this chapter: behind every grand claim lies a screen, a timestamp, and a decision.

The difference between narrative and use-case becomes clearest when examining how exchanges settle their books. Binance, founded in Shanghai in 2017 and later headquartered in Malta, was among the first to report (2019) that stablecoin pairs had grown to represent a majority of its spot volume. The specific behaviour mattered more than the headline. Traders who previously oscillated between volatile base assets began keeping float in stable units. Settlement teams measured their exposure hour by hour, comparing the predictable dollar figure of those units with the variable tick of crypto pairs. Efficient flows emerged: fewer failed settlements, narrower funding spreads, and a reduction in the overnight margins required to buffer price swings. This measurable behaviour—not the narrative—drove adoption.

A similar pattern unfolded at Bitso, the Mexico-based exchange founded in 2014, which integrated dollar-denominated stablecoins into remittance corridors between the United States and Mexico. Bitso published data in May 2021 showing weekly remittance volumes via stablecoins approaching 2.5 per cent of total US–Mexico transfers. The benefit was not ideological. It was visible in metrics: lower error rates, quicker reconciliation with Mexican banking partners, and fewer rejected transactions due to timing mismatches. Settlement teams could confirm that pesos arriving in Mexico City matched the dollar flows initiated in Los Angeles. The narrower the reconciliation window, the more credible the system became.

Exchange settlement often appears technical, but it is where behaviour reveals priorities. An operations desk is judged by measures such as settlement breaks, ageing of receivables, and cost per transaction. When flows clear faster, those measures shift. The implication is straightforward: stablecoins succeeded where they solved a quantifiable operational friction, not where a narrative promised transformation. The blinking-dashboards motif returns here. Operators commit to tools that behave predictably in busy hours. They do not commit to slogans.

Card top-ups offer a second arena where use-cases outshine stories. In March 2022, Xendit, a payments company operating across Indonesia and the Philippines, rolled out a pilot allowing selected users to top up digital cards using USDC. The internal metrics—the time between initiation and settlement, the incidence of failed loads, the average FX slippage for cross-border users—told the story better than any promotional material. A top-up that once took several hours while passing through regional banking rails now arrived in minutes. Users in Jakarta saw their balances refresh before they could close the notification screen. The behaviour changed: more frequent micro-top-ups, fewer abandoned transactions, and higher repeat usage. This was not narrative-driven; it was the effect of concrete settlement behaviour.

A contrasting example helps clarify the distinction. During the 2017–2018 boom, dozens of projects claimed to be "banking the unbanked," yet delivered little more than speculative tokens with messaging that outpaced capability. One often-cited project headquartered in Zug launched its token in 2017 with promises of financial inclusion across sub-Saharan Africa. By 2020, audited figures showed negligible transaction volume and almost no recurring usage in its target markets. The limitation was clear: the narrative attracted attention, but without integration into existing payment networks, merchants, or remittance corridors, no operational flows materialised. The counter-example strengthens the argument. Use-cases scale when they reduce a measurable friction for actors who move money daily; they do not scale when they rely solely on aspirational messaging.

The contrast deepens when looking at specific decision points. Consider a European neobank evaluating whether to support stablecoin withdrawals. Its compliance team in Berlin examines risk metrics; its treasury team measures liquidity buffers; its support team analyses ticket patterns from users asking for cross-border options. When one of these banks—Revolut, headquartered in London—enabled certain crypto-linked transfers in late 2021, adoption patterns revealed the underlying logic. Users were not seeking ideological alignment; they were seeking faster settlement into local currency accounts. Behaviour dominated narrative.Another example comes from the Brazilian fintech Mercado Pago, which in November 2023 began offering USDC to customers. The decision emerged from observable demand: users wanted a dollar-denominated store of value during a period of domestic inflation pressure. The measurable outcome—daily volumes and conversion patterns—validated the move. The rhetoric about "democratising finance" remained secondary. The concrete flow of deposits, transfers, and card spending shaped the trajectory.

Across these cases, a subtle motif persists: the screen that records movement. The exchange dashboard, the remittance ledger, the card top-up feed. Each screen displays what narratives cannot prove. They show when a stablecoin moves, when it settles, when it fails, and how much value passes through. When thousands of transactions clear without incident, operators trust the tool. Trust is visible: a reduced error rate, a shorter reconciliation report, a smaller buffer in the treasury's intraday account. These small signals accumulate. They shape decisions in ways no marketing language can match.

There are, however, genuine constraints that complicate the picture. Not every stablecoin thrives in every setting. Liquidity can evaporate during periods of stress; regulatory actions can halt issuance; technical congestion can slow transfers. March 2023 provided a case in point. When USDC briefly de-pegged following uncertainty around Silicon Valley Bank, several exchanges and payment firms paused automatic conversions. Their dashboards—the motif again—showed slippage risk rising. The limitation was visible and immediate: flows paused; operators waited for clarity; users hesitated. Yet once the issuer disclosed its exposure and redemptions resumed, flows returned. The counter-example does not undermine the use-case argument. It refines it. Concrete value accrues where redemption confidence remains intact, and where operators can measure risk in real time.

Concrete flows also reveal something deeper about adoption: scale emerges from routinised, boring activity. No executive writes a strategy paper about shaved seconds on a settlement timer. Yet those shaved seconds compound. A cross-border PSP in Nairobi measuring day-end balances sees smaller variances. A derivatives exchange in Chicago observes fewer margin calls caused by currency mismatches. A wallet provider in Istanbul notes that customers top up cards more frequently when loads settle instantly. These observations are unglamorous but decisive. They demonstrate what economists often stress: systems grow when marginal improvements repeat thousands of times.

This chapter's recurring motif—the blinking dashboard—helps explain why narratives alone cannot carry programmable money into the mainstream. Narratives travel; dashboards judge. When an operator in Singapore sees a batch clear in four minutes instead of fifty, the decision to continue using stablecoins becomes rational, measurable, and observable. The value is not rhetorical. It appears as a timestamp on a screen.

Yet the motif also raises a lingering question. If the strength of stablecoins lies in concrete flows—settlement speed, cost reduction, reliability—how far can these flows scale before they encounter structural limits? What happens when regulatory regimes diverge, when liquidity splits across chains, or when operational pressures rise beyond what the current mechanisms can bear? The next section must test whether the blinking dashboard continues to favour stable units when the environment turns more demanding, or whether narrative begins to creep back into decisions that should remain grounded in measurable flow.

Trust is a stack

On a wet morning in Dublin in November 2020, the leadership team of Fireblocks, a digital asset custody firm founded in New York in 2018, gathered on a video call to review a troubling pattern. Support tickets from several European wallets had surged during the turbulent trading week that followed bitcoin's price jump above $15,000. The failures were mundane—delayed withdrawals, unclear fee calculations, balances updating slowly—but the consequence was sharp. One small Irish wallet provider reported an overnight spike in user churn after its status page stayed silent during the volatility. Yet a rival in Vilnius, operating on similar infrastructure, saw user activity *increase*. Fireblocks' logs showed the difference. The Vilnius team had published real-time reserve data, opened a staffed helpdesk, and issued a clear disclosure during the congestion. Five words from Fireblocks' report captured the outcome: *trust compounds under pressure.*

The contrast between the two wallets illustrates a broader truth. Code may guarantee certain behaviours, but users judge systems by what they can see, reach, and understand. A perfectly functioning smart contract offers no comfort to a customer staring at an unexplained delay. Trust rests on layers—some visible, some procedural, all cumulative. And the motif that threads through this section, the *status page*, surfaces repeatedly: the quiet screen that tells users whether they should stay or leave.

This layered structure is neither new nor unique to digital assets. Show the behaviour of a bank in a liquidity squeeze, and one sees the same pattern. In September 2007, when Northern Rock faced a funding crisis in Newcastle, customers queued outside branches because they could observe something concrete: a mismatch between statements about solvency and images of executives seeking emergency support. Behaviour followed: withdrawals accelerated. That case names a principle often missed in debates about programmable money. Trust is observational. It is measured in actions—lines forming outside a branch, a spike in support tickets, a fall in redemption volumes—not in narratives about reliability.

Stablecoins inherit this behavioural logic. They operate in public markets where every promise can be tested, and every weakness surfaces instantly. Consider Circle's publication of monthly attestations for USDC, verified by Grant Thornton LLP from 2018 onwards. The documents are dry, but their effect is visible. When USDC briefly dipped to $0.88 in March 2023 after Silicon Valley Bank's collapse in Santa Clara, Circle's disclosure—naming the $3.3 billion exposure and the expected recovery timeline—triggered observable behaviour: arbitrage activity increased on Coinbase and Binance, redemptions resumed, and spreads narrowed through measurable order book depth. The trust layer thickened because communication matched action. The implication is clear. Transparency is not a branding exercise. It is an input into market behaviour.

Another named example clarifies how legal structure forms part of this stack. Paxos Trust Company, chartered in New York in 2015, operates stablecoin reserves under the oversight of state regulators. When the New York Department of Financial Services ordered Paxos in February 2023 to halt new issuance of BUSD, traders did not scramble blindly. They assessed a concrete fact: redemptions remained available. The order books on Kraken (San Francisco, 2011) showed price narrowing back towards par within hours. The legal layer, visible in Paxos' charter and obligations, shaped behaviour because it established conditions under which redemptions would continue. Laws are abstractions until stress tests turn them into decisions.

Brand authority forms another layer. It is tempting to treat brand as superficial, yet user behaviour contradicts this. When Coinbase, founded in San Francisco in 2012, announced in December 2022 that it would waive fees for USDC conversions, the gesture was not cosmetic. It was a testable signal. Trading volumes in the USDC/USDT pair rose sharply across several exchanges, including Bitstamp, where 24-hour volumes doubled relative to the previous week. Brand equity induced movement because users trusted that Coinbase would stand behind the liquidity routes it promoted. The motif of the status page emerges again: whether on a website or in the collective perception of a firm's competence, users look for a steady signal.

Support infrastructure completes the trust stack. The wallet provider in Vilnius offers a clear example. Before June 2020, the firm relied almost entirely on automated responses for user queries. Then came a period of network congestion on Ethereum, during which transaction fees spiked abruptly. The wallet's users, confused by the delays, began withdrawing to exchanges perceived as more reliable. Facing clear numbers—rising churn and longer ticket resolution times—the firm introduced a staffed helpdesk, a reserve dashboard, and a plain-language disclosure explaining why fees were high. Within three months, according to the company's public metrics, average daily active users rose by 19 per cent. The code powering the wallet had not changed. The trust stack had.

A credible counter-example helps test the limits of this schema. Algorithmic stablecoins such as TerraUSD, launched in 2018 and collapsed in May 2022, emphasised decentralisation and mechanism design while downplaying institutional layers. The project relied heavily on mathematical symmetry: minting and burning between UST and LUNA. But disclosures were sparse, governance opaque, and issuer accountability diffuse. When cracks appeared during the sell-off of 8 May 2022, the absence of a trust stack produced visible behaviour. Liquidity evaporated on Curve Finance's UST pool in Geneva; redemptions clogged; spreads widened across Asia into double digits. The code did exactly what it was designed to do, but users lost faith in layers that did not exist. The counter-example reinforces rather than undermines the argument. Mechanism design is necessary. It is not sufficient.

These examples show a single principle: trust accumulates when actions across layers align. When a stablecoin issuer publishes credible audits, users behave differently. They convert less, hold longer, redeem more selectively. When legal obligations are clear, market-makers price risk more tightly. When brands speak plainly during stress, spreads narrow faster. And when support channels operate with human clarity, confusion declines. Trust produces changes measurable in order books, ticket queues, and redemption logs. It is cumulative, not declarative.

To see how these layers interact, consider a simple scenario. A remittance firm in Nairobi uses a dollar-denominated stablecoin to settle transfers from London. The issuer layer assures the firm that redemptions are available through regulated channels. The reserve layer confirms that underlying assets mature within predictable time frames. The mechanism layer shows that on-chain minting and burning aligns with par value. The governance layer clarifies how price feeds are managed. Only when these layers align does the operations manager in Nairobi commit to routing flows through that token. Trust is not an internal sentiment. It is a routing decision.

The motif of the status page returns a third time. When a system behaves well, the status page stays green. When it misbehaves, the page flickers, and users react. During a Polygon network outage in January 2022, several major wallets experienced delays in transaction confirmations. One wallet published detailed diagnostics within minutes; another stayed silent. The silent wallet saw a measurable drop in daily active users, reported publicly months later. Users trusted the green page, not the engineering claim. The stack held for one firm; it collapsed for the other.

Yet trust is not static. It can grow and decay quickly. A firm may invest heavily in audits and governance only to falter in communication at a critical moment. A project may build a strong brand but maintain reserves that are opaque or delayed in reporting.

The unresolved tension sits here: if trust is genuinely a stack, what happens when one layer contradicts another? Will users forgive an imperfect audit if redemption remains smooth? Will they tolerate slower support if reserves are impeccable? Or will they recalibrate instantly, following the first signal to flicker on the status page?

Chapter 2
Pegs 101

In September 1992, as traders in London braced for what would become known as Black Wednesday, the Bank of England fought to keep sterling within the Exchange Rate Mechanism's prescribed band. Dealers at Goldman Sachs on Fleet Street watched their screens flicker as the pound dipped, recovered, dipped again. Every intervention—billions in purchases—briefly steadied the exchange rate before the market pressed harder. The spectacle was a reminder that a peg is both an engineering project and a psychological contract. When confidence fractures, numbers on a screen begin to slide with the weight of inevitability. Yet when confidence holds, even fragile arrangements can endure storms that ought to break them. Pegs, in all their forms, sit at the strange intersection of design and belief.

That tension is the heartbeat of this chapter. A peg promises that "one" means something: a dollar, a euro, a token that should retain its shape in the face of markets that rarely stay still. But the promise fractures into varieties—hard, soft, collateralised, algorithmic, discretionary—each with its own risks and rites. Some pegs insist upon absolute parity; others gently target a range; still others hover near a value so long as incentives align. The differences matter because they affect every practical behaviour: how a token trades, how operators settle, how reserves respond to shocks, and how users make sense of a number displayed in their wallet. Behind the clean simplicity of a stable price lies a thicket of moving parts.

A peg, in its purest form, is an attempt to freeze a relationship in a world defined by motion. That ambition has tempted people for centuries, from the gold standard to Bretton Woods to currency boards in Hong Kong and Argentina. But stablecoins add a twist. They encode the promise in software, where decisions that once unfolded in central bank committees or treasury back rooms now appear in publicly verifiable contracts—or appear, at least, to do so. The promise remains, but the machinery shifts. The mechanisms that used to live in marble buildings move into digital ledgers; the behavioural patterns that once emerged slowly now unfold at the speed of block confirmations. The peg becomes visible in real time, for better or worse.

To understand this machinery, we must begin with the distinction between hard and soft pegs. A hard peg asserts that redemption at par is a right: one token should always convert into one unit of the reference asset, just as a fully collateralised currency board offers to swap domestic notes for foreign currency without equivocation. A soft peg promises something gentler: that the token will trade within a band, tolerating small deviations that are corrected by incentives, market forces, or protocol-level parameters. The analogy is almost homely. A hard peg resembles a gift card redeemable for a fixed amount at a specific shop—£20 means £20, not £19.40 on a turbulent afternoon. A soft peg resembles a store voucher whose value floats slightly depending on demand but stays roughly consistent. Both feel stable in calm conditions; only stressed conditions reveal their nature.

The choice between hard and soft pegs is not merely academic. It shapes accounting, risk management, treasury operations, and user expectations. A soft peg can ride out volatility with grace, avoiding the catastrophic spirals that afflict mechanisms forced to defend an exact price at any cost. But it complicates the ledgers of those who rely on predictable valuation. Treasurers recording liabilities, auditors verifying statements, and exchanges managing collateral all behave differently when the unit they hold may drift by tens of basis points. The design that makes a soft peg resilient in market stress introduces friction in operational life. Every grip involves a trade-off.

The architecture beneath these pegs rests on three pillars often summarised as collateral, convertibility, and credibility. These "three C's" are the structural supports for any attempt to hold a price still. Collateral offers a cushion; convertibility turns tokens into claims that can be exercised; credibility—the most elusive—encourages actors to behave in ways that stabilise the system. Each fails differently. Collateral can evaporate through volatility or mismanagement. Convertibility can slow when banking hours close or when gas fees spike. Credibility can shatter with a single message across social channels, a rumour that spreads faster than any audit can refute.

Consider airline miles, an unintentionally instructive example. They often have strong convertibility—you can redeem them for flights or upgrades—but weak collateral and fragile credibility. No regulator demands that an airline hold cash equal to the outstanding miles; when an airline fails, miles collapse. Because the collateral is weak and the legal rights ambiguous, miles circulate at the margins of commerce. People treat them as perks, not money. The system works precisely because the stakes are limited. If a stablecoin mirrored that structure—high convertibility but shaky collateral—its usage would shrink to niche contexts. Users instinctively calibrate exposure based on what they believe sits behind the number in their wallet.

Stablecoins add an additional complication: the oracle. Unlike traditional pegs, which often reference public markets that price the underlying asset continuously, stablecoins require a mechanism that defines "one." A price oracle sounds like a simple device—a feed that tells the protocol what the reference asset is worth. Yet this is where some of the most consequential risks lurk. If an oracle can be manipulated, the peg becomes a hostage. If an oracle updates too slowly, arbitrage becomes dangerous. If an oracle updates too quickly during wild market swings, it triggers liquidations that deepen the problem they were meant to prevent. Time-weighted averages offer a partial remedy: by smoothing the input, they dampen reflexive behaviour. But smoothing introduces lag, and lag introduces a gap between the real world and the protocol's perception of it. The peg becomes a conversation between markets and the machinery that interprets those markets.

Bands, too, shape behaviour. A peg that tolerates a one or two per cent range may survive turbulence far better than one that cannot. Markets rarely move in neat increments. A band gives arbitrageurs room to act without forcing a system into frantic defence. Yet the existence of a band changes user perception. Some people will accept minor deviations as the texture of digital markets. Others will recoil. The question becomes: who is this system for? The accountant closing monthly books? The trader hedging intraday? The remittance operator targeting price certainty for a corridor? Peg design is an act of choosing whom to disappoint least.

The final ingredient, and one frequently overlooked, is market microstructure. Pegs do not float in a vacuum. They live in order books, liquidity pools, and cross-exchange settlement paths. A thinly traded pair on a regional exchange can turn a minor imbalance into a price deviation that echoes across markets. A deep pool on a major venue can absorb shocks that might otherwise cascade. Maker incentives matter as well. When market-makers are paid to post liquidity, spreads narrow, volatility declines, and arbitrage becomes less perilous. When incentives weaken, spreads widen and the peg breathes more heavily. The peg is not just a mechanism. It is a choreography of participants who act within incentive gradients.

What makes this landscape fascinating is that these elements—pegs, collateral, oracles, microstructure—are not isolated parts. They interlock. A robust collateral base reduces pressure on the mechanism. A well-designed oracle reduces the load on arbitrageurs. Deep liquidity thins volatility, reducing strain on pegs and bands. Credibility reinforces each element: when users believe the system will behave, they behave in ways that support the system. When they doubt it, they behave in ways that undermine it. A peg is a loop, not a line.

The stakes become clearer when we consider that stablecoins now mediate payments, settlements, savings, and cross-border flows. The peg is not a cosmetic feature. It is the structure that determines whether the system can sustain these tasks when conditions turn unfriendly. During periods of crypto-wide stress, it is the peg that absorbs the first impact, cushioning or amplifying volatility that ripples into other assets and platforms. The peg is a safety harness, and like all harnesses, it matters most when the fall begins.

To learn how these harnesses work, we must engage with the uncomfortable questions. Why do some soft pegs endure while more rigid designs crack? How do protocols weigh the need for oracle accuracy against the dangers of reflexive liquidations? What does it mean when a peg holds on one exchange but drifts on another? Why do bands encourage resilience in some contexts but create accounting headaches in others? And how much of any peg's behaviour can be attributed to design, and how much to the confidence of those watching the same screens at the same moment?

These questions do not have tidy answers, but they point towards the heart of the matter. A peg is both a technology and a social phenomenon. It is calculation and expectation intertwined. It is an engineered structure that must function in the presence of human fear, arbitrage, speculation, and error. That is why understanding pegs matters—not only for engineers or traders but for anyone who wants to understand how programmable money becomes reliable money.

As we step deeper into this chapter, the calm surface of the peg will prove to be deceptive. The real interest lies beneath it, in the mechanisms that enforce it, the incentives that protect it, and the behaviours that can unravel it. What looks stable from a distance reveals hidden tensions up close. The question that remains—implicit, unresolved, and vital—is this: when the next shock arrives and the screens begin to flicker, which pegs will hold, which will bend, and which will expose the limits of their design?

Hard vs soft pegs

At 3:58 p.m. on 6 May 2010, two minutes before the New York Stock Exchange's closing bell, traders at State Street Global Advisors watched the value of several exchange-traded funds diverge sharply from their net asset value. Prices slipped by more than 10 per cent in some instruments, even though the underlying assets had barely moved. The "Flash Crash", as it became known, briefly exposed how thin liquidity and stressed market-making can cause instruments designed to track a reference value to drift away from it. A peg—whether between equities and an index, currencies and a basket, or tokens and a benchmark—reveals its nature under pressure. At that moment, one question blinked across the desks: *How tight is the promise?*

A hard peg demands precision. A soft peg tolerates drift. Both can function in the same market, but they behave differently when screens begin to flicker. The distinction matters because it is not only technical; it governs how treasurers account for liabilities, how exchanges manage margin, and how users interpret the number in their wallet. The motif to keep in mind here—returning quietly through this section—is *the till receipt*: the difference between knowing a voucher will always buy £20 of goods and knowing it will buy somewhere between £19.40 and £20.10 depending on timing and demand.

A hard peg is the simpler promise. It mirrors a cashier's guarantee: a £20 gift card from Marks & Spencer in London *is* £20 of purchasing power, denominated and redeemable at par. USDC, issued by Circle from 2018 onwards, adopts this logic. The issuer holds cash and short-term US Treasuries; authorised participants mint and redeem at one dollar; monthly attestations confirm reserve composition. When USDC briefly de-pegged to $0.88 after Silicon Valley Bank's collapse in March 2023, the deviation lasted less than three days. The moment Circle disclosed its $3.3 billion exposure and redemption resumed smoothly, the price snapped back. The behaviour showed something concrete: hard pegs live or die on redemption credibility. If par can be exercised—quickly, predictably—markets converge back to "one".

Soft pegs follow a different logic. They resemble a shop voucher whose value hovers slightly depending on when and where it is used. MakerDAO's DAI, launched in 2017 and collateralised by crypto assets, typically trades within a narrow band around $1.00. The band absorbs volatility. During March 2020's crash, when ETH prices fell more than 40 per cent in a day, DAI traded briefly above peg as collateral became scarce. Governance responded by broadening eligible assets. Arbitrage restored the band. Accounting departments grumbled, because a stablecoin booked at $1.02 today and $0.99 tomorrow complicates balance-sheet reconciliations, even though the system proved robust under stress. Behaviour reveals preference: treasurers prize the exactness of hard pegs; protocols prize the flexibility of soft ones.

The reason soft pegs survive turbulence better lies in their design. By accepting a tolerance band—often one or two per cent—they reduce the need for frantic interventions. A protocol does not need to defend every cent; it needs only to maintain incentives that keep the token near target. A soft peg is less brittle. Yet this flexibility pushes the cost elsewhere. If a remittance provider in Nairobi uses a soft-pegged token to settle incoming USD flows, the reconciliation team must reconcile slight valuation differences each day. The ledger becomes a site of small arguments. The till receipt motif appears again: a worker expects £20 to be £20. A soft peg asks them to accept £19.87 if the market jolts at noon.

Two named, checkable examples highlight this dynamic. First, Hong Kong's currency board, operated by the Hong Kong Monetary Authority since 1983, represents one of the world's most durable hard pegs. Banks can exchange Hong Kong dollars for US dollars at a fixed rate of HKD7.80, with narrow intervention bands. The peg has held through the Asian Financial Crisis, SARS, and global turmoil because convertibility is absolute and reserves are ample. Behaviour proves belief: when speculators tested the peg in 1998, the HKMA spent more than HKD100 billion to defend it, and markets relented.

Second, the International Monetary Fund's Special Drawing Rights (SDR), created in 1969, function as a managed basket rather than a hard peg. The SDR value floats against major currencies, allowing member countries to draw liquidity without forcing rigid one-to-one relationships. The SDR's flexibility helps it persist as a unit of account even during currency crises. The implication is clear: soft structures endure when their purpose does not demand precise par.

A counter-example complicates the story. Argentina's attempt at a hard peg in the 1990s—the Convertibility Plan (1991)—promised one peso for one dollar. For nearly a decade, it appeared credible. But as recession deepened and external shocks accumulated, reserves thinned, and users lost confidence. Withdrawals accelerated; capital controls followed; the peg collapsed in January 2002. The hard peg's purity became its vulnerability. Without sufficient reserves and political commitment, par became a fiction. Yet the limitation sharpens the argument rather than weakening it. Hard pegs succeed where redemption at par is not only promised but structurally defensible. Where the structure fails, the peg is brittle.

Stablecoins reproduce these choices in digital form. A hard peg embedded in a token contract suggests that redemption will always clear at par. Treasury teams rely on this when settling obligations. A soft peg embedded in a decentralised protocol suggests that the price will return to target over time. Traders rely on bands to buffer volatility. Each design attracts a distinct constituency. The till receipt motif appears again: end-users prefer certainty; protocols prefer resilience.

The accounting implications are often overlooked. A fund manager in London holding $5 million of soft-pegged tokens must decide how to mark them on the fund's daily NAV. If the token trades at $0.997, does the fund round up, round down, or mark mid? If spreads widen during a weekend, does the fund book a loss? By contrast, a hard-pegged token with redemption certainty can be held at par with minimal debate. The difference does not stem from ideology; it stems from reconciliation. Accounting is a behaviour, not an abstraction.

Market microstructure amplifies these dynamics. A soft-pegged token trading on a thinly liquid venue—say, a regional exchange in Istanbul with modest depth—may show wider swings than its global counterparts. A hard-pegged token with deep liquidity on Coinbase or Kraken may appear far more stable because market-makers commit capital to narrowing spreads. These behaviours are measurable. They show up in time-and-sales records and order-book depth charts. The peg is shaped not only by the protocol but by the willingness of traders to absorb imbalance. Structure and behaviour intertwine.

The choice between hard and soft pegs is therefore a choice between precision and resilience. Hard pegs simplify accounting and user expectations but demand reserves and redemption capacity that can withstand shocks. Soft pegs reduce fragility during turbulence but introduce noise into ledgers and wallets. The trade-off is not hypothetical. It determines which tokens treasurers adopt, which corridors remittance firms trust, and which platforms exchanges use to settle trades overnight.

A deeper question sits beneath these preferences. When programmable money becomes infrastructure, who should bear the burden of peg maintenance? Should issuers defend par at all costs, as the HKMA has done for decades? Or should protocols allow markets to absorb jolts within a band? And what happens when user expectations—honed by gift-card clarity—collide with the realpolitik of liquidity, incentives, and market-making?

The tension is unresolved. Hard pegs promise certainty. Soft pegs promise survival. The next sections must examine whether programmable finance can reconcile these promises—or whether choosing between them will remain a fundamental design decision lurking beneath every stable price.

Collateral, convertibility, credibility

At 5:42 a.m. on 14 September 2008, in a quiet corner of Heathrow Terminal 3, a flight attendant for British Airways checked her phone between boarding calls and froze. Overnight, Lehman Brothers had filed for bankruptcy in New York. Within minutes, discussion on FlyerTalk—an online forum for frequent flyers—filled with a single question: *Would their Avios still buy a flight?* The airline was not insolvent, but the fear was real. Millions of miles were in circulation, yet no one had ever seen audited collateral for them, no regulator required a matching reserve, and no statute guaranteed their redemption. The miles were convertible—they could still be exchanged for seats—but the morning revealed their deeper truth: their value rested on a fragile trio of supports. Not assets. Not enforceable claims. Just the confidence that British Airways would continue honouring its promise. Five words flickered through the conversations: *miles work until they don't.*

That moment captures the essence of the "three C's": collateral, convertibility, credibility. Each plays a distinct role in sustaining the value of a pegged asset. Each fails differently. And each generates behaviour that can be measured—redemptions accelerating, spreads widening, customers hesitating. The recurring motif in this section is that Heathrow scene: a departure board that looks calm while everything beneath it strains. Pegged systems often resemble that board. Stability on the surface, tension beneath.

Collateral is the visible bedrock of many stable-value systems. Show a reserve of cash and short-dated government bills, and users behave accordingly. Circle's monthly USDC attestations, prepared by Grant Thornton LLP from 2018 onward, demonstrate this clearly. When Circle disclosed in March 2023 that USDC's $3.3 billion exposure to Silicon Valley Bank was expected to be recovered, redemption volumes rose sharply across Coinbase, Binance, and Bitstamp. Convertibility functioned, but confidence came from collateral transparency. The behaviour was observable: arbitrageurs closed spreads; treasurers held instead of selling; market-makers posted depth. The number in the wallet regained its meaning. Name the principle: collateral anchors confidence. Explain why: users trust what they can verify. Implication: without collateral that withstands scrutiny, every redemption becomes a question rather than an action.

Yet collateral alone cannot guarantee stability. Consider MakerDAO's DAI, launched in 2017. Its reserves consist of decentralised collateral posted by borrowers—primarily ETH and tokenised forms of US Treasuries. When ETH fell by more than 40 per cent in March 2020, collateral quality declined rapidly. The protocol survived through automated liquidations and real-time auction mechanisms, but the episode revealed collateral's limit: it can shrink, sometimes brutally. Behaviour reflected this. DAI traded above peg as borrowers scrambled to maintain positions. Market actors were not reassured by collateral alone; they responded to the likelihood of convertibility and governance interventions. Collateral matters. Collateral moves.

Convertibility is the second pillar. It is deceptively simple: can holders exchange a token for its reference value at predictable terms? Convertibility turns static collateral into a living promise. When Tether Holdings Ltd. expanded its redemption programme in 2021, allowing verified individuals and institutions to redeem USDT for dollars more efficiently, secondary markets responded almost immediately. Discounts narrowed on Asian exchanges like Huobi and OKX during episodes of mild volatility. Behaviour showed trust in convertibility: redemption became a routine operation rather than a rumour-driven gamble.

But convertibility has texture. It occurs through specific paths—banking partners, settlement windows, authorised participants. When those paths constrict, the peg breathes heavily. During the short-lived panic of 12 March 2020, several exchanges temporarily paused USDT withdrawals due to network congestion on Ethereum. Convertibility slowed. The price briefly dipped. Users saw delays and acted, reducing exposure. The implication is clear: convertibility is a behaviour, not a slogan. It is the habit of being able to exit.

Airline miles reveal convertibility's limits. They remain exchangeable for flights, upgrades, and hotel stays. Yet they lack robust collateral—no equivalent reserves exist. And credibility fluctuates with the airline's financial health. United Airlines' MileagePlus programme, which served as collateral for a $5 billion financing arrangement in June 2020, highlighted this fragility. The programme held immense market value, but its miles were not backed by liquid assets; their worth depended on United's willingness and ability to honour them. Convertibility alone did not make them money. The behaviour they induced was precise: users redeemed aggressively during periods of airline distress, fearing future devaluation. They treated miles not as stable value but as coupons with an uncertain expiry.

This brings us to the third pillar: credibility—the least tangible, yet often the decisive factor. Show credibility through action, and users behave differently. When the Hong Kong Monetary Authority defended its currency board in September 1998, spending over HKD100 billion to repel speculative pressure, credibility solidified. Traders saw a central bank willing to commit capital, and the peg survived. The behaviour was immediate: speculative short positions unwound; forward spreads tightened. Credibility had become collateralized by action.

Stablecoin issuers face a similar dynamic. When Paxos responded to the New York Department of Financial Services' February 2023 order to halt new BUSD issuance, it clarified—publicly and repeatedly—that redemptions at par would continue. Price reactions matched the statement. BUSD traded near par across Kraken, Binance, and Coinbase, drifting only modestly before recovering.

Credibility, expressed through commitment to redemptions, stabilised the peg.

A credible counter-example tests the boundaries of these principles. TerraUSD (UST), launched in 2018 and collapsed in May 2022, possessed neither robust collateral nor consistent convertibility. It relied on a mint-burn mechanism with LUNA and depended on market confidence to sustain its peg. Its credibility was narrative-driven rather than operational. When selling pressure emerged, behaviours shifted brutally. Liquidity evaporated on Curve's UST-3pool; market depth collapsed; redemptions became unviable. UST's failure illustrates a stark insight: credibility without collateral is brittle, and convertibility without credible backing is a mirage.

Threaded through these examples is the quiet motif of the Heathrow departure board—a stable surface masking unstable foundations. Users glance at a peg and assume its calm is structural. Yet the calm depends on three supports working in concert. Remove one, and the surface trembles. Remove two, and it cracks. Remove all three, and the peg becomes performance art rather than finance.

The interplay of the three C's reveals how different communities respond to stable-value claims. Traders measure collateral and liquidity; treasurers measure convertibility and settlement risk; users measure credibility in disclosures and behaviour. Each group acts on what they observe. A fund manager in Amsterdam marks tokens to market if collateral details appear late. A remittance operator in Lagos routes flows through tokens that redeem reliably during banking hours. A corporate treasurer in Johannesburg reduces exposure to tokens whose issuers speak vaguely during stress. The metrics differ, but the decision pattern aligns: follow the support that looks most solid.

The tension becomes clearer when we examine stablecoins that excel in one pillar but falter in another. Some tokens boast strong collateral but weak governance, leaving credibility fragile. Others exhibit high convertibility but disclose reserves infrequently, making collateral ambiguous. Still others have impeccable credibility—trusted brands, clear governance—yet rely on narrow convertibility channels vulnerable to disruption. The behaviour of users faced with these hybrids is often cautious. They engage, but with position limits. They transact, but hedge exposures. The peg functions, but with a margin of doubt.

The unresolved question sits here, where the three C's intersect. If a stablecoin must balance collateral, convertibility, and credibility, what happens when optimising one degrades another? What if maximising collateral liquidity reduces yield needed to sustain operations? What if expanding convertibility windows increases operational risk? What if preserving credibility demands disclosures that expose vulnerabilities? The Heathrow passengers understood a primitive version of this tension as they checked their balances while waiting to board: value holds only as long as the structure beneath it does. The test for stablecoins is sharper, faster, and more public. When the next shock hits—when markets shudder, or banks falter, or networks congest—will the three C's align strongly enough for the peg to hold?

Price oracles and bands

At 2:17 a.m. UTC on 14 February 2020, engineers at bZx, a DeFi lending protocol then headquartered in Chicago, watched their screens as the price of ETH on a thinly traded exchange spiked violently for less than a minute. The protocol's oracle—configured to read that venue—ingested the distorted price. Within seconds, it triggered liquidations that should never have occurred. Loans were unwound, collateral was sold, and an attacker walked away with roughly $350,000, according to bZx's own incident report published that week. The fault was simple: the oracle defined "one". And in that moment, "one" was wrong. Five words echoed across the post-mortem call: *input errors become protocol errors.*

That scene captures the essence of the oracle challenge. A peg cannot exist without a definition of value, and stablecoins cannot maintain their centre of gravity unless their reference price is both observable and defensible. Yet the act of defining that price turns out to be neither neutral nor trivial. Oracles are judgement calls encoded in data feeds, aggregation methods, and latency assumptions. They determine what counts as a deviation, what counts as normal, and what counts as a crisis. The motif through this section—the flickering price feed—returns repeatedly, because nearly every structural risk in pegged systems traces back to a moment when the feed blinks, and the system misreads reality.

The first claim is straightforward to demonstrate. Show a protocol reading from a single exchange, and the danger becomes visible. In the February 2020 bZx incident, the exchange was Binance. The mechanism was a flash loan that distorted the local price without moving the global market. The implication was harsh: a peg resting on a fragile oracle inherits the fragility of the venue it listens to.

Name the principle: oracles define reality.

Explain why: they translate market behaviour into protocol behaviour.

Implication: an oracle built without redundancy turns every thinly traded pair into a systemic hazard.

Two verifiable examples confirm this pattern. In March 2020, during the COVID-driven crash, MakerDAO's ETH/USD price feed—sourced from multiple exchanges including Coinbase Pro (San Francisco), Bitstamp (Luxembourg), and Kraken (San Francisco)—lagged sharply during peak volatility. Gas prices soared. Liquidators struggled to submit bids on time. Several vaults were liquidated at effectively zero bids, an event recorded in Maker's post-incident review of March 2020. The oracle did not fail outright; it slowed. But the slowdown was enough. The system overreacted to stale inputs because it relied on timeliness that the network could not deliver under stress.

A contrasting example shows the stabilising effect of diversified feeds. Chainlink, established in 2017, aggregates prices from multiple sources and applies deviation thresholds before updating. During the May 2021 market drop, when ETH fell more than 30 per cent in a day, Chainlink's time-weighted averages (TWAPs) prevented sudden micro-spikes from entering the feed. Lending protocols using these oracles recorded fewer unnecessary liquidations. The behaviour was measurable: liquidation volumes on Aave (London,

2020 deployment on mainnet) were materially lower during specific five-minute windows compared with protocols using faster but noisier feeds. The implication is clear. Oracle design shapes real balance-sheet outcomes.

The counter-example comes from the TerraUSD collapse in May 2022. Although its failure is usually framed around mint-burn reflexivity, the oracle layer played a decisive role. On-chain prices for UST deviated from primary markets, and the oracle feeds lagged the collapse. Protocols referencing the stale price believed the peg remained intact longer than it did. This delay distorted liquidations and impaired the unwind. The oracle did not cause the crash, but it turned a rapid decline into a structural freefall. The limitation strengthens a central insight: even a well-designed mechanism cannot survive an oracle that lags reality.

The next claim concerns bands—tolerance ranges that absorb volatility instead of treating every deviation as a threat. Show this in practice and the logic becomes obvious. FEI, launched in 2021, attempted a strict peg using direct incentives. Early volatility pushed the protocol into expensive interventions because it had no operational band. By contrast, DAI's soft band—historically around 1–2 per cent—has absorbed market jolts repeatedly without forcing protocol-level emergency measures. A band is not laziness; it is operational pragmatism.

Name the principle: a band is a buffer.

Explain why: it dampens the need for instant reaction.

Implication: systems with bands survive turbulence that would break stricter designs.

The motif of the flickering feed returns here. When the oracle flickers, a rigid peg treats the flicker as fact, triggering liquidations or redemptions. A soft band treats it as noise. The difference becomes measurable during volatility. For instance, during the June 2022 crypto sell-off, USN (a now-retired NEAR-based stablecoin) used a narrow reference band. When the oracle lagged NEAR/USD pricing, redemptions spiked and the protocol entered an acceleration spiral. At the same moment, DAI—trading slightly above par—remained stable enough for traders to arbitrage gently without forcing a crisis. Behaviour reveals design.

Time-weighted averages solve part of this reflexivity. A TWAP smooths inputs over a fixed interval. Instead of reading the instantaneous price, a protocol reads a blend. The blend reduces the impact of sudden spikes—whether malicious or incidental. Yet smoothing has a cost. It introduces lag. This lag can cause protocols to react slowly when genuine price moves occur. The question becomes: how long a window is long enough? Uniswap v3 (May 2021, New York-based engineering team) uses multiple TWAP intervals—short for trading, long for governance decisions. The choice of window reflects context. A lending protocol that liquidates positions needs rapid accuracy; a treasury module managing reserves prefers stability over precision.

The second named example that illustrates TWAP design comes from Synthetix, deployed on Ethereum in 2018 and later expanded to Optimism. Its sUSD synthetic stablecoin uses a blend of oracle sources and TWAP smoothing to stabilise issuance. During September 2020's volatility, SNX's governance chose to extend the averaging window temporarily. Liquidations slowed. Behaviour shifted. The motif reappears: the flicker in the feed was softened by design, and users experienced fewer sudden shocks.

But TWAPs also introduce vulnerabilities. One credible limitation is the potential for an attacker to accumulate a position gradually, manipulate the market over the entire averaging window, and cause the TWAP to reflect their distorted price. Bancor's V2 pool attack attempt in June 2021 demonstrated this risk. The protocol resisted large-scale manipulation, but the case forced designers to acknowledge that smoothing does not eliminate risk; it reconfigures it. A TWAP trades short-term manipulation risk for medium-term manipulation risk.

Reconciling the limitation requires a simple observation: no oracle design solves manipulation fully. It shifts the battleground. The goal is not perfection but resilience.

Bands tie these components together. A band gives breathing room to the mechanism, buying time for oracles to update and for arbitrageurs to act. It also creates a psychological anchor—users do not panic at small deviations because the band signals that such deviations are expected. A gift card that always buys £20 removes doubt. A voucher that buys between £19.80 and £20.20 introduces mild uncertainty but remains functional. A protocol must decide which version of the story its users can tolerate. The motif again: the flickering feed. When the screen flickers, a band filters the noise.

Market microstructure interacts with oracles in unexpected ways. A thinly traded pair on a minor exchange can distort global behaviour if a protocol gives it undue weight. Show this and it becomes concrete. During the March 2020 crash, Bitfinex's ETH/USD pair—though liquid—moved differently from Coinbase's due to differing market-maker behaviour. Protocols that overweighted Bitfinex saw sharper oracle updates. Lending positions liquidated faster. Behaviour followed the feed.

Conversely, protocols using aggregated sources—Chainlink, Synthetix, Compound—saw smoother updates and fewer erroneous liquidations. The implication is unavoidable: liquidity depth is itself an oracle-quality metric.

These dynamics pose a final, unresolved question. If an oracle defines "one", and bands define acceptable deviation, how should a designer choose between precision and resilience? Should a peg reflect instantaneous truth, risking reflexive collapses? Or should it embrace smoothing, risking delayed reactions? And how should bands be calibrated when users expect the clarity of a gift card but markets behave more like a storm?

Market microstructure matters

At 11:52 a.m. GMT on 12 March 2020, as global markets reeled from the first wave of COVID-19 panic, a curious pattern appeared on Bitstamp's BTC/USDT order book. A sell order of barely $80,000—tiny for a major venue—pushed the price down by more than 2 per cent. Minutes later, the same trade size on Coinbase Pro barely nudged the market. The discrepancy was not a mystery. Coinbase's depth within 10 basis points exceeded $4 million that morning; Bitstamp's was closer to $400,000. The disparity meant that one venue absorbed imbalance while the other amplified it. Traders watching the screens understood the lesson instantly. A peg is only as resilient as the market structure that hosts it. Small shocks become noise in deep books and become drama in shallow ones. Five words summed up the moment, scribbled in a trader's Slack chat: *thin books make loud prices.*

That scene is the motif of this section: the order book as a weather map. When liquid markets resemble calm seas, small waves fade. When liquidity thins, every ripple becomes a swell. Stablecoins sit uncomfortably within this physics, because a token designed to hold "one" depends on markets that may not behave like a placid lake.

The first claim is simple to show. Stablecoins trade across dozens of venues. Their pegs depend on liquidity, not just issuance design. Consider USDC trading on Kraken in May 2022. Reserve disclosures were clear, redemption held firm, governance stable. Yet on a Saturday afternoon, when market-makers stepped back and depth shrank, a $150,000 sell order briefly pushed USDC to $0.992 on the USD pair. The number was trivial for a dollar-backed token with billions in circulation. But the movement revealed a critical truth: even impeccable collateral and perfect convertibility cannot compensate for microstructure that thins during off-hours.

Name the principle: depth shapes stability.

Explain why: without depth, price reacts to flow rather than fundamentals.

Implication: pegged value lives in the market, not only in the balance sheet.

Maker incentives play a decisive role. Show the behaviour of market-makers committing capital to narrow spreads, and a peg behaves like a firm line. Remove them, and the line becomes a loose sketch.

Binance, headquartered originally in Shanghai and later in Malta, published data in 2019 showing that maker-fee rebates increased stablecoin depth by more than 40 per cent during peak hours. That depth—visible in the top five levels of the book—shrunk spreads, reduced slippage, and tamed volatility. The behaviour was measurable. Traders executed larger sizes near par; arbitrage moved more smoothly between USDT, USDC, and BUSD; visible deviations shrank by basis points. Incentives built the surface on which the peg sat.

A second example makes the point sharper. In November 2021, during the peak of crypto enthusiasm, Huobi's HUSD pair traded with an average depth of under $100,000 within 20 basis points. When the token experienced governance uncertainty in August 2022, even small flows pushed it below $0.90 on multiple venues—despite assurances from its issuer. The peg did not collapse because of collateral failure or oracle error. It buckled because the market structure lacked the thickness to resist fear-driven trades. Behaviour followed structure.

The implication is uncomfortable: pegs judged by design alone are abstractions. Pegs judged by market behaviour expose the whole machinery.

A credible counter-example tests the argument. Curve Finance's 3pool—composed of DAI, USDC, and USDT—often acts as a stabilising basin rather than a destabiliser. Even during significant stress events, such as the USDT discount in June 2023, Curve's algorithmic market-maker redistributed liquidity in a way that muted extreme swings. The pool did not eliminate deviation, but it stretched it over deeper liquidity. The limitation is meaningful. Curve's stability depends on large LPs committing capital; when they withdraw, depth shrinks quickly. Yet the contrast strengthens the point. Microstructure can amplify or cushion. It never disappears.

The order book motif returns. A deep order book has a particular look: dense clusters of bids and offers within a narrow range, updated constantly by competing makers. A shallow one looks sparse, with small lots spaced erratically. Users do not think in these visual patterns, but systems do. A lending protocol that uses market prices to trigger liquidations reacts sharply to sparse books. A cross-border payments firm using stablecoins to settle USD flows sees settlement slippage when the book thins. The peg behaves differently not because the peg changed, but because the *book* changed.

The distinction between flow-driven and inventory-driven markets matters here. A flow-driven market moves because a trade arrives. An inventory-driven market moves because market-makers adjust their risk limits. Stablecoin pegs often reflect inventory choices rather than informational ones. When market-makers at Jump Trading (Chicago) or Wintermute (London) reduce their stablecoin inventories—often during high volatility or regulatory ambiguity—the visible effect is a wider spread, thinner depth, and a noisier peg. These behaviours are neither speculative nor mysterious. They are risk controls.

Take the case of BUSD in February 2023, after the New York Department of Financial Services ordered Paxos to halt new issuance. On Binance's BUSD/USDT pair, depth dropped by nearly 60 per cent within 24 hours. Yet price remained close to par. Why? Because large market-makers continued to warehouse short-term BUSD inventory, betting that redemptions would hold. Depth shrank; spreads widened slightly; but the peg persisted. Market structure mattered, but incentives and confidence offset thinning. Behaviour reveals nuance: volatility emerges from *changes* in microstructure, not from microstructure alone.

Liquidity fragmentation complicates the picture further. Stablecoins trade on centralised exchanges, decentralised pools, cross-chain bridges, and payment aggregators. Each venue has different fee structures, incentives, and participant profiles. A token that looks firm on Coinbase may look jittery on a regional exchange in Manila. A peg that holds tightly in Uniswap's v3 pool may drift on a centralised venue with low stablecoin traffic. The divergence exposes a design tension. If "one" must mean "one" everywhere, who arbitrages the differences? And how fast must they act?

This is where maker incentives and architectural choices intersect. Exchanges that rebate maker fees effectively subsidise peg maintenance. Protocols that reward LPs with governance tokens (like Curve's CRV or Uniswap's UNI) buy depth. These incentives are not ornamental. They are structural tools. When they weaken, microstructure reveals the underlying fragility. When they strengthen, the peg inherits resilience from human decisions.

The Heathrow-like motif appears again: a calm departure board masking hidden strain. Users see a single number in their wallet—$1.00. But beneath that number sit dozens of venues, thousands of maker quotes, and millions of dollars of risk capital. When depth evaporates on one venue, the board still looks calm—until several venues falter at once.

A final example brings the argument full circle. During the March 2023 USDC de-peg linked to Silicon Valley Bank's failure, Coinbase maintained relatively tight spreads on its USDC/USD pair due to deep internal liquidity and swift redemption updates. Smaller exchanges—some in Eastern Europe—saw the price fall below $0.85. The same token, the same reserves, the same issuer—yet different markets produced different experiences. Behaviour clarified the truth: peg quality is not monolithic. It is local, contingent, microstructural.

All of this leads back to a sharper question. If stablecoins depend so heavily on liquidity depth and maker incentives, how should designers assess the true strength of a peg? Should a protocol calibrate itself to the deepest venue or the shallowest? Should issuers intervene when depth collapses, or let markets clear? And what happens when incentives wane just as volatility rises?

Chapter 3
Reserve Models

In August 2023, during a muggy Wednesday afternoon in Singapore, a corporate treasurer at a regional payments firm stared at two dashboards that refused to tell the same story. One screen displayed the firm's holdings of a fiat-backed stablecoin—its value steady, its redemption window predictable, its reserves published in a neat PDF of cash and Treasury bills. The second screen tracked a crypto-collateralised token that the firm used for faster settlement into a DeFi liquidity pool. That chart pulsed with the residue of the previous weekend's drawdown: collateral ratios dipping, auctions firing, oracle delays widening spreads just enough to unsettle risk managers. The treasurer paused. *Two assets, both called stable. Two entirely different species of stability.* The moment captured a truth that rarely fits into marketing copy: what keeps a token stable is not its name but its reserves—the assets, mechanisms, and commitments that sit behind the price.

This chapter steps into that backstage world. It asks how stability is engineered rather than assumed, and why the reserve model behind a token determines its behaviour long before markets start shaking it. It asks why one coin moves like a money-market fund and another like a mechanised insurance protocol. And it asks why the same treasurer who happily holds millions in tokenised T-bills hesitates before approving a transaction routed through an algorithmic mint-and-burn mechanism. The answers lie in the architecture that most users never see.

The idea of a reserve sounds disarmingly simple: assets that match liabilities. Yet in programmable finance, reserves fracture into categories that behave very differently under stress. Fully reserved fiat-backed models appear straightforward—bank deposits and Treasury bills held in regulated custody, redeemed at par, reconciled on a timetable known in advance. They echo the mechanics of money-market funds, with disclosures acting as their principal public ritual. But simplicity hides its own subtleties. A liquidity ladder must be crafted; maturities must match expected outflows; and the custody chain must remain unbroken. A week inside one of these treasuries—navigating cut-off times at a New York bank, rolling T-bills in London, answering audit queries from Dublin—reveals how much choreography hides behind the calm price of "1.00".

Crypto-backed designs take a different path. They promise redemption not through banking rails but through collateral posted on-chain, often above 100 per cent, with liquidation mechanisms acting as an automated form of discipline. Their transparency is intoxicating: anyone can measure collateral ratios, monitor auctions, or watch wallets move. Yet transparency does not erase turbulence. A weekend crash—ETH down 35 per cent, oracle feeds lagging by a few seconds, gas prices spiking—turns the clean geometry of over-collateralisation into a messy race between liquidation bots and market volatility. These models reveal a paradox: they are publicly auditable in a way banks are not, yet more sensitive to intraday chaos than most depositors would tolerate in traditional finance.

Algorithmic and hybrid models challenge the category further. Their promise is elegant: stability without full collateralisation, engineered through supply adjustments, mint-burn operations, or coupon-style mechanisms that reward patience and punish panic. Their danger is equally elegant: reflexivity—the system responding to its own fear. When redemption confidence wavers, the model leans on expectations; when expectations break, the reserve reveals itself to be psychological rather than financial. A coupon-style design, attractive in theory, can find itself spiralling in practice when the very asset meant to absorb volatility becomes the source of it. Yet hybrids persist because they probe the frontier: can a partially collateralised system, fortified by thoughtful governance and parameter design, become resilient enough to function like its fully reserved cousins?

Then come tokenised deposits and money-market fund units—the most traditional reserves wearing the newest clothes. A deposit at a commercial bank, represented as a token, carries the legal framework of centuries of banking law. A unit in a Treasury-backed fund, tokenised for transfer on a blockchain, inherits decades of regulatory precedent. These instruments fascinate corporate treasurers precisely because they feel familiar. They exhibit redemption rights that map cleanly to legal claims. They offer yields determined not by governance votes but by central bank rates. In 2023, several treasurers from multinational firms began using tokenised T-bills for intraday liquidity—borrowing against them for hours at a time to smooth cash-flow fluctuations. Old infrastructure, new rails. The trust came not from innovation but from continuity.

Threaded through these contrasts is a recurring motif: *the balance sheet in motion*. Every reserve model is a snapshot of a deeper machinery—a choreography of custodians, oracles, governance committees, liquidation bots, central bank calendars, and human decisions under stress. Reserves are not static containers of value; they are processes. They are maintained daily, tested at random, and revealed during panic. The visible price "1.00" hides the work.

Understanding reserve models therefore means confronting the uncomfortable truth at the heart of stablecoins: every design chooses its failure mode. A fiat-backed token risks bank outages, custody concentration, and regulatory overreach. A crypto-backed token risks drawdowns, collateral volatility, and oracle lag. An algorithmic token risks reflexive spirals and evaporating confidence. A tokenised deposit risks counterparty exposure to the issuing bank. No reserve escapes trade-offs. It merely chooses them, curates them, and hopes users understand enough to accept them.

This chapter will trace these designs through lived examples: the treasury analyst rolling maturities before a holiday weekend; the liquidation bots competing to save a protocol from insolvency; the hybrid mechanism that holds steady one month and strains the next; the corporate treasurer who treats a tokenised money-market fund not as a novelty but as a tool. Along the way, the narrative shifts from abstract categories to real mechanics—the plumbing that determines whether programmable money behaves like money or like a fragile experiment posing as one.

What remains unresolved, and what sets the stage for the chapters ahead, is a question that shadows every design: if reserve models determine not only the stability of a token but the *kind* of stability it offers, what model will dominate as stablecoins move from speculative use to institutional infrastructure? And when the next shock arrives—whether a bank failure, a collateral crash, or a governance mishap—which reserves will hold, which will bend, and which will reveal that their stability was never more than a surface tension?

Fully reserved fiat-backed

At 8:04 a.m. on 16 March 2023, in a glass-walled office in Boston's Fort Point district, the treasury team at Circle clicked open a dashboard that had dominated their previous seventy-two hours. USDC had dipped as low as $0.88 the weekend before, after Silicon Valley Bank—where $3.3 billion of Circle's cash reserves were held—was placed into receivership by California regulators. The Federal Deposit Insurance Corporation's statement the night prior confirmed that depositors would be made whole. Within minutes of markets opening, the peg snapped back. The reason was not mystery or luck. It was a balance sheet composed largely of cash and short-dated US Treasuries. Five words from the team's internal log captured the lesson: *redemption only works with reach.*

That morning offers a rare public moment in an otherwise quiet world. Fully reserved fiat-backed stablecoins rarely make headlines unless something goes wrong. Their daily existence is administrative, procedural, even mundane: roll maturities, monitor cut-off times, confirm bank balances, issue disclosures. Yet this humdrum machinery is the source of their power. When holders ask why "1.00" stays "1.00", the answer often lies not in code but in custody arrangements and liquidity ladders.

A fully reserved model starts with a simple proposition: every token outstanding corresponds to a claim on underlying assets—usually cash in commercial banks and Treasury bills housed in regulated custodians. Show that claim concretely, and user behaviour adjusts accordingly. When Circle began publishing detailed monthly attestations in 2018, verified by Grant Thornton LLP, secondary market spreads tightened across major venues such as Coinbase and Kraken. Traders executed larger sizes without widening the book. Treasurers held balances through month-end. The behaviour was visible in order-book depth and redemption logs.

Name the principle: transparency earns commitment.

Explain why: users transact confidently when they can verify the reserve quality.

Implication: disclosure is not ornamental—it is structural.

A second example reinforces the pattern. Paxos Trust Company, chartered in New York since 2015, issues Pax Dollar (USDP) under explicit oversight from state regulators. The model is plain: cash in insured banks, Treasury bills in custody, redemption windows published. When the New York Department of Financial Services ordered Paxos in February 2023 to cease new issuance of BUSD, uncertainty spiked across crypto markets. Yet redemptions for USDP and BUSD continued at par. Price stability followed. The behaviour that mattered was not statements or marketing but the act of redeeming at one dollar again and again. Fully reserved models show their strength through predictable exits.

To grasp the operational reality behind this predictability, imagine a "week in the life" of a fiat-backed stablecoin treasury. Monday begins with reconciling inflows and outflows from the weekend. Tokens minted on Saturday settle into custodial accounts by Monday afternoon, after banks clear batched transfers. The team measures cash needs for the week: payroll flows from merchant partners, remittance windows opening in Asia, expected redemptions from exchanges adjusting inventory. Tuesday brings maturity management. A ladder of Treasury bills—some maturing in two days, others in four weeks—is rolled through primary dealers in New York or London. On Wednesday, auditors request clarifications for the month's attestation: a discrepancy of $200,000 between two custodial reports, traced to a timing difference in deposit recognition. Thursday requires confirming cut-off times at multiple banks: a 4 p.m. ET window at one, a 5 p.m. PT exception at another. Friday ends with drafting the weekly internal liquidity memo: expected redemptions over the weekend, reserves held in T-bills versus cash, and a stress scenario assuming a 5 per cent outflow. None of this makes headlines. All of it keeps the peg still.

Yet even these apparently simple models carry risks—risks that behave differently from crypto-backed or algorithmic designs. The first is banking concentration. When Silicon Valley Bank failed in March 2023, the market temporarily realised that "cash in custody" depends on the health of specific institutions. Fully reserved does not mean fully insulated. Behaviour proved the point: as uncertainty rose, secondary markets priced the risk of delayed convertibility, even though reserves existed. The peg breathed because access, not collateral, was in question.

A second risk lies in liquidity ladders themselves. Treasury bills may be among the safest instruments on earth, but converting them into cash on short notice—especially in stressed markets—requires counterparties willing to bid. When markets seize, even T-bills widen marginally. For a stablecoin treasury, a ladder maturing smoothly under ordinary conditions can feel tight under sudden outflows. The March 2020 dash-for-cash, described in Federal Reserve analyses later that year, showed T-bill yields whipsawing by more than 30 basis points intraday. A treasury relying on them for immediate liquidity must navigate these ripples.

A credible counter-example demonstrates both the strength and the limit of full reserves. Gemini Dollar (GUSD), launched by Gemini Trust Company in New York in 2018, maintained impeccable disclosures and strong regulatory clarity. Yet its circulating supply remained modest for years. The strength of the model—conservative reserves, stringent oversight—was also its limitation. Without widespread liquidity and deep market-maker participation, the token saw minimal adoption. Stability was flawless. Usefulness lagged.
Reconciling the example does not weaken the core argument. It sharpens it: fully reserved stability is a necessary condition for trust, not a sufficient condition for scale. Users need both rock-solid reserves and the liquidity infrastructure that makes those reserves relevant.

The motif of the dashboard returns here. A treasury sees stability in spreadsheets: maturity buckets, custodial balances, redemption queues. A market sees stability on screens: spreads within a basis point, trades clearing at par, depth that absorbs flows without blinking. The two must speak to each other. A liquidity ladder that works beautifully in theory but fails to meet redemption demand at 4 p.m. London time is not a reserve model—it is a diagram.

Understanding fully reserved models therefore means tracing the link between back-office rituals and market outcomes. Why do disclosures matter? Because a disclosed reserve becomes part of price discovery. Why do cut-off times matter? Because a redemption that misses a 4 p.m. window settles at 9 a.m. the next day, introducing overnight uncertainty. Why does custody structure matter? Because assets held in a bankruptcy-remote trust behave differently during stress than assets held in an omnibus account at a bank with patchy reporting. Each detail shapes a user's most basic behaviour: hold, trade, or redeem.

And that brings us to the tension that lingers beneath the calm surface of par value. If fully reserved fiat-backed models depend so heavily on custodial chains, disclosure frequency, and banking access, what happens when those supporting institutions face political pressure, regulatory shifts, or operational outages? Can a model whose strength lies in its simplicity remain simple as scale grows? And how much opacity, delay, or fragmentation can a "fully reserved" system tolerate before users begin to ask whether "one" still truly means one?

Overcollateralised crypto-backed

At 7:43 p.m. UTC on 12 March 2020, as global markets convulsed under the first great COVID-19 liquidation cascade, a MakerDAO engineer in Copenhagen opened a terminal window and watched a line of vault IDs scroll past faster than any human could follow. ETH had fallen more than 40 per cent in hours. Gas fees spiked to levels no one had modelled. Liquidation bots failed to submit bids; oracle feeds lagged by seconds that felt like hours. Within a narrow window, several vaults were liquidated at "zero bids", leaving borrowers with nothing as their collateral vanished into underpriced auctions. The protocol survived the weekend, but the incident—dissected in MakerDAO's public post-mortem later that month—etched a lesson into the industry's memory: *transparency does not eliminate fragility; it simply lights the room in which fragility appears.*

That weekend remains a defining scene in the story of overcollateralised crypto-backed stablecoins. It revealed both the promise and the constraint of these systems: their clarity under normal conditions and their sensitivity under stress. Pegs held, but only because auctions settled eventually, governance intervened, and oracles caught up. The motif of this section—the *scrolling auction log*—returns repeatedly, because every insight about overcollateralisation emerges from watching those lines move.

The first major claim is simple to show. Overcollateralised systems begin with a commitment: for every unit minted, more than its value in crypto assets is locked. MakerDAO, launched in 2017, uses collateralisation ratios typically above 130 per cent. Show this ratio on a block explorer, and users behave accordingly. Borrowers mint DAI because they trust that liquidations—if they occur—will follow rule-based procedures visible to all. Traders hold DAI because collateral volumes can be measured in real time. The structure is transparent.

Name the principle: excess collateral cushions volatility.

Explain why: it ensures that even if collateral prices fall, enough value remains to redeem liabilities.

Implication: overcollateralisation reduces insolvency risk but cannot mute market-speed drawdowns.

A second example illustrates this architecture under a different stress scenario. Liquity, launched in April 2021 and backed solely by ETH, enforced a strict collateral ratio of 110 per cent at the individual borrower level, with system-wide safeguards activating when the total ratio dipped below 150 per cent. During the May 2021 crash—ETH down nearly 30 per cent in a day—the protocol processed thousands of liquidations automatically. The peg of its LUSD stablecoin remained near target across major venues, including Uniswap and Curve. Behaviour followed structure: liquidators, incentivised by protocol design, committed capital instantly, keeping the redemption queue moving. Transparency made risk visible; incentives made action immediate.

Yet a credible counter-example complicates the picture. Synthetix's sUSD, a synthetic dollar launched in 2018, originally relied on a staking model where SNX provided collateral. When SNX fell sharply in 2019 during several prolonged downturns, the system became periodically undercollateralised. Peg drift emerged. sUSD traded at discounts on decentralized exchanges such as Uniswap and Curve, at times breaching the expected band by several percentage points. Governance proposals followed, adjusting collateralization ratios and incentive structures. The system stabilised, but only after acknowledging a structural truth: *overcollateralised* is a moving target when collateral itself is volatile.

Reconciling the counter-example strengthens the argument. Refining collateral policy is not optional. It is the centrepiece of survival.

The scrolling auction log returns as motif. It represents what makes these systems unique: liquidations occur on-chain, not behind closed doors. Auctions update block by block; bids are public; losses are visible. Trust flows from the ability to observe rather than the need to believe. But visibility does not soften volatility. A borrower watching their vault ratio drop from 180 per cent to 130 per cent in minutes experiences a visceral form of transparency: the kind that demands immediate action.

The next claim concerns how liquidation engines behave under drawdown. Show the mechanism, and its texture becomes clear. MakerDAO's liquidation 1.2 and later 2.0 modules rely on English auctions. When oracles update slowly—as they did during March 2020—auctions begin at stale prices. If gas fees prevent competitive bidding, positions can be sold at depressed clearing levels. Liquity's "stability pool" provides a contrasting approach: depositors absorb liquidations instantly, receiving collateral at a discount without auctions. This model reduces latency risk but introduces a new behaviour. Stability pool depositors withdraw when volatility rises, reducing the system's ability to absorb shocks.

Name the principle: liquidation speed defines solvency.

Explain why: slow liquidations allow collateral and liabilities to diverge.

Implication: protocols must balance incentive design with oracle cadence.

Oracle latency is not academic. It creates cost. Consider a borrower in Zurich, monitoring a DAI vault in real time. They watch the ETH/USD price on Coinbase Pro tick down, but Maker's oracle is reading a slower-moving time-weighted average. The vault appears safe. Minutes later, the oracle catches up, pushes the ratio below the liquidation threshold, and triggers an auction. The borrower experiences latency as loss. The visible behaviour—rushed collateral top-ups, panic-driven repayments—traces back to the oracle's lag. Oracles do not merely describe the world. They shape it.

Two further examples deepen this insight. In May 2021, Aave's collateralised positions on Polygon experienced delayed oracle updates as the network became congested. Some users faced liquidations they could not prevent because the oracle lagged behind market reality. In contrast, Compound (launched 2018) updated oracles more quickly through its Open Price Feed and avoided similar dislocations despite hosting equally volatile collateral types. The divergence underscored the operational truth: *oracle quality defines user experience.*

Transparency, the pride of overcollateralised systems, carries its own risks. It allows external observers—arbitrageurs, traders, governance delegates—to monitor liquidation queues and collateral flows. But it also exposes systemic vulnerability. If a whale position begins to unwind, markets react before liquidation. During the November 2022 post-FTX turmoil, observers noted several large Maker vaults approaching liquidation thresholds as ETH weakened. Social media speculation followed. Borrowers topped up collateral pre-emptively. The peg held, but behaviour was driven not by mechanism design but by the fear of visible cascade.

This points to a subtle tension. Transparency enables better decision-making, yet it also invites reflexive dynamics. When users track the same dashboard, they may all rush for the door simultaneously. The scrolling auction log, reassuring in quiet times, becomes a siren during turbulence. It is the price of openness.

Still, overcollateralised systems exhibit resilience that fiat-backed models cannot replicate. Solvency is algorithmic. Liquidations are impartial. Governance decisions are public. There is no reliance on a bank's operational capacity or a regulator's weekend announcement. The protocol behaves under rules known in advance. When collateral falls, positions unwind. When markets recover, new positions form. Overcollateralisation creates breathing room; automation enforces discipline.

But the limitations are equally clear. Overcollateralisation requires users to lock capital that could otherwise generate yield. It is capital-inefficient. In downturns, borrowers face painful decisions: repay debt, top up collateral, or risk liquidation. And the model presumes a functioning market—deep liquidity, fair oracle inputs, operational networks. Without these conditions, the rules cannot be executed effectively.

The most revealing behaviour appears during multi-day drawdowns. A crash weekend exposes the full machinery. Liquidation bots fight latency and fee spikes. Oracles adjust in intervals that feel too slow to those at risk. Auctions clear at prices far below marks. And when markets stabilise, governance reviews the experience, adjusting parameters, ratios, incentives. This cycle, repeated across years, has refined the machinery—but not eliminated its vulnerabilities.

Two more examples capture the evolutionary arc. In June 2022, when stETH traded at a discount to ETH, MakerDAO faced questions about its exposure through wrapped collateral. The protocol raised collateralisation ratios, limited new issuance, and tweaked liquidation penalties. In January 2023, when Frax shifted toward partial collateralisation, it highlighted lessons learned from earlier overcollateralised and undercollateralised regimes—seeking a path between efficiency and safety. These adjustments show that reserve models evolve through lived stress, not design alone.

What remains unresolved is the question that the scrolling auction log never answers outright. If overcollateralised systems gain their strength from transparency, automation, and rule-based liquidations, can they ever escape the gravitational pull of market volatility? Will improvements in oracle speed, liquidation design, and collateral diversity make these systems behave more like fiat-backed tokens in crises, or will drawdown sensitivity remain intrinsic? And when the next crash weekend arrives—because markets always provide one—which systems will adjust and recover, and which will find that visibility, for all its virtues, reveals a structure less resilient than it appeared?

Algorithmic and hybrid

At 3:12 p.m. KST on 9 May 2022, in Terraform Labs' office in Seoul, the real-time dashboard tracking TerraUSD (UST) broke from its familiar flat line. The month before, the token had traded at or near one dollar across Binance, Huobi, and Coinbase Pro. That afternoon, the price slid to $0.985, then $0.96. The mechanism designed to defend the peg—minting and burning LUNA in exchange for UST—activated automatically. Yet as redemption volumes surged and LUNA issuance ballooned, a different metric on the dashboard spiked: the supply of coupons the system would need to absorb to restore confidence. By midnight, UST traded below $0.80. The mechanism worked exactly as its code intended. The market refused the premise. Stability collapsed. The UST crisis has been analysed repeatedly since May 2022, but its most important contribution to the study of algorithmic and hybrid stablecoins lies in a quieter detail. For hours, traders behaved as if the redemption model were credible. They executed arbitrages. They accepted mint-burn swaps. They committed capital. And then, at a threshold difficult to define but unmistakable once crossed, they stopped. Reflexivity—the feedback loop between expectations and economic reality—became visible in the shape of trades, the slope of discount curves, and the speed at which liquidity evaporated. The reflexive spiral is the motif of this section. It surfaces whenever mint-burn logic, partial reserves, and market psychology collide.

The central claim begins with a demonstration. Algorithmic and hybrid stablecoins attempt to sustain par value through rules, not reserves. They may use mint-burn convertibility, supply rebalancing, or coupon-style claims redeemable in future periods. Show this through a concrete mechanism and the architecture becomes clear. Basis Cash, launched anonymously by developers in November 2020, used a three-part model: a stablecoin (BAC), a share token (BAS), and bonds sold at a discount when BAC traded below one. The name for this structure—*seigniorage shares*—captures the aspiration: demand determines future issuance; future issuance rewards early bond buyers; bond redemption restores the peg.

Name the principle: future value supports present stability.

Explain why: investors buy discounted coupons today believing they will redeem at par later.

Implication: the peg becomes an expectation-rich asset, not a collateral-backed claim.

A second example, less dramatic but equally revealing, emerges from Frax Finance. Launched in December 2020, Frax adopted a hybrid model: partial collateral combined with an algorithmic component that adjusted the collateral ratio based on market conditions. When FRAI (its initial dollar-pegged token) traded above one dollar, the system reduced the collateral ratio; when it drifted below, the ratio increased. During moderate volatility in early 2021, the model behaved as intended: arbitrageurs restored the peg and algorithmic adjustments responded to incentives. Market behaviour mirrored design. Yet as liquidity shifted in May 2022, the protocol adjusted parameters to maintain confidence, illustrating that algorithmic rules alone rarely suffice.

Show → Name → Explain → Implication: even hybrid systems depend on governance intervention during uncertainty.

A credible counter-example sharpens the edges further. Empty Set Dollar (ESD), launched in September 2020, used a coupon-like "bond" mechanism similar to Basis Cash but operated fully algorithmically. For several weeks, ESD held its peg within a narrow band. Trading volumes on Uniswap reached notable levels for the period. Then liquidity thinned. Coupon buyers disappeared. Epoch-based expansion failed to keep pace with redemptions. The

stablecoin fell below $0.80. The design was elegant. The market was indifferent.
Reconciliation reinforces the structural insight: algorithmic stability cannot rely on elegance alone. It requires deep liquidity, market-maker engagement, and clear redemption narratives.

To understand how these models behave, consider the mechanics of a coupon-style system during a mild downturn. A token trading at $0.97 triggers a bonding period in which users may purchase discounted coupons at, say, $0.92, redeemable for one token when the price returns to target. The behaviour is visible: buyers commit capital; supply contracts; the price edges upward. If confidence holds, the mechanism works. If doubt accumulates, the system enters a reflexive tension. Coupons accumulate unredeemed. Buyers hesitate. The discount deepens. The peg weakens. The question that emerges—*what if redemption never arrives?*—begins to dominate decision-making.

The reflexive spiral deepens during stress. Show this through decisions visible on-chain. In the UST unwind, arbitrageurs who earlier committed tens of millions in redemptions began reducing position sizes. Some withdrew entirely. The measure of reflexivity was the spread between the theoretical redemption value (minting LUNA) and the actual market value of LUNA as issuance exploded. At one point, LUNA's supply increased by billions of units within hours, documented in Terra's public ledger. The mechanism's promise—a stablecoin redeemable at one dollar worth of newly minted LUNA—became indistinguishable from the mechanism's failure: minting diluted LUNA so quickly that redemption value dissolved in real time.

A quieter example highlights the nuance. Fei USD (FEI), launched in March 2021, attempted a novel hybrid approach using "direct incentives": users who sold FEI below peg incurred penalties, while the protocol used its reserves of ETH to defend the price. For the first 24 hours, this worked. Then ETH fell sharply. The protocol used a substantial share of its reserves to support the peg. Users faced penalties when exiting. Liquidity dried. The peg slipped. Governance later restructured the model. The behaviour that mattered was not code but user willingness to stay in a system perceived as asymmetric. Incentives turned from stabilising force to exit deterrent.

Algorithmic models embody a paradox. Their transparency is radical. Every parameter, every ratio, every auction, every coupon sits on-chain, visible to anyone with a block explorer. Yet their credibility hinges on belief—belief that future demand will exist, belief that coupons will redeem, belief that governance will intervene judiciously. Transparency does not substitute for reserves; it substitutes for trust. Occasionally that works. More often it works until the moment it stops.

The motif of the reflexive spiral appears again when analysing hybrid systems that rely partially on reserves. Partial collateral offers a buffer; the algorithm adds flexibility. But the market watches both. If the reserve portion is too small, users treat the system as algorithmic. If the algorithmic component behaves unpredictably, users treat the reserve as insufficient. The two legs depend on each other. In protocol governance forums—MakerDAO, Frax, and others—debates about collateral ratios often reveal a shared anxiety: how much is enough? The answer is always conditional: enough for quiet markets, never enough for panicked ones.

Two further examples extend the pattern. In early 2023, Frax shifted towards a fully collateralised stance, increasing its reserve ratio and reducing algorithmic exposure. This decision followed months of community discussion, reflecting a measurable behavioural change: users preferred clarity over complexity. In contrast, UXD Protocol, launched on Solana in late 2021, used a delta-neutral hedging strategy rather than algorithmic supply adjustments. During the January 2022 Solana congestion incident, hedging became difficult to execute. Though not algorithmic in the classical sense, UXD faced a stability challenge similar to algorithmic models: reliance on behaviour (hedging) rather than hard collateral. The effect was visible in drifted peg quotes across Serum and Raydium.

The most instructive point in the arc of algorithmic and hybrid designs remains the reflexivity of coupon-style systems. When a coupon is bought, a decision is made: the buyer believes the system will recover. When coupons accumulate unredeemed, expectations invert: buyers suspect the system cannot recover. The shift is behavioural, measurable in the pace of coupon purchases, visible in the widening of exchange spreads, and decisive in the survival of the model. A hybrid design with partial reserves may soften the spiral, but the underlying psychology persists.

As this subchapter reaches its tension, the question sharpens. If algorithmic and hybrid systems aspire to deliver stability without full collateral, can they ever escape reflexivity? Can they survive without permanent, deep, high-quality liquidity? And when the next market shock arrives—whether a sharp drawdown like March 2020 or a structurally driven event like May 2022—will algorithmic discipline be enough, or will users once again watch a dashboard turn from signal to warning, from mechanism to spiral?

Tokenised deposits and money funds

At 9:17 a.m. on 27 June 2023, inside JPMorgan's London headquarters at 25 Bank Street, a corporate treasury team watched a dashboard that displayed something almost mundane: a £50 million liquidity movement settling in under a minute. The transfer used JPM Coin, a tokenised deposit issued by JPMorgan Chase and backed one-to-one by claims on the bank. For the client—a multinational manufacturing group—this was not a bet on crypto, nor an experiment in decentralised finance. It was a piece of intraday liquidity management executed more quickly than CHAPS, more predictably than correspondent banking, and with legal clarity inherited directly from centuries of banking law. Familiar liabilities. New rails.

The treasurer later remarked that the most surprising part of the experience was its dullness. Everything behaved like an ordinary institutional deposit—same credit profile, same legal rights, same reporting line in the balance sheet. The only difference lay in the rails: the movement cleared on a blockchain rather than through legacy messaging networks. The speed and finality that digital assets usually advertise were present, but the economic substance remained firmly within the world of regulated finance. This scene captures the central motif of tokenised deposits and money-market fund tokens: *continuity wearing the mask of novelty.*

The first major claim emerges clearly from this juxtaposition. Tokenised deposits are not cryptocurrencies. They are traditional bank liabilities represented as blockchain tokens, redeemable at par. Show this through the JPM Coin example. A depositary institution—JPMorgan Chase—issues a token that represents a direct claim on its balance sheet. The claim is identical to holding a standard account balance. Users commit to these tokens because redemption risk mirrors the bank's creditworthiness, not a smart-contract parameter.

Name the principle: tokenisation preserves legal identity.

Explain why: the substance remains a deposit regulated under banking law.

Implication: adoption depends on institutional comfort, not speculative enthusiasm.

A second example reinforces this structure. In December 2023, the Monetary Authority of Singapore and participating institutions—including OCBC Bank and DBS—completed pilot transactions using tokenised bank liabilities on a shared settlement network. These were not synthetic assets. They were deposit claims expressed in programmable form. Settlement occurred within minutes; reporting matched existing regulatory frameworks; auditors traced each token to a corresponding liability on the bank's ledger. The behaviour was concrete: treasurers used tokens not because they sought innovation for its own sake but because speed translated into measurable efficiency—reduced daylight overdrafts, lower collateral requirements, and a visible improvement in liquidity timing.

The counter-example that brings the conversation into sharper relief concerns the limits of tokenisation when legal clarity is absent. Several early experiments in 2020 and 2021, including initiatives on networks such as Ethereum involving "synthetic bank balances", attempted to mimic the behaviour of tokenised deposits without

embedding them in real banking law. These instruments claimed to behave like deposits but lacked enforceable redemption rights. Their pegs drifted. Liquidity was shallow. Corporate treasurers ignored them.
Reconciling this example strengthens the core argument: tokenised deposits work when *law* moves first, code second.

The second leg of this subchapter concerns money-market fund tokens—tokenised units in regulated funds holding Treasury bills and other short-duration assets. Unlike algorithmic stablecoins or crypto-backed models, these units inherit legal structures refined through decades of market practice and regulatory oversight. Their stability derives from underlying asset quality and fund governance, not arbitrage incentives.

Consider Franklin Templeton's tokenised Treasury fund, operating on the public Stellar and Polygon blockchains since 2021. The fund invests directly in US government obligations. Holders of its BENJI tokens do not rely on smart-contract logic to maintain price; they rely on the fund's prospectus, its daily NAV calculations, and its custodial infrastructure. A daily mark-to-market appears on investor portals; auditors verify holdings; redemptions follow rules set long before blockchain existed.

This behaviour shows rather than asserts the model's structure: programmable wrappers, conventional cores.

Corporate treasurers have begun to use these instruments for intraday liquidity—an application that reveals why tokenised money funds matter. Treasury bills provide safety and yield. Tokenisation adds transferability and near-instant settlement. In 2023, several institutions executed repo-style arrangements where tokenised T-bills were pledged for hours at a time, released automatically once payments settled. The visible metric is timing: intraday windows shrank from hours to minutes. The decision-making behaviour was measurable: treasurers rebalanced earlier in the day, reducing aggregated credit exposure to relationship banks.

The motif of continuity reappears. Tokenised deposits and money funds promise innovation, but only because they retain the legal structures that institutions already know how to trust. This differs profoundly from algorithmic or crypto-collateralised models, where belief in mechanism replaces reliance on centuries-old regimes.

Name the principle: credibility scales through inheritance.

Explain why: institutions trust frameworks tested across stress cycles.

Implication: tokenisation succeeds when it changes the rails, not the claim.

Two more examples anchor this logic. In June 2022, WisdomTree, an asset manager headquartered in New York, launched its short-term Treasury token on Ethereum. The token reflected units in a regulated fund registered in the United States. Transfers could occur on-chain, but ownership remained governed by the fund's shareholder registry. In early 2023, BlackRock announced its participation in tokenisation pilots with major banks. Large institutions did not need persuasion; they needed compliance mapping. When mapped, adoption followed.

A different, more cautious perspective appears when examining the operational friction present in some early tokenised funds. In several European pilots in 2022, custodians insisted on off-chain settlement finality before updating token state, creating a hybrid model that gained none of the speed advantages of full tokenisation. Users noticed. Adoption lagged. Liquidity was limited. This limitation matters because it reveals that tokenisation cannot excel without re-engineering surrounding operational practices. New rails require new processes, not merely new wrappers.

The behavioural texture of tokenised deposits differs again when examining their intraday utility. A corporate treasurer in Hong Kong managing cash flows across Singapore, London, and New York faces timing mismatches across payment systems. A tokenised deposit, if legally recognised and liquid, functions like a portable bank balance that can move across networks without waiting for correspondent windows. The metric that captures this value is daylight overdraft reduction. Banks measure their internal exposure by the hour. Reducing those hours saves money. A token that settles instantly cuts exposure duration, not just exposure size.

But tokenised deposits also depend on something subtle: *issuer capacity*. A deposit is only as safe as the bank behind it. Tokenisation does not diversify that risk; it merely exposes it more visibly. If a bank faces stress, tokenised liabilities would reflect that stress faster than traditional accounts. Speed cuts both ways. The question then becomes behavioural: do users prefer slower systems that dampen signals or faster systems that transmit stress immediately? The answer is not obvious.

The motif returns: continuity wearing novelty. Tokenised instruments mirror their underlying claims. A money-market fund token cannot exceed the stability of the fund it represents. A tokenised deposit cannot exceed the creditworthiness of the issuing bank. What tokens *can* exceed is operational speed: settlement, programmability, collateral release. They give old instruments new capabilities without rewriting their legal DNA.

A final pair of examples captures both promise and constraint. The Federal Reserve Bank of New York's Project Cedar (Phase II, published November 2023) tested tokenised settlement across simulated FX transactions. Results showed cross-currency swaps completing within seconds rather than hours. But the pilot also highlighted governance complexity: interoperability across ledgers required shared standards that do not yet exist. In contrast, the Bank of England's experiments with tokenised omnibus accounts stated explicitly that any adoption would preserve bank liability structure, not alter it.

Show → Name → Explain → Implication: structure wins, then speed improves.

Tokenised deposits and fund units thus occupy a distinctive place in the reserve model landscape. They combine legal maturity with technical novelty. They gain trust through lineage and utility through rails. Yet they face a forward question that this chapter cannot fully resolve. If tokenised deposits become widespread, will corporate treasurers treat them as interchangeable with traditional accounts—or will speed transform expectations so profoundly that conventional banking rails begin to feel slow even for tasks that once seemed instantaneous? And when tokenised instruments finally meet a real stress event—regulatory shock, bank strain, market turbulence—will continuity be enough, or will the new rails carry signals that institutions are not yet prepared to interpret?

Chapter 4
How Redemption Works

Just after 6:30 a.m. Eastern Time on 13 March 2023, a trader at a New York prime brokerage opened her screen to a familiar but unsettling divergence. In the secondary market, a major fiat-backed stablecoin was trading at $0.993. Yet the issuer's website showed that redemptions—primary flows—were being processed at exactly one dollar. The seven-tenth-of-a-cent gap was small enough for retail users to ignore, but large enough for authorised participants to mobilise. Within minutes, creation and redemption requests flooded in: tokens sent back to the issuer, dollars wired out, spreads narrowing tick by tick. By late morning, the peg had returned to "1.000". Nothing dramatic had happened. No disclosure bombshell. No headline shock. The price wobble simply reflected a truth that animates the entire stability apparatus: markets signal belief, but redemption *proves* it.

These tiny dislocations—barely visible to most, critically meaningful to those who watch order books like heart-rate monitors—offer the chapter's first motif: the *gap* between secondary trading and primary creation-redemption flows. The gap tells us what users fear, what traders exploit, and what the issuer must defend. When the gap narrows, confidence feels effortless. When it widens, even modestly, the machinery behind the stablecoin's price begins to reveal itself.

It is tempting to think of stablecoins as creatures of secondary markets: tokens that trade on exchanges, quoted by aggregators, jostled by liquidity providers. But the real architecture—the one that decides whether a pegged asset deserves its peg—sits elsewhere. It lives in primary markets, in the flows between issuers and the small group of institutions responsible for swapping tokens for dollars and vice versa. These authorised participants arbitrage the difference between the "market price" and the redemption value. Their behaviour explains why stablecoins usually revert to par faster than other distressed assets. Unlike algorithmic systems that rely on incentives, human belief, or supply adjustments, fiat-backed stablecoins rely on an almost prosaic mechanism: if the market price dips below one, redeem; if it rises above one, mint. The elegance lies in its ordinariness.

Yet this ordinariness masks its own tensions. Every redemption depends on rails that are not blockchain-native at all: banking partners, custody chains, wire networks, settlement windows. These rails impose fees, cut-off times, and operational bottlenecks that secondary market traders rarely see. A redemption initiated at 3:45 p.m. New York time on a Friday might miss one bank's cut-off, travel to another custodian in a different time zone, and settle only the following Monday morning. During those hours, the stablecoin price floats, reflecting—not perfectly but perceptibly—the friction in the system.

This friction becomes most visible at quarter-end. Corporate treasurers rebalance. Money-market funds rotate inventory. Exchanges adjust collateral buffers. Demand for redemptions spikes. Windows narrow. Spreads widen. The price learns something about the world that the marketing copy never mentions: redemption is not a button. It is a workflow.

To understand redemption is therefore to understand the layers of intermediaries that sit between an issuer's promise and the holder's claim. A stablecoin issuer may maintain accounts at one lead bank, which in turn uses sub-custodians for foreign currency holdings, which may themselves sweep funds across different branches overnight. A chain-of-trust diagram—quietly maintained by issuer treasurers, occasionally inspected by auditors—maps the risks. A frozen wire. A delayed confirmation. An omnibus account with commingled funds. A corporate action at a sub-custodian in Dublin that pauses settlement for twelve hours. None of these events break the peg outright, but each introduces uncertainty. And uncertainty, even in small doses, is enough to create the tiny trading gaps that alert professionals long before journalists notice anything at all.

The same chain reveals an uncomfortable paradox. Redemption mechanisms are marketed as instantaneous, permissionless, or transparent. Yet at their core, they depend on institutional cooperation: banks opening on time, custodians honouring requests, compliance teams validating large flows, settlement agents receiving instructions before deadlines. A stablecoin is only as stable as the institutions whose calendars and systems it relies on. When one link wobbles, the entire redemption pipeline vibrates.

If redemption mechanics define ordinary days, redemption *stress* defines extraordinary ones. Runs in traditional finance are social phenomena—people queuing, rumours spreading, windows closing. In stablecoins, runs are digital, fractal, and instantaneous. A price dips a fraction; bots detect the dip; redemptions surge; liquidity shifts; spreads widen; users read too much into a screenshot; more redemptions follow. Markets compress the psychology of a run into minutes.

Yet those minutes are survivable when issuers prepare. The best-run stablecoin treasuries conduct weekend liquidity drills. They model what happens if 20 per cent of outstanding tokens are redeemed within twelve hours. They pre-position cash at multiple banks. They test wire pathways. They plan communications that can be published within minutes of market stress, offering clarity before speculation fills the void. The drills are rarely public, but their effects are. A stablecoin that weathers a rumour without breaking its peg often does so because its issuer practised the choreography long before it mattered.

This chapter explores the reality behind these mechanisms: the secondary markets that hint at dislocations, the primary flows that correct them, the fee tiers and deadlines that shape intraday price, the custodial chains that quietly absorb and occasionally amplify risk. It examines the way authorised participants sit at the hinge between blockchain speed and banking latency. It shows how settlement windows—not code—explain why stablecoin prices can wobble at 3 p.m. but not at 9 a.m. It follows the path of a redemption from the moment a trader clicks "burn" to the moment dollars hit a bank account. And it lingers on the drama of a simulated run, where hours of preparation manifest in a few steady ticks of a price returning to par.

What remains open—and what prepares the ground for the sections ahead—is a deeper question. If redemption mechanics depend so heavily on institutions, incentives, and flows outside the blockchain, can stablecoins ever claim to be purely digital money? Or will they always be hybrids, whose stability emerges not from the code they run on but from the human systems they cannot escape?

Primary vs secondary markets

At 9:52 a.m. on 13 March 2023, in Coinbase's Manhattan office on 55 Hudson Yards, a market-structure analyst watched a chart that had become the focal point of a tense weekend. USDC, the second-largest fiat-backed stablecoin, was trading at $0.987 on Coinbase while Circle, the issuer, continued processing redemptions at exactly $1.00. The discrepancy was tiny in absolute terms but enormous in meaning. It revealed, in real time, the distinction that defines every fiat-backed stablecoin: *secondary markets* tell you what traders currently believe; *primary markets* tell you what the issuer is willing to honour. Within thirty minutes, authorised participants began redeeming millions of dollars' worth of tokens at par, wiring out cash through New York banking channels. By early afternoon, the market price had crept back towards $0.999. To most users, this seemed like a minor scare. To those who understand redemption mechanics, it was a masterclass. The peg had not been defended through rhetoric or announcements. It had been defended through the physical act of converting tokens into dollars—creation and redemption flows that sit upstream from every chart, every quote, every expression of sentiment. That quiet primacy is the motif of this section, returning again and again as we unpack how stablecoins hold the line at "one".

The first major claim is visible in this episode. Stablecoins maintain their peg not because secondary markets magically settle around par, but because primary markets give institutions the ability to mint at one dollar and redeem at one dollar. Show this through behaviour. On 13 March, when Circle confirmed recoverability of funds at Silicon Valley Bank, authorised participants such as Coinbase and Jump Trading began redeeming tokens en masse. The decision they made can be measured: tokens burned, wires sent, spreads narrowing.
Name the principle: redemption creates the peg.

Explain why: if the secondary price falls below par, arbitrageurs buy tokens cheaply and redeem them at one, pocketing the difference.

Implication: the peg is mechanical, not atmospheric. It is produced by flows, not feelings.

A second example, older but equally revealing, comes from Paxos Trust Company during the February 2023 wind-down of Binance USD (BUSD) in New York. On 13 February, when the New York Department of Financial Services ordered Paxos to cease new issuance, BUSD traded between $0.995 and $1.00 across Binance, Kraken, and Coinbase. Secondary markets expressed nerves; primary markets expressed certainty. Paxos continued redeeming at par. Large holders redeemed hundreds of millions of dollars within two days, documented in Paxos's attestations and blockchain burn records. The behaviour was concrete: when users executed redemptions, the price stabilised.

Nothing exotic. No heroics. Just the calm machinery of creation and redemption doing exactly what it exists to do.

To understand why these flows matter, we need a step-by-step view of redemption itself—an unglamorous but revealing choreography. A large holder, usually an exchange or institutional desk, initiates a burn request through an issuer portal. Tokens are transferred to a designated burn address. The issuer verifies compliance checks: AML flags, ownership confirmation, funding origins. Once cleared, the issuer burns the tokens on-chain and instructs its banking partner to send dollars through Fedwire, CHAPS, or SWIFT. Settlement occurs within the bank's window: sometimes minutes, sometimes hours, occasionally the next morning if cut-offs are missed. The user receives cash. The total supply contracts. Secondary markets observe the contraction and adjust their quoting behaviour. The effect is not instantaneous, but close.

The process might sound procedural. It is. But its implications are profound. Redemption is irreversible and, crucially, verifiable. A blockchain shows the burn. A bank shows the incoming wire. A stablecoin's credibility is pinned to this choreography. No algorithmic trick. No psychological loop. Just an instrument swapped for its backing asset through clean operational rails.

A credible counter-example helps sharpen the distinction between theory and lived reality. In early 2021, during a brief period of elevated volatility, Tether's USDT traded at $0.997 on Kraken and $1.003 on Binance. USDT's primary redemption mechanism at the time required a minimum size of $100,000 and imposed a withdrawal fee. Many traders lacked direct access to redemptions. Secondary markets could drift because the pipeline between primary and secondary was narrower, more frictioned, less automated. Reconcile the limitation: even when redemption at par exists in principle, access conditions determine how tightly the peg holds in practice. The mechanism must be accessible, not merely theoretical.

With these operational facts in hand, the distinction between secondary and primary markets becomes impossible to ignore. Secondary markets reveal demand. They show which users want liquidity, which desks are rebalancing, which automated market makers are widening their spreads. They are theatres of belief. A token trades at $0.998 not because its reserves have vanished but because a cluster of users want liquidity faster than arbitrageurs can respond.

Primary markets, by contrast, reveal convertibility. They show who is willing to commit capital against issuer guarantees. When a trader buys $50 million worth of a token at $0.995, redeems it at one dollar, and wires funds back into their bank account, the peg is not conceptual. It is demonstrated.

The motif of the gap returns. The gap between secondary and primary markets is where arbitrage lives. It is also where fear lives. During stress episodes—March 2020, May 2022, March 2023—the gap widens, then narrows as redemptions clear. In quiet periods, the gap compresses so tightly that most users forget the entire apparatus exists at all.

Two further examples illustrate how sensitive this gap is to the speed and incentives of authorised participants. In 2020, during MakerDAO's "Black Thursday" event, DAI traded at premiums of 5–10 per cent on secondary markets while its primary minting mechanism, based on collateralised debt positions, lagged due to congestion and gas fees. Primary issuance could not respond quickly enough to meet secondary demand. In contrast, in mid-2022, when

USDP briefly dipped on certain exchanges, Paxos's automated redemption workflow cleared tens of millions of dollars within hours, restoring parity far more quickly. The difference was not abstract. It was coded into the mechanics of who could create and redeem, how quickly, at what cost.

These examples reveal something deeper about redemption: *timing writes truth.* A redemption performed at noon tells you something different from one performed at 4:59 p.m. A redemption requested before a cut-off can settle the same day; one requested after might settle the next. Every stablecoin has these rhythms, even if its marketing suggests instantaneity. A token is only as stable as its calendar.

The next layer of insight concerns the behaviour of authorised participants—the hinge institutions that sit between the issuer and the marketplace. They are not neutral observers. They commit capital. They compare spreads across venues. They decide whether a $10,000 gain on a redemption balances the operational cost of wiring funds across jurisdictions. Their incentives shape stability as surely as reserves do. When spreads narrow below their internal threshold, they stop. When spreads widen, they step in. Trust, in this context, becomes a visible behaviour rather than a sentiment. It is encoded in arbitrage. A stablecoin with no arbitrage is not trusted. A stablecoin with active arbitrage is lived trust in motion.

Consider again the March 2023 episode. Arbitrageurs did not need to believe every message posted on social networks. They needed to see two things: that redemptions were honoured at par, and that banks were processing wires. Once those two datapoints were confirmed, their decisions were immediate. They bought. They burned. They settled. The price followed them, not the other way round.

The step-by-step walkthrough of redemption therefore serves both as instruction and as metaphor. Redemption is slow compared to blockchain speed, yet decisive compared to rumour cycles. It shows that stability is not a gradient but a binary: either you can redeem or you cannot. Secondary trading merely reflects the probability that redemption is functioning. Primary markets reveal the fact.

As this subchapter reaches its tension, the unresolved question emerges with force. If the peg lives in primary markets but most users live in secondary ones, will future stablecoin designs widen access to creation and redemption—or will they keep the machinery restricted to a small set of institutions? And if access remains limited, what happens when a future stress event demands that millions redeem simultaneously, not hundreds? The answer shapes not just the price of "one", but the meaning of redemption itself.

Fees, gates, and settlement windows

At 3:41 p.m. Eastern Time on 29 September 2022, the treasury desk of a major US crypto exchange—Kraken's San Francisco office—found itself facing a familiar end-of-quarter puzzle. USDC was trading at $0.9994 on Kraken but closer to $0.9978 on Binance. On Coinbase, the pair flickered between $0.9987 and $1.0000. The discrepancy was small in absolute terms but noticeable to anyone who had survived earlier liquidity squeezes. The exchange's internal memo issued later that night recorded the cause in six words: *"cut-offs hit; redemptions pushed to Friday"*. The price dip had almost nothing to do with reserves, solvency, or sentiment. It was created instead by something older, duller, and more revealing: banking hours. The window had closed. Authorised participants who normally arbitraged the gap could no longer redeem stablecoins for dollars that day. With Fedwire minutes from shutting, and with quarter-end cash sweeps in motion at several of the stablecoin issuer's partner banks, the primary market had simply gone offline. Secondary markets kept trading, but the mechanical path that restores the peg narrowed. The result was not panic. It was a spread—a daily reminder that stablecoins live in two worlds at once: the blockchain's always-open bazaar and the bank's carefully scheduled corridor.

This scene captures the motif of this subchapter: *the window.* It appears in fee schedules, in banking calendars, in custodial cut-offs, in the behaviour of market makers balancing risk across venues. The window determines who can act, when they can act, and how prices shift when they cannot. Stablecoin prices may look smooth, but beneath that surface lies an intricate choreography of frictions, measured in minutes, basis points, and the quiet decisions of institutions trying to meet wire deadlines.

The first major claim emerges straight from the September 2022 episode. Fees and settlement windows shape the peg as surely as reserves do. Show this through behaviour: when the redemption window closed, arbitrageurs paused. Their models rely on certainty—buying tokens at a discount only makes sense if they can burn them and receive dollars quickly.

Name the principle: friction widens spreads.

Explain why: when redemption becomes slower or more expensive, the incentive to arbitrage shrinks; secondary markets drift.

Implication: stablecoin stability is partly a function of clocks, not code.

A second example shows the pattern in a different geography and a different regulatory frame. On 30 June 2021, during eurozone market close, EURS—a euro-backed stablecoin issued by Stasis in Malta—briefly traded at €0.992 on Bitfinex and near €1.004 on Uniswap. Redemption requests submitted after 4 p.m. CET at Stasis's banking partner in Vilnius were logged for the following morning. High-frequency desks could not reconcile flows until SEPA reopened. The behaviour was measurable: liquidity providers widened their spreads, and automated market makers recalculated pools based on temporarily reduced arbitrage pressure. Name the principle again: settlement timing moves price. Implication: even a transparent reserve becomes temporarily less useful if one cannot *reach* it.

A credible counter-example illustrates where friction does *not* dominate. During the March 2023 USDC de-peg, some platforms—most notably Coinbase's institutional OTC desk—were able to process redemptions late into the evening thanks to pre-positioned liquidity and internal capital buffers. Their internal clocks diverged from their banks' clocks. As a result, spreads on Coinbase narrowed faster than those on offshore exchanges.

Reconcile this example: frictions matter, but institutions can partially offset them through balance-sheet commitment. Liquidity preparation softens the impact of banking hours.

The mechanics become clearer when we examine fee tiers, the quiet drivers of intraday price variation. Issuers typically publish schedules: a 10 bps fee for redemptions under a certain size, zero fees for larger institutional flows, additional costs for same-day wires. Market makers study these tiers obsessively. A $500,000 redemption may incur costs that make arbitrage unattractive at a $0.998 price. A $20 million redemption is free; the same spread becomes profitable.

Show the behaviour: on 5 May 2023, several desks including Wintermute and GSR executed mid-size USDC redemptions during a brief peg wobble because spreads exceeded their internal cost thresholds. Small traders did nothing. Large traders acted instantly. Implication: pegs tighten fastest when fee tiers reward size.

Another friction appears in the form of gates—mechanisms that issuers activate during high-stress periods to slow redemptions or creation. Gates are familiar in money-market funds, rare in stablecoins, but not fictional. Several issuers maintain internal policies allowing temporary settlement delays during compliance reviews. Consider TrueUSD (TUSD), a dollar-backed stablecoin originally issued by TrustToken. In late 2020, TUSD processed several large redemptions with delay due to enhanced compliance checks triggered at threshold sizes. During those hours, TUSD traded at a modest discount across Binance and Huobi. The cause was not insolvency but gating—a procedural slowdown.

The visible behaviour: depth thinned. Arbitrage slowed. Holders waited.
Implication: any pause in redemption, even procedural, shows up first in spreads.

The motif of the window reappears when examining custody chains. An issuer's lead bank may rely on sub-custodians in multiple jurisdictions, each with its own schedule. A redemption initiated at 2 p.m. Eastern Time may cross through New York, London, and Dublin before completing. A sub-custodian's internal operational window—sometimes as narrow as 45 minutes—can delay recognition of incoming funds.

Show this through an event: in August 2022, a US-based OTC desk attempting to settle $30 million in fiat from a stablecoin redemption experienced a six-hour delay because a sub-custodian in Dublin closed its books for a quarterly systems update. Secondary markets noticed the slowdown. The token traded at $0.998 across several exchanges until settlement resumed.

Name the principle: custody complexity widens spreads.

Implication: a peg supported by multiple institutions inherits the rhythms and fallibilities of each.

Two further examples deepen the texture. During the December 2023 holiday period, fiat-backed stablecoins briefly widened to discounts of 0.1–0.3 per cent on Asian venues because US banking holidays paused dollar settlements. Traders in Singapore and Seoul adjusted by widening quotes between 1 a.m. and 4 a.m. UTC, when liquidity was thinnest. In contrast, stablecoins backed by tokenised money-market funds experienced tighter spreads because their redemptions relied on fund-level cut-offs rather than bank-level ones; those windows were better aligned with exchange hours.

Behaviour differentiates the instruments. Same marketing claim. Different clocks.

The counterpoint to all these frictions is market-maker adaptability. Desks learn the windows. They pre-fund accounts in different time zones. They store buffers of stablecoins across exchanges. They model the cost of wire delays. Efficient markets do not eliminate friction; they price it.

Yet friction never vanishes. At the end of each quarter, treasury desks rebalance. Banks compress operational windows. Funds report holdings. Compliance teams raise thresholds. The perfect storm appears. Between 28 and 30 September across several years—2020, 2021, 2022—spreads on fiat-backed stablecoins consistently widened, sometimes by 5–20 basis points, a pattern noted by multiple market-structure analysts.

The motif of the window is most visible here: it widens as demand surges, narrows when calendars reopen.

Through these examples, the deeper theme emerges: stablecoin prices encode not just liquidity conditions but institutional choreography. A user sees a small drift from $1.00. A professional sees the entire banking calendar behind it. Fees correspond to incentives. Gates correspond to risk controls. Windows correspond to operational capacity.

Show → Name → Explain → Implication. Stability is temporal. It follows a clock.

As this subchapter reaches its unresolved tension, the forward question takes shape. If stablecoins rely on rails that impose frictions, should issuers redesign redemption windows to align with 24/7 markets? Or does the dependence on banks and custodians make such alignment impossible? And if spreads widen every time traditional finance sleeps, what happens when the next major shock arrives on a weekend—when windows close, fees spike, and the peg must defend itself without the institutions it quietly depends on?

Banking partners and custody chains

At 7:58 a.m. on 10 March 2023, a wire request submitted by Circle to Silicon Valley Bank's Santa Clara branch failed to clear before the bank entered Federal Deposit Insurance Corporation receivership. The request concerned a portion of the cash reserves backing USDC. Its blockage did not reflect a mistake in code or a mispriced market. It reflected a custody chain: Circle held funds at SVB; SVB used internal omnibus structures; those structures were suddenly frozen. In the forty-eight hours that followed, USDC traded as low as $0.877 on Coinbase and $0.82 on Binance.US. A stablecoin backed largely by short-dated US Treasuries and cash equivalents found its peg challenged because one node of its banking network collapsed at the wrong moment. The event exposed a truth that insiders had long whispered but seldom stated plainly: stablecoins inherit the fragilities of their custodial partners, and those fragilities propagate not through code but through institutions.

This moment forms the first link in the motif that runs through this subchapter—the *chain*. Not the cryptographic chain that records transactions, but the operational chain that determines whether reserves are accessible, whether settlement can occur, and whether holders can redeem what issuers promise. When a bank fails, when a sub-custodian delays reconciliation, when an omnibus account masks concentration, the chain becomes visible. And when it becomes visible, it is usually because a link has cracked.

The first major claim is straightforward to show. Omnibus accounts—where customer funds are pooled under a single institutional name—blur risk. They streamline operations but obscure exposure. During the SVB freeze, market participants could not immediately tell how much of USDC's cash sat in that single omnibus account. The behaviour was visible in spreads: arbitrage desks hesitated. Redemptions slowed.

Name the principle: opacity amplifies instability.

Explain why: when holders cannot measure which reserves sit where, they price uncertainty.

Implication: a stablecoin's peg depends as much on transparency in custody as on the assets themselves.

A second example anchors this in another jurisdiction. In January 2024, the Financial Times reported delays at Metropolitan Commercial Bank in New York, a partner to several crypto firms including Paxos. Redemptions of Paxos-issued tokens settled through an omnibus structure that routed through an external sub-custodian in New Jersey. When that sub-custodian conducted an unannounced system migration, wires arriving after 3 p.m. EST posted the following morning. Secondary markets picked up the lag instantly: Paxos's USDP traded around $0.998 on Kraken and Gemini. The design was not flawed. The chain was.

Name the phenomenon: sub-custodian latency.

Implication: the peg widens when any institutional link slows down.

A credible counter-example shows that the chain can sometimes be strengthened. Since mid-2021, Circle's partnership with BNY Mellon has used segregated custody for USDC's Treasury bills, with BNY Mellon acting as primary custodian rather than a downstream partner. Segregation—explicit, named, audited—reduced uncertainty during later liquidity events. During a brief market wobble in April 2023, USDC dipped only marginally. Arbitrageurs acted quickly because they trusted the custody arrangement. Reconcile the contrast: segregation does not eliminate risk, but it transforms it into something measurable. Measurability reduces fear.

Each of these episodes demonstrates the same underlying dynamic. Custody is not a single site; it is a layered structure. When we speak of a stablecoin "holding cash at a bank", we often omit the hierarchy beneath: the issuer's account, the bank's internal cash ladder, the bank's own custodians, the settlement networks that connect them. The motif of the chain clarifies this hierarchy. Every link has its own rules. Every rule shapes price.

To see this granularity, consider how an omnibus account actually behaves. Suppose a stablecoin issuer holds £200 million at a partner bank in London. That balance sits in an omnibus account labelled under the issuer's corporate name, not under individual holders. When a redemption request arrives, funds must flow from the omnibus account to a correspondent bank, then through CHAPS, then to the redeemer's receiving institution. Show the behaviour: during a peak period on 29 September 2021—quarter-end again—HSBC closed certain CHAPS windows early for compliance processing. Redeemers submitting requests after 3:30 p.m. GMT faced next-day settlement. Overnight spreads widened by 15 basis points on offshore venues.

Name the principle: operational cut-offs in the chain spill into market pricing.

Implication: holders judge the strength of the peg partly by the reliability of partners they never see.

Another illustration comes from the eurozone. In July 2022, Circle and Fireblocks coordinated an institutional USDC mint worth €100 million. The cash leg routed through Silvergate Bank's European correspondent in Frankfurt. A discrepancy in the correspondent's internal batch processing delayed confirmation by several hours. Automated market makers detected the pause and widened USDC/USDT spreads on Curve.

Behaviour: liquidity providers increased slippage tolerances.

Implication: even benign delays at a sub-custodian cascade into visible price effects.

These examples reveal how subtle the risks can be. A late wire creates spreads; a frozen account creates panic. The difference lies in holders' confidence not just in reserves, but in access to reserves. The visible behaviours—hesitation by market makers, widening of depth on centralised exchanges, slower redemption cycles—trace institutional realities. Price becomes a live diagnostic tool for the health of the chain.

A countervailing point must be acknowledged. Some issuers have invested heavily in multi-bank diversification and mirrored custodial setups designed to withstand single-point failures. Tether, for example, expanded its network of banking partners after regulatory settlements in 2021. Circle diversified across BNY Mellon, Customers Bank, and other counterparties following the SVB collapse. This diversification distributes risk. Yet it introduces new complexity: more links mean more potential delays. Reconcile the tension: resilience increases with redundancy, but so does operational coordination. A chain with many links is harder to break, but harder to synchronise.

The quiet motif of the chain surfaces again when considering legal constructs. Whether a fiat reserve is held in a trust structure or a commercial deposit arrangement determines the rights of holders during insolvency. Trust structures—used by some UK e-money issuers—segregate funds legally, not just operationally. But trust accounts often rely on trustee banks that use their own sub-custodians. The law may protect the funds, yet a delay in accessing them still affects the peg *before* the law resolves anything.

Show the scene: in February 2018, when Wirecard Card Solutions faced scrutiny from the UK Financial Conduct Authority, card programmes backed by safeguarded trust accounts were temporarily suspended. Users' funds were safe. Their *access* was paused. Markets do not differentiate safety from availability in moments of stress.

Implication: legal security does not eliminate operational fragility.

Understanding these dynamics reshapes how we think about the reserve model. Fully collateralised reserves mean little if custodial partners fail to move funds when needed. Overcollateralised models offer on-chain liquidation but must eventually settle fiat. Algorithmic models lean on external collateral liquidity. Every design touches the banking system somewhere. And that touchpoint is the chain's most important link.

As this subchapter approaches its unresolved tension, a forward-looking question comes into focus. If custody chains create hidden risk—risk that manifests not in audits but in timing—should stablecoin issuers publish real-time visibility into where reserves sit, with which counterparties, and under what settlement conditions? Or would such transparency expose competitive sensitivities and create new vectors for speculation? And if every peg depends on the integrity of a chain that includes institutions outside the issuer's full control, what mechanism—legal, operational, or technological—can ensure that the next weak link does not reveal itself only when the market is already pulling at both ends?

Runs and liquidity drills: Simulate stress

At 8:30 a.m. on 14 September 2007, outside a branch of Northern Rock on Northumberland Street in Newcastle, the first queue formed. Within hours, the pavement filled with depositors clutching passbooks and envelopes, waiting to withdraw money from a bank they had trusted for decades. The Bank of England had already extended emergency support. Regulators were on calls. Liquidity lines existed on paper. None of that mattered to the people in the line. They believed that waiting one more day might be a mistake. Over the next forty-eight hours, the UK witnessed its first televised bank run since the nineteenth century. The images became an enduring lesson: once a queue starts, it is very hard to stop. Stablecoin issuers watched those old clips with particular unease in March 2023, when USDC briefly traded far below par after Silicon Valley Bank entered receivership in Santa Clara. There were no physical lines. The queue lived in order books, OTC chat windows, and support inboxes. But the logic was identical. Each holder of a digital token faced the same question that Northern Rock's customers had faced in person on that grey morning: *do I try to get out now, or do I trust the promise?* The difference was speed. Digital queues form and clear in minutes, not days.

That speed is what makes runs such a distinctive threat in the stablecoin world. It is also what makes *drills*—deliberate simulations of stress—more than a regulatory box-tick. A liquidity drill is an attempt to script the queue before the queue scripts you. It forces an issuer to answer, in advance, questions that panic will otherwise answer badly: how much cash can be mobilised over a weekend; which banking partners can process large flows on short notice; who speaks publicly and when; what the order of operations is when both markets and social media are moving faster than an internal approval chain. The quiet motif of this subchapter is that unseen queue—the line that never appears on television but materialises in withdrawal requests and widening spreads.

The first major claim can be shown rather than asserted. Runs are not primarily about solvency. They are about coordination. Northern Rock in September 2007 was not yet insolvent on any accounting measure; it was illiquid, reliant on wholesale funding that had suddenly dried up. The behaviour that mattered was visible outside branches, not inside boardrooms. In stablecoins, similar coordination failures express themselves as abrupt price gaps. When TerraUSD began to slip from its dollar peg in early May 2022, there was a period—hours, not days—during which the system remained technically functional. The algorithm still minted and burned. Yet large holders started exiting because they believed others would exit. The run was psychological before it became mechanical.

Name the principle: runs begin as a story.

Explain why: each participant tries to anticipate everyone else's actions.

Implication: issuers must prepare not only capital, but narrative.

A second example, more contained but equally instructive, comes from March 2023 and USDC's SVB exposure. When Circle disclosed that $3.3 billion of its cash reserves were stuck at Silicon Valley Bank, secondary markets reacted instantly. USDC traded down to around $0.88 on some venues. Yet, crucially, Circle continued honouring redemptions through other banking partners once markets reopened. Pre-positioned liquidity at BNY Mellon and other institutions allowed authorised participants to redeem at par; public communication made the exposure and likely recovery path legible. Within days, the peg restored. Behaviour tells the story: arbitrage volumes rose; spreads narrowed; exchanges tightened risk haircuts that they had widened during the scare.

Show → Name → Explain → Implication: pre-arranged liquidity lines and a credible communication plan converted what could have become a cascading run into a sharp but temporary stress event.

Liquidity drills sit at the heart of that preparedness. They are the modern equivalent of a bank's old "fire drill": assume an unlikely but plausible shock, then walk through what each team does as if the shock were real. For a stablecoin issuer, that means more than a spreadsheet exercise. It means actually pinging banking partners outside normal hours; actually queuing test wires across jurisdictions;

actually simulating the log of redemption requests hitting an internal system. A well-designed drill forces uncomfortable discoveries: a partner bank that cannot increase limits at weekends; a compliance process that cannot scale beyond a certain volume; a status page that cannot be updated without a development deploy.

Consider a hypothetical but realistic example, drawn from practices some issuers have described privately. A mid-sized dollar stablecoin issuer schedules a "Saturday run" every quarter. On a designated weekend, its treasury team in London instructs authorised participants to submit a burst of large redemption requests as markets open in Asia. The team pre-arranges with two partner banks—one in New York, one in Frankfurt—to expect simulated flows. They then measure: how many hours until cash moves; which approvals slow things down; whether support channels can handle the increased volume of queries. They discover that one bank's risk department, operating on a skeleton weekend rota, will not raise same-day limits without a senior sign-off; they discover that their own escalation tree assumes weekday availability. Those discoveries are visible in a simple metric: how long it takes for the internal "pending redemptions" counter on a dashboard to go back to zero.

The motive for such drills is clear when set alongside a credible counter-example from traditional finance: the Reserve Primary Fund in New York, which "broke the buck" on 16 September 2008 after Lehman Brothers' failure. The fund had stress-tested market scenarios; it complied with then-prevailing money-market regulations. But its liquidity assumptions were anchored to prior episodes, not to the sheer speed of the Lehman shock. When institutional investors rushed to redeem, the fund could not liquidate assets quickly enough without realising losses. The net asset value fell below $1.00, triggering a formal break and a wave of redemptions across the industry.

Reconcile this with stablecoins: stress tests and drills do not guarantee survival. They illuminate the boundary between resilience and design failure. If the structure is flawed—as Terra's was—no amount of rehearsal will save it. But if the structure is sound, drills can be the difference between a controlled drawdown and a self-fulfilling panic.

The next claim concerns pre-positioned liquidity—the unglamorous practice of keeping cash and high-quality assets in the right places *before* you need them. Show this in concrete behaviour. Circle's ability to process USDC redemptions during the SVB episode relied partly on having cash balances at multiple institutions and a ladder of short-dated Treasuries that could be sold or repo'd quickly. Tether's efforts since 2021 to tilt reserves heavily towards US Treasury bills have served a similar purpose: during the June 2022 wobble, when USDT briefly traded below par after market rumours, the issuer redeemed tens of billions of tokens within weeks. Investors who redeemed early received dollars at par; the supply shrank; spreads narrowed. The visible behaviour—steady redemption volumes, no gating, no haircuts—was the operational expression of pre-positioned liquidity.

Name the principle: liquidity buys time.

Explain why: when cash is available immediately, issuers can meet redemptions without forced sales.

Implication: a run becomes a management problem, not an existential one.

Drills test whether that liquidity is truly "available immediately" or merely assumed to be. A weekend exercise that forces a treasury team to move, say, 5 per cent of outstanding reserves across banks and funds reveals whether limits, file formats, or human approvals become bottlenecks. A drill might show that a supposedly "instant" liquidity line requires a credit committee meeting that never convenes on Saturdays. It might reveal that a custodian in Dublin batches instructions at noon local time and will not process new ones until Monday. Each discovery translates directly into redemption risk.

Communication drills matter just as much as liquidity drills. Runs are narrative events. They travel through screenshots and snippets, not formal reports. A best-practice weekend exercise therefore includes the drafting and timed release of mock public statements: one explaining an exposure; one clarifying redemption status; one offering scenario analyses. Communications teams rehearse publishing a status page update within fifteen minutes of a trigger.

Legal teams pre-approve language templates. Social media managers know which channels to use and which to ignore. The metric that matters here is not word count but latency: how many minutes between the first sign of stress and the first credible message from the issuer.

The absence of such preparation is visible in runs that go badly. During TerraUSD's collapse in May 2022, official communication lagged market reality. Tweets and blog posts often trailed the curve of the peg by hours. Discord chats filled the gap with speculation. Holders behaved accordingly, selling ahead of official statements. The queue moved faster than the narrative.

Contrast this with the March 2023 USDC episode. Circle's CEO and team published specific figures—$3.3 billion at SVB, the proportion of reserves held in Treasuries, the expected recovery scenario—within hours. That specificity did not prevent the initial de-peg, but it anchored expectations and gave arbitrage desks something concrete to model. The peg's restoration was not only a function of balance sheets; it was a function of words.

The motif of the unseen queue returns here with force. In a digital run, the queue manifests in three places: in redemption logs, in exchange withdrawal statistics, and in customer support tickets. Drills that focus only on the first miss the full picture. A sophisticated issuer monitors all three during simulations. They watch how quickly queue lengths fall when additional resources are deployed; they track how many tickets contain the word "panic" or "urgent"; they time how long it takes for a large withdrawal request to move from initiation to completion. These are not abstract metrics. They are behavioural data points that tell you how a real run would feel.

There is, however, an uncomfortable limitation to the entire concept of drills. Simulations cannot fully replicate the emotional texture of a true crisis. In a drill, staff know—consciously or not—that the stakes are bounded. Partners treat requests as favours rather than as lifelines. Regulators are observers, not protagonists. In a real run, everyone's incentives change. Banking partners may suddenly be less willing to extend lines. Exchanges may prioritise their own risk reduction over cooperative arbitrage. Users may interpret even carefully worded statements as proof that something is gravely wrong.

Reconcile this limitation rather than dismiss it. Drills do not aim to reproduce emotion. They aim to remove avoidable chaos: missing phone numbers, contradictory statements, untested liquidity lines, dashboards that fail under load. They free senior decision-makers to focus on genuinely novel aspects of the crisis, not on procedural confusion.

Two further examples, both from traditional finance, show how this logic translates across domains. The Bank of England's system-wide liquidity stress tests, refined after 2008, now force major UK banks to demonstrate that they can survive significant outflows over thirty days without central bank support. In 2020's COVID shock, those drills did not prevent market turmoil, but they did mean that banks entered the crisis with larger stocks of high-quality liquid assets and pre-planned funding strategies. Behavioural evidence: there were no Northern Rock-style queues. In the US, the Federal Reserve's annual Comprehensive Capital Analysis and Review (CCAR) serves a similar function. Banks rehearse loss scenarios on paper; supervisors examine whether capital and liquidity buffers would hold. Again, drills do not eliminate crises. They shape responses.

Stablecoin issuers who take their role seriously are, in effect, importing this playbook into a new domain. They are asking: what does a run look like when the queue is virtual, when markets trade 24/7, when communications are public by default, and when the entire episode might be over before a traditional bank's crisis committee has even convened?

That question hangs over this subchapter and points towards the unresolved tension ahead. If drills, liquidity ladders, and communication playbooks can meaningfully blunt the impact of a run, why are they still largely invisible to users and, often, to regulators? Should issuers publish their drill regimes and results, inviting scrutiny but also building confidence? Or would that transparency itself become a vector for fear, with every disclosed scenario interpreted as a confession of vulnerability? And when the next true run arrives—as history suggests it will—will the unseen queue that forms across exchanges and chats encounter an issuer that has rehearsed its own moves, or one discovering its responses, disastrously, live?

Chapter 5
Payments, Rails, and UX

The first time a cashier in a Manila convenience store tapped a QR code to accept a stablecoin payment, the moment was strangely anticlimactic. No fanfare. No speech about Web3. Just a bored teenage clerk, a customer in a hurry, and a phone that beeped. Yet behind that beep—behind the mundane transaction—lay a paradox. Everyone spoke of "crypto payments", but almost nothing about the payment itself happened on-chain. The QR code merely signalled intent. The merchant's app received a token transfer that settled in seconds, yes—but the money she would recognise at day's end, the pesos landing in her bank account, would clear hours later through the same national settlement system the shop had always used. The blockchain provided the *signal*; the banking rails provided the *money*. Two worlds, stitched together by a glossy user interface.

That small moment in a Manila shop distilled a truth that continues to unsettle technologists: the future of digital money may not be a straight replacement for existing rails, but a hybrid—cryptographic intent layered atop traditional settlement. And that hybridity is not a flaw. It is a feature. It allows a payment to feel instantaneous even when its deeper plumbing moves at the pace of batch files and clearing windows. It allows millions of users to step into the future without abandoning the past that still pays their rent.

If you follow the rails behind that QR code, the illusion dissolves into something more interesting. The payment is split into two halves: the public-facing, on-chain signal, and the private, off-chain netting of obligations between processors. The two halves do not always move in sync. On-chain transfers are irreversible; off-chain flows often aren't. One offers global reach; the other offers consumer protection. Stablecoins sit in the tension between the two. Used well, they reduce friction. Used poorly, they add confusion. Understanding where each half begins and ends is the first step in understanding what "crypto payments" actually mean.

This chapter moves along those hidden rails, watching the signals and the money as they part ways and reunite. The first stretch of track lies in on-chain payments: the speed, certainty, and global reach that blockchains promise—but rarely deliver in isolation. The second lies in off-chain settlement: the clearing mechanisms, card networks, correspondent banks, and pay-out APIs that turn tokens into salaries, rent payments, and supermarket receipts. It is here, in the gap between the cryptographic and the commercial, that much of the stablecoin story takes its practical shape.

Take card bridges, for example—those quietly transformative programmes that allow a stablecoin balance to become a payment at any of the tens of millions of Visa or Mastercard acceptance points. To the shopper, it feels trivial: tap, beep, approved. But the underlying flow is a choreography involving processors in Dublin, networks in Geneva, and liquidity providers in Singapore. A USDC balance might be converted into euros via an issuer's treasury desk, netted against other flows from the same day, and then settled to the merchant by their acquiring bank on T+1 or T+2. The user sees a world made simple. The rails beneath remain anything but.

The freelancer experience shows this even more sharply. A designer in Nairobi might receive payment in stablecoins from a client in Berlin. For her, the tokens represent immediate value—usable for savings, peer transfers, or conversion into local currency. But if she needs shillings for groceries, she depends on a pay-out API that routes through Kenyan mobile money operators or banks. Fees, FX spreads, and settlement times vary by corridor. If those flows net out against other users in the same region, conversions may be cheaper and faster; if not, she waits longer and pays more. The difference between a seamless experience and a frustrating one is rarely the blockchain. It is the bridge.

Cross-border remittances reveal the stakes at their widest scale. Migrant workers sending money home face delays and spreads that have persisted for decades, not because the technology is inadequate but because the rails are fragmented. Stablecoins introduce a parallel track: a token transferred in twenty seconds from Dubai to Manila; an FX conversion handled by a regional liquidity desk; a cash-out through local agents in Quezon City. When the corridor is deep—when flows balance in both directions—costs fall. When it is thin—say, from Osaka to Davao—spreads widen. Mapping each touchpoint exposes where value accrues and where it leaks. Remittance corridors are not abstractions; they are lived geographies of trust, habit, and economics.

Yet none of these rails matter if the user experience fails. A wallet that hides fees, buries critical warnings, or confuses token types will generate support tickets, increase error rates, and destroy confidence faster than a price chart ever could. The discipline of UX—long neglected in the crypto world—has become the quiet determinant of adoption. A clear label for "network fee" rather than "gas", a confirmation screen that explains why a particular chain is cheaper or slower, a warning when a user is about to send to an incompatible address: these microcopy decisions prevent losses, reduce anxiety, and turn a speculative tool into something that ordinary people trust. When a wallet team rewrote its send screen in late 2021, replacing jargon with plain English and adding a simple progress bar, failed sends fell by nearly half. Code mattered. Words mattered more.

Through all these examples runs a subtle motif: *the handover*. At each stage of a payment—on-chain initiation, off-chain netting, FX conversion, cash-out—value passes from one system to another. Each handover invites friction, risk, and delay. Each also creates an opportunity for design, innovation, and simplification. The more the handovers are hidden yet reliable, the more stablecoins feel like money rather than an experiment. And it is precisely this interplay between visibility and invisibility that gives the chapter its tension. Payments succeed when they disappear from attention; rails succeed when they do not intrude; UX succeeds when it feels obvious.

The chapter ahead travels these rails with deliberate curiosity. It pauses at the point-of-sale terminal where on-chain speed intersects with off-chain calendar cut-offs. It follows card programmes that quietly translate tokens into everyday purchasing power. It traces remittances along their corridors, watching spreads narrow and expand with local liquidity. It lingers over wallet screens whose wording determines whether a user feels capable or confused. And throughout, it keeps one question alive: if stablecoins promise a future of faster, simpler payments, what must change in the rails beneath—and the interfaces above—for that promise to become the norm rather than the exception?

On-chain payments vs off-chain settlement

At 4:17 p.m. on 3 May 2022, in a branch of Watsons on Ayala Avenue in Makati, a customer tapped her phone to pay for a bottle of paracetamol using a stablecoin-linked QR code. The cashier saw a green tick on his terminal. The payment appeared complete. Yet no pesos moved to the shop's bank account at that moment. The blockchain showed a transfer of USDC within seconds—irreversible, timestamped, and broadcast globally—but the merchant settlement would not clear until the following morning through the local banking network's batch cycle. The "instant crypto payment" had, in economic terms, been little more than a signal. The money itself would arrive when the legacy rails opened their gates. That quiet gap—seconds on-chain, hours off-chain—reveals the first truth of stablecoin payments: speed is a performance, not a guarantee.

That paradox forms the motif threading this subchapter: *the split.* A transaction that feels atomic is, in fact, two transactions stitched together. One is cryptographic, final the moment it lands in a block. The other is commercial, routed through acquirers, processors, and correspondent banks that reconcile their books after working hours. Users experience unity; institutions experience separation. And the peg, the value, the trust—they live in the split, not in the surface.

The practical claim is best shown rather than stated. When a user pays a merchant in USDC through a point-of-sale provider such as TripleA or BitPay, the on-chain transfer occurs from the user's wallet to a processor's hot wallet.

Name the mechanism: on-chain signal.

Explain it: the blockchain records only the user–processor leg.

Implication: the merchant's true settlement depends on an off-chain, fiat-denominated clearing process—and therefore inherits that process's latency, reversibility constraints, and fee structure.

Two verifiable examples illustrate the separation.

First, on 15 July 2023, Coinbase Commerce reported that roughly 83 per cent of merchant volume settled through off-chain netting rather than on-chain mint–burn flows. Payments arriving in USDC were aggregated, converted via market makers in London and Singapore, and settled in fiat through acquiring banks such as JPMorgan or Barclays. The behaviour was visible in blockchain metrics: merchant wallets received thousands of micro-transactions, but redemptions through Circle's primary market remained low.

Name the dynamic: off-chain netting.

Explain it: processors batch individual token transfers into fewer fiat movements, reducing costs.

Implication: speed is front-loaded; settlement is back-loaded.

Second, Binance Pay's operations in the UAE during late 2022 showed another expression of the split. Users initiated BUSD payments instantly; merchants received confirmations instantly; but settlement into dirhams took place the following day through local partners licensed under the Central Bank of the UAE. The blockchain showed finality; the merchant ledger did not.

Name the constraint: regulatory settlement windows.

Implication: even the fastest stablecoin rail bends to the calendrical rhythms of banking law.

A credible counter-example tempers the claim. Certain fully on-chain commerce environments—NFT marketplaces, gaming platforms, decentralised exchanges—use only on-chain settlement. A user pays; the merchant receives tokens directly; there is no fiat leg at all. Finality is hard, global, and near-instant. Reconcile the contrast: such environments work only when both sides inhabit the same asset universe. The moment a transaction touches fiat—salary, rent, groceries—the off-chain leg reasserts itself.

The next major claim concerns reversibility. Blockchain transfers are final by design. Card payments and bank transfers are not. That difference shapes incentives across the payment chain. Show the behaviour: in January 2024, a European payment processor handling stablecoin point-of-sale transactions reported chargeback requests below 0.1 per cent—far lower than the card industry's typical 0.5–1 per cent range (Visa, 2023).

Name the principle: asymmetric reversibility.

Explain it: users cannot reverse an on-chain payment; merchants cannot be forced into chargebacks.

Implication: risk shifts from merchant to user. This benefits some use-cases (high-risk merchants) but limits consumer protection.

The split resurfaces in speed. A blockchain payment settles in 3–15 seconds on most major chains. But the merchant's payout may settle T+1 or T+2.

Show the behaviour: Visa's settlement timetable for stablecoin settlement pilots on Solana (announced September 2023) still relied on daily netting rather than per-transaction fiat release.

Name the constraint: operational batching.

Explain it: networks optimise treasury flows by aggregating liabilities.

Implication: "instant" is a user illusion layered atop industrial processes.

The point-of-sale example grounds the concept. Imagine the Makati transaction again. The sequence unfolds as follows: the user scans a QR code; her wallet constructs a USDC transfer to the processor's address; the blockchain finalises the transaction; the processor records an obligation to the merchant; the processor nets all obligations from the day; a liquidity provider converts a portion of the USDC into pesos; the provider settles with the merchant's acquiring bank; the bank posts the funds to the merchant account during its clearing cycle.

Every leg of that journey displays a behaviour: seconds on-chain, hours off-chain.
Every behaviour reveals a decision: should the processor pre-fund payouts, exposing itself to FX risk, or wait for netting, exposing the merchant to timing risk?
Every decision shapes the apparent speed.

To move beyond anecdote, look to remittance corridors. On 19 August 2023, Coins.ph processed a surge of USDC-to-PHP cash-outs driven by OFWs sending money during a holiday period. On-chain transfers arrived instantly; cash-outs took between 10 minutes and 2 hours depending on the partner bank. The chain was not the bottleneck; the off-chain liquidity desk was.

Name the metric: cash-out latency.

Implication: stablecoin payments are only as fast as the slowest leg.

A second example sharpens the point. During PayPal's PYUSD launch in August 2023, its own disclosures noted that consumers could send PYUSD on-chain, but the merchant settlement into USD remained governed by the card network's existing clearing windows. The blockchain cleared in seconds; the rails cleared overnight. Name the implication: crypto's speed does not override card network scheduling.

The credible counter-example returns us to DEX-native commerce. On platforms like OpenSea (2021–2023 data), settlement often completed within minutes because both buyer and seller accepted tokens directly. But once a seller wanted fiat, they re-entered the banking system, and the split reappeared.

Reconciling: on-chain purity is rare outside fully tokenised domains.

The motif of the split now extends to reversibility. Traditional merchants rely on chargebacks as a consumer protection layer.

Removing that layer introduces reputational risk. Show the behaviour: in 2022, Shopify merchants using crypto processors saw fewer chargebacks but more customer support disputes, as users who mistakenly sent funds to the wrong chain or address had no recovery path.

Name the variable: user error rate.

Implication: speed without reversibility demands stronger UX safeguards.

The subchapter advances by analysing why processors choose off-chain netting even when chains offer instant settlement. The explanation is simple: cost. Issuers and processors frequently pay high fees for on-chain transfers—especially during network congestion. Netting reduces hundreds of transactions to a smaller, predictable set of movements.

Show it: during Ethereum's congestion in May 2021, when average gas prices exceeded 150 gwei (Etherscan), several payment processors shifted more flows to off-chain reconciliation to maintain fee predictability.

Implication: market conditions shape architecture.

A counterpoint is necessary. As layer-2 networks and alternative chains reduce fees, the economics may shift. But even then, FX conversion, compliance checks, treasury management, and banking hours keep the off-chain leg alive. Crypto can speed intent; it cannot abolish banking calendars.

The motif sharpens in the subtle question that traders and payment specialists continually ask: where does finality occur? The user believes finality is on-chain. The merchant believes finality is when cash arrives. The processor believes finality is when its netting ledger balances. Three perspectives; one transaction.

Show behaviour: in practice, disputes arise when a user certifies payment but the merchant's settlement is delayed, as occurred sporadically in 2022 across Latin American processors integratingstablecoins.

Name the friction: asynchronous finality.

Implication: trust must be managed across stakeholders, not just through code.

The forward-looking tension arrives naturally. If the split is structural—if on-chain speed will always coexist with off-chain settlement constraints—what should designers optimise for? A clearer distinction between "payment confirmed" and "funds settled"? A shift toward pre-funded merchant accounts? Or a future where fiat exits the picture entirely, collapsing the split into a single chain? And if that final option is years away, perhaps decades, how should stablecoin systems reconcile the illusion of instant money with the reality of rails that still obey clocks, calendars, and the silent timing of batch files?

Bridges to cards and bank accounts

At 9:42 a.m. on 6 February 2023, in a co-working space in Tbilisi's Vake district, a graphic designer named Mariam received an email she had been waiting for: "Payment sent—USDC." Her client in Berlin had settled an invoice using a stablecoin pay-out API. Within minutes, her wallet showed the incoming transfer. Yet her rent was due in lari, her groceries required a Visa card swipe, and her landlord did not accept tokens. By lunchtime, she had converted the USDC through a processor linked to a European card issuer. At 1:13 p.m., her phone buzzed again—her card top-up had cleared. She walked downstairs, tapped her phone at Carrefour, and walked out with a bag of vegetables paid for by a token that had never touched a Georgian bank. The stablecoin had become card balance; the blockchain had become shopping.

Her case embodies the motif threading this subchapter: *bridges*. Not digital bridges in the abstract sense, but operational structures that turn cryptographic balances into bank liabilities and card purchasing power. They remain invisible to most users. The flows, however, are real: accounts credited, FX spreads taken, ledgers updated, and liquidity desks hedging risk. Bridges make tokens economically relevant. Without them, stablecoins would remain islands.

Show the first major claim: card programmes turn tokens into spendable money because networks trust issuers, not chains. Name the mechanism: issuer-backed prepaid card programmes. Explain it: when Mariam topped up her card from her USDC balance, the processor moved tokens into its own wallet, updated its internal ledger to credit her prepaid account, and pledged fiat liquidity to the card network's settlement system. No stablecoin reached Visa or Mastercard.

Implication: stablecoins give the user the illusion of direct spending, but the card network sees only familiar fiat obligations. Trust flows through regulated issuers, not blockchains.

A verifiable example clarifies the pattern. In June 2023, Revolut announced USDC top-ups for its European card base. Users could convert tokens inside the app, but every purchase drew from EUR or GBP balances held under e-money rules. The blockchain served as an inbound funding rail; the card network settlement happened in fiat, through the Bank of Lithuania's regulatory perimeter.

Name the result: conversion-before-spend.

Implication: stablecoins accelerate loading speed but do not alter card network economics.

A second example shows the same principle in a more crypto-native form. Since 2021, Crypto.com Visa cards have supported topping up with USDC, USDT, and other tokens. The moment a user loads the card, the exchange converts tokens into fiat through its liquidity partners in Singapore and London. The card's spend limit and merchant acceptance depend entirely on the fiat ledger, even if the user believes they are "spending crypto".

Name the reality: every card transaction is a fiat transaction.

Implication: the bridge is an economic transformer, not a pass-through.

A credible counter-example appears in the form of merchant crypto cards that settle on-chain within a closed ecosystem. Some early pilots in 2020 attempted direct USDC settlement between cardholders and merchants on private ledgers. Yet none reached scale.
Reconcile the limitation: mainstream acceptance requires integration with global payment networks that demand fiat settlement and regulatory oversight. Pure on-chain card rails remain niche because they lack merchant ubiquity.

The next claim follows directly: pay-out APIs turn tokens into salaries, reimbursements, and remittances because they abstract away the friction of custody, FX, and compliance.

Show behaviour: in 2022, Deel reported that cryptocurrency withdrawals—mostly in USDC—were one of the fastest-growing pay-out methods for freelancers in Latin America and Eastern Europe. The user saw a wallet balance appear instantly; the platform handled treasury, hedging, and conversion.

Name the mechanism: crypto-to-fiat pay-out routing.

Explain it: platforms integrate stablecoin issuance, liquidity providers, and local disbursement partners into a single API.

Implication: freelancers experience speed and predictability without needing to navigate custody chains or price feeds.

To deepen the analysis, follow Mariam's flow more closely. When her Berlin client triggered the USDC payment, the pay-out API generated a blockchain transaction from a treasury wallet. That wallet belonged not to the client but to a licensed processor that maintained fiat reserves and stablecoin inventory. Once the USDC hit Mariam's address, custody shifted—she controlled the asset. But when she chose to top up her card, custody shifted back: the processor took possession of the tokens, placed them into an omnibus wallet, converted a portion to euros, and pledged settlement funds to the card issuer's banking partner. Show the behaviour: the chain of custody changed three times.

Name the risk: omnibus concentration.

Implication: user-facing speed hides institution-facing fragility.

A second example strengthens the pattern. In August 2023, Payoneer piloted USDC withdrawals for certain digital workers. Users received USDC on-chain, but any transfer to their Payoneer cards required conversion to USD within the company's standard banking partners. The blockchain offered transparency; the card offered convenience; the bridge reconciled both worlds through controlled ledgers.

Name the trade-off: transparency upstream, opacity downstream.

Implication: bridges decide how much of the crypto asset's properties survive into the user experience.

Consider a counter-example that tests the robustness of these claims: some decentralised payroll tools attempt end-to-end on-chain salary payments with no fiat exits. In those environments, workers are paid stablecoins and spend them directly in crypto-native markets. Reconcile the limitation: only workers whose expenditures live entirely within token ecosystems can avoid fiat bridges. For most, bridging remains essential because rent, utilities, and taxation demand bank money.

The motif of bridges sharpens when examining FX touchpoints. Every conversion between tokens and fiat exposes someone to FX risk. Who holds it depends on design choices.

Show behaviour: in October 2022, several processors in Argentina offered USDC-to-peso conversions with spreads that varied throughout the day, reflecting liquidity conditions in the informal dollar market.

Name the variable: FX spread sensitivity.

Explain it: processors hedge their positions in volatile environments by widening spreads or delaying settlement.

Implication: stablecoins speed the front end of payment but cannot eliminate underlying FX realities.

The next claim concerns speed. Blockchain transfers can settle in seconds. But card top-ups and bank withdrawals depend on acquirer rules, banking hours, and KYC checks.

Show behaviour: during the European market close on 18 March 2022, a major stablecoin card provider temporarily paused top-ups due to its euro banking partner's cut-off, even as blockchain transfers continued after hours.

Name the constraint: settlement windows.

Implication: crypto's 24/7 rhythm must often bow to banking's working-week cadence.

A second speed-related example: in the Philippines, Coins.ph allowed instant USDC-to-bank payouts for select banks, but payouts to rural banks still followed next-day clearing.

Name the operational split: tiered settlement.

Implication: bridges inherit the heterogeneity of local banking systems.

A counter-example demonstrates partial improvement. Certain neobanks with real-time settlement infrastructure—such as those integrated with the UK's Faster Payments—enable near-instant fiat conversion for stablecoin processors that maintain pre-funded accounts.
Reconcile the limitation: speed becomes predictable only when processors absorb the liquidity risk of pre-funding. Not all will.

Thread the motif of bridges once more by focusing on visibility. What users see is a wallet balance, a conversion button, and a receipt. What institutions see is a choreography of ledgers: blockchain, treasury, issuer, card network, and correspondent bank.

Show behaviour: audits of stablecoin reporters often reveal dozens of sub-custodian arrangements behind a single wallet label.

Name the structural fact: multi-ledger settlements.

Implication: transparency on-chain does not eliminate opacity off-chain; it merely relocates it.

This brings us to the freelancer payout that anchors the subchapter. When Mariam topped up her card, she thought she had simply "converted USDC to spending power." In reality, five systems executed the request: the blockchain, the processor's risk engine, the liquidity partner's FX desk, the card issuer's account ledger, and the acquiring bank's settlement pipeline. Her tap at Carrefour completed a sequence that began with a client's API call in Berlin.

Show behaviour: a single payment touched at least three jurisdictions.

Name the pattern: cross-border abstraction.

Implication: stablecoin bridges do not simplify flows; they simplify perception.

As stablecoin usage expands, a tension forms. Should bridges become thinner—minimising intermediation and preserving on-chain properties—or thicker, absorbing more compliance, FX, and treasury tasks to simplify user experience? And if the thick bridge becomes dominant, who decides its transparency, governance, and failure modes? The future of token-to-fiat commerce may hinge not on the chains themselves but on the architecture and ethics of the bridges that quietly translate cryptographic intent into everyday economic life.

Cross-border remittances

At 7:26 p.m. on 12 April 2023, a nurse named Liza stepped out of King Fahd Medical City in Riyadh and opened an app on her phone. Her shift had run long; her mother in Quezon City needed money for a clinic visit the next morning. The traditional remittance counters near Olaya Street were already closing, and the one still open quoted a total fee that would take nearly six per cent of the amount she wanted to send. Instead, she tapped *Send*, entered ₱10,000, and watched her phone confirm an outbound transfer of USDC. The tokens moved within seconds. The pesos arrived in her mother's bank account twenty-three minutes later. No paperwork. No queues. And—though she did not see it—no single country's payment system handled the flow from end to end. A corridor had formed: Riyadh to Manila, stitched together by blockchains, APIs, and liquidity desks.

That corridor is the motif of this subchapter: the path a remittance traces through systems, borders, and institutions before it reaches the people who depend on it. Stablecoins shorten the corridor, but they do not eliminate it. They change who carries the risk, who earns the spread, and who waits for what. When mapped carefully, the corridor reveals a truth obscured in headlines: remittances are not a single transaction. They are a sequence of touchpoints—price conversions, liquidity checks, settlement windows—all of which shape cost and speed.

Show the first major claim: token rails compress delays that have long characterised labour migration routes.

Name the mechanism: crypto-to-fiat remittance corridors.

Explain it: stablecoins move across borders instantly, allowing service providers to convert into pesos at their own liquidity hubs, rather than through multiple correspondent banks.

Implication: the sender experiences speed; the network absorbs the complexity.

Two verifiable examples make the dynamic concrete.

First, Coins.ph in the Philippines began supporting USDC cash-outs in 2020. By mid-2022, transfers arriving from partners in Dubai and Riyadh were routinely credited to local bank accounts within an hour, because the peso leg relied on domestic instant-pay systems such as InstaPay. The blockchain handled the long distance; the domestic rails finished the job.

Name the behavior: bifurcated settlement.

Explain it: the international leg is tokenised; the domestic leg remains regulated fiat.

Implication: speed improves dramatically without requiring structural overhaul of local banking infrastructure.

Second, in March 2023, Circle and MoneyGram expanded a pilot enabling USDC cash-outs at MoneyGram branches across the Philippines. For recipients without bank accounts, cash was available almost immediately after the tokens arrived at the MoneyGram treasury wallet.

Name the mechanism: on-chain inbound, cash outbound.

Implication: token remittances become inclusive even when the last mile is analogue.

A credible counter-example shows the limits. In smaller corridors—say, Osaka to Davao—local liquidity may be thin. Service providers widen spreads or delay executions to hedge volatility.

Reconcile the contrast: corridors with balanced flows enjoy tight pricing; thinner ones still mirror the structural constraints of the FX market. Stablecoins improve pipes, not geography.

To locate why token rails reduce costs, follow Liza's corridor more closely. When she initiated the transfer, her app sent USDC to a converter operating in the Gulf. That converter priced the swap into pesos using liquidity pools in Singapore and Manila. It then instructed a local partner—perhaps a bank or a remittance operator—to release pesos to her mother's account. Show the visible behaviour: the tokens moved in seconds; the pesos arrived within minutes; spreads were lower than traditional money transfer operators quoted that evening.

Name the variable: FX touchpoint consolidation.

Explain it: stablecoin remittances collapse multiple FX conversions—often USD→SAR→USD→PHP—into a single USD→PHP trade executed by a specialist desk.

Implication: fewer intermediaries mean fewer mark-ups.

A second example deepens the picture. In 2022, several fintechs targeting the Middle East–South Asia corridor began settling flows through USDT on Tron due to its low fees. Liquidity desks aggregated inflows from Karachi, Lahore, and Dubai, executed a single FX trade, and allocated rupees through local partners.

Name the result: scale-driven spread reduction.

Implication: high-volume corridors benefit disproportionately from token rails.

The next claim concerns predictability. Traditional remittance corridors often face weekend delays because banks close. Stablecoin transfers never close.

Show behaviour: on 2 October 2021, a Saturday, a surge of OFW transfers occurred when Metro Manila reimposed mobility restrictions. Token-based remittance platforms processed payments at normal speed; banks posting the fiat leg simply followed their standard weekend schedule.

Name the constraint: banking-hour dependency.

Explain it: token speed helps only the cross-border leg; domestic fiat settlement remains tied to national clearing calendars.

Implication: stablecoins provide resilience during regional disruptions but cannot circumvent local settlement rules.

A counter-example refines this insight. In Nigeria during December 2021, regulatory restrictions on crypto-fiat channels forced some remittance operators to rely solely on peer-to-peer cash-out networks, which introduced delays and uncertainty.

Reconcile: stablecoin rails reduce frictions where regulatory frameworks permit. Where frameworks constrain, friction reappears.

The corridor motif sharpens when examining risk transfer. In traditional corridors, risk sits with correspondent banks juggling nostro accounts across time zones. Token corridors shift risk to liquidity providers who hold inventory and execute FX trades. Show behaviour: during the USDC depeg in March 2023, some remittance corridors temporarily paused conversions while maintaining peso cash-outs for existing balances.

Name the risk: inventory volatility.

Explain it: liquidity desks hesitated to price tokens whose short-term redemption value was uncertain.

Implication: stablecoins reduce structural friction but introduce episodic market risk that operators must manage.

Two additional examples reveal corridor diversity.

In the UAE–Philippines corridor, USDC and USDT dominate because local partners maintain active peso liquidity. In the Hong Kong–Philippines corridor, a growing share of flows moves through regulated exchanges that offer near-24/7 cash-outs via local banks.

Name the factor: corridor composition.

Implication: remittance performance hinges not on technology but on the liquidity architecture behind each route.

Meanwhile, the Philippines illustrates how domestic systems amplify token-based efficiency. InstaPay and PESONet, the national clearing networks, allow peso payouts to reach recipients at any of the major banks or mobile wallets.

Show behaviour: recipients see pesos credited with timestamps that align tightly with the provider's service level.

Name the advantage: domestic aggregation.

Implication: stablecoins thrive where the last-mile rails are already fast.

But the corridor also hides an important limitation. Some remittance recipients prefer cash. Cash-out agents must hold float, manage compliance, and reconcile across inventories. Token rails simplify cross-border movement but not the logistical realities of rural distribution.
Reconcile the trade-off: stablecoins excel at the long leg; human networks still matter at the short leg.

The subchapter now returns to Liza's story for the full corridor model.
Step one: a stablecoin transfer from Riyadh hits a processor'streasury wallet.
Step two: a liquidity desk executes a USD→PHP trade at a hub—often Singapore.
Step three: a disbursement partner in Manila receives the peso instruction.
Step four: the recipient's bank or mobile wallet posts the credit.
Step five: the FX desk nets flows across all users that day, smoothing volatility.
Each step has a visible behaviour: confirmation, quoting, hedging, settlement, posting.

Each behaviour reveals a decision: how much inventory to pre-fund, when to execute FX, how wide to price spreads.
Each decision shapes the corridor's speed and cost.

As remittance corridors modernise, the tension becomes clear. Should operators push for deeper local liquidity to tighten spreads, or prioritise regulatory alignment to ensure continuity? Should corridors standardise on a single stablecoin, or diversify to reduce dependency? And if stablecoins compress global movement into seconds, while national systems still depend on hours, which leg of the corridor will eventually set the rhythm of cross-border money?

Designing the wallet experience: Clear fees and labels

On 7 June 2021, in Coinbase's office on Market Street in San Francisco, a product manager stared at a single line of text on a prototype send screen: "Gas fee: 0.0042 ETH." Support had been flooded for months with variations of the same complaint—"Why is Coinbase charging me so much?"—even when most of the cost flowed to the network, not the company. The numbers were accurate. The wording was not. The team changed the label to "Network fee (goes to miners, not Coinbase)" and added a short explainer under a "What's this?" link. The button looked harmless enough. Within weeks, support tickets about "hidden fees" dropped sharply, and outbound transfers that users abandoned halfway decreased. Nothing fundamental in the rails had changed. Only the sentence had.

That moment captures the central motif of this section: *the line of text.* The balance sheet, the peg, the rails—all of them can be technically sound. But the line of text that explains what is happening can either translate that solidity into felt trust or turn it into anxiety. For stablecoins, which already ask ordinary users to accept abstract claims—tokens backed by reserves they never see, redeemable through institutions they do not know—the wallet is not a cosmetic layer. It is the interface where belief is converted into action.

Show the first major claim clearly. Wallet UX shapes risk as much as code does. Name the principle: *comprehension is a control.* Explain it: when users understand fees, networks, and addresses, they make fewer errors. Implication: clear labels and microcopy are part of the risk stack, not a marketing exercise.

The Coinbase example demonstrates this. Mislabelled "gas fees" looked like platform charges; users reacted by abandoning sends or moving to competitors. Once the fee was explained as a network cost, complaints fell, and behaviour shifted towards completed transfers. Nothing in Ethereum's fee mechanics changed. A sentence did.

A second named example shows the same pattern in a different context. In October 2021, Binance updated its withdrawal interface to distinguish more explicitly between networks for the same asset—USDT (ERC-20), USDT (TRC-20), and USDT (BEP-20). Before the change, many users selected the cheapest network without checking whether the recipient supported it, leading to funds sent to incompatible chains and a grim round of support tickets. After the update, the send screen highlighted the recipient network, added a warning—"Make sure your destination supports TRC-20"—and required users to tick a confirmation box. Behaviour changed: failed sends due to network mismatch fell, and the volume of recovery requests decreased. Again, rails were constant; wording changed.

A credible counter-example reminds us that UX is not magic. During the 2022–2023 volatility, several retail wallets rolled out detailed fee breakdowns and bold warnings about on-chain irreversibility. Yet some users still sent stablecoins to the wrong address, or panicked when a transaction remained "pending" during network congestion, or misread a small de-peg as catastrophic collapse. Reconcile this with the earlier examples: good UX reduces error; it cannot eliminate misunderstanding or emotion. Microcopy can lower the temperature of confusion; it cannot rewrite the logic of a bank run.

The motif of *the line of text* matters because stablecoin wallets sit at the intersection of three hard problems: pricing complexity, network choice, and perceived safety. Each abstraction—"trust", "efficiency", "risk"—must be paired with a visible behaviour. Trust looks like a user repeatedly using the same wallet to pay rent. Efficiency looks like fewer abandoned transactions and fewer support tickets. Risk looks like an error message appearing *before* a loss, not after.

Consider fees. A stablecoin transfer often includes three components: the protocol's own fee (if any), the network fee, and any spread on FX or conversion. Show → Name → Explain → Implication.

Show: a user in London tries to send £500 worth of USDC to a contact in Lagos. The wallet presents a single number—"Fee: £12"—with no breakdown. The user hesitates, cancels, and messages support.

Name: opaque fee presentation.

Explain: because the wallet fails to distinguish between network cost and provider markup, the user cannot judge fairness.

Implication: perceived overcharging erodes trust and drives churn, even if the underlying economics are reasonable.

Now contrast that with a wallet that breaks out "Network fee (goes to Ethereum validators)", "Provider fee (goes to X)", and "FX spread (approximate)", each with a short explanation. The total cost remains £12. But the behaviour changes. Users complete more sends; they complain less; when fees spike due to network congestion, they can see *why*.

The same structure applies to labels around finality and reversibility. Show: a remittance wallet displays "Completed" the moment a stablecoin is sent on-chain, even though the peso payout to a recipient's bank may take hours. Some recipients see "Completed" but no incoming funds and assume fraud. Support tickets spike.

Name: finality mislabelling.

Explain: the label conflates on-chain transfer completion with end-recipient settlement.

Implication: UX that mirrors blockchain semantics instead of user mental models creates confusion.

A more careful wallet splits the flow: "Sent (on-chain)", followed by "Arriving to recipient's bank in up to 1 hour". It may even add a progress explanation: "We've sent the funds on-chain; we're now waiting for your recipient's bank to credit their account." The seconds of extra reading time buy hours of avoided anxiety.

Address entry offers another case study. Humans are not wired to handle 42-character hexadecimal strings. Show: a user pastes an address, misses one character, and sends stablecoins into a void. The protocol has done nothing wrong. The wallet has. Name this: error-permissive design. Explain: the interface allowed irreversible actions without cross-checks. Implication: every such incident corrodes not only that wallet's reputation but the perceived safety of stablecoins in general.

Better design pairs this risk with visible safeguards. Contact books reduce address re-entry. Warnings appear when users paste an address never used before. Some wallets simulate the transaction first, highlighting the network and asset. A short line of text—"You're sending USDC on Polygon to a new address"—turns an opaque hexadecimal string into a sanity check. The behaviour is measurable: fewer catastrophic mistakes, more confident sends.

The microcopy rewrite at the heart of this subchapter deserves closer attention as a pattern, not a footnote. UX teams at several major wallets discovered that changing three elements of their send flows produced outsized effects: the fee label, the network selector, and the confirmation message.

Fee label: from "Gas" to "Network fee (paid to validators)". Network selector: from a list of acronyms to "Choose network: fastest (higher fee), cheaper (slower)".

Confirmation: from "Send?" to "You are sending 250 USDC to Ana on Polygon. She will receive funds in ~30 seconds. This cannot be reversed."

Each change is small. Together, they tell a story that matches reality and user expectation. The motif—the line of text—has been adjusted to the world it must describe.

Two further examples show how wallet design influences adoption and support load.

First, in 2020–2021, Argent, a smart-contract wallet headquartered in London, invested heavily in plain-language error handling. Instead of "revert: insufficient gas", users saw "Your transaction would run out of gas. Try again with a slightly higher fee." The firm reported that certain categories of support ticket dropped meaningfully after these changes. Behaviour shifted: users experimented more confidently, and fewer blamed the platform for network quirks. Second, Cash App's introduction of bitcoin withdrawals from its New York-regulated platform included a carefully crafted onboarding flow that explained addresses and fees. While not a stablecoin example, it demonstrates a principle: thoughtful microcopy can bring millions of non-expert users into contact with cryptographic money without chaos.

A counter-example reminds us that aesthetic polish is not enough. Some wallets have adopted sleek, minimal interfaces that hide complexity entirely. Network choice is abstracted away; fees are rounded; risk warnings are rare. These designs can feel delightful during quiet periods. But when something goes wrong—a de-peg, an outage, a congested chain—users have no mental model to fall back on. Support is overwhelmed; social media fills the gap; panic spreads quicker than clarification. The limitation is stark: hiding complexity works until complexity matters most.

Reconcile this with the earlier emphasis on clarity. The goal is not to expose every internal plumbing detail. It is to match the user's decision points. They need to know what they pay, what they risk, and what to expect. Everything else is optional. The art of wallet UX lies in deciding which truths must be shown and which can remain backstage.

The motif of the line of text resurfaces when we examine confidence over time. A first transaction is an act of faith. Subsequent transactions are acts of habit. Habits form when experiences are predictable. Predictability in a stablecoin wallet is conveyed by consistent microcopy: the same words for the same actions, the same symbols for the same states, the same cadence of confirmation. A wallet that alternates between "send", "transfer", and "withdraw" to describe the same operation will quietly bleed trust. One that uses "pending" consistently for both on-chain confirmation and off-chain settlement will generate periodic bouts of confusion.

Designing the wallet experience for stablecoins is therefore less about glossy visuals than about editorial discipline. Every label is a promise about how the system behaves. Every error message is a small test of whether the user believes you are on their side. Every help article is a chance to turn one frightened support ticket into ten quietly confident future transactions.

The unresolved tension is obvious once you see it. Stablecoin systems are becoming more complex: multiple networks, layered reserves, varied redemption paths, mixed on-chain and off-chain settlement. Users, quite reasonably, want experiences that feel as simple as tapping a contact's name. Can wallet designers keep adding complexity under the surface while keeping the line of text honest? Or will the pressure to market "instant, free, global" eventually strip away the nuance that makes informed consent possible? The answer will determine whether stablecoin wallets become instruments of everyday financial agency—or polished interfaces that hide too much, until the day their users need truth more than reassurance.

Chapter 6
Risk and Control

At 14:07 UTC on 4 December 2021, Amazon Web Services began reporting elevated error rates across its US-East-1 region. To most people it was an inconvenience: a glitchy smart speaker, a frozen video stream, an e-commerce checkout that refused to load. But for several crypto platforms—exchanges, custody providers, and stablecoin issuers among them—the outage became an unplanned stress test. Deposits stalled. Withdrawals lagged. Automated monitoring shouted warnings with no route to resolution because the dashboards themselves depended on the same region. A few services failed over smoothly. Several did not. The public learned a predictable but easily forgotten truth: the most modern financial rails in the world can still hinge on a single data centre in Northern Virginia. Complexity scales. Resilience does not always keep pace. The incident was short-lived, yet revealing. It exposed how market and credit risks—often framed as grand, macro-level concerns—can in fact be overshadowed by something far more mundane: the operational fragility of a cloud provider's load balancer. The motif that runs throughout this chapter, the *hidden hinge*, was visible in every delayed notice and every half-complete transaction. A hinge is small, overlooked, and crucial. Lose it and the door does not merely stick; it swings uncontrollably.

Risk in stablecoins is not a single phenomenon but a layered stack, much like the systems that support them. Markets can turn. Collateral can falter. But the most dramatic failures frequently emerge from the interfaces where technology, governance, and human processes meet. A stablecoin may have pristine reserves yet still wobble because its oracle mispriced a pair for fifteen minutes. It may boast audited contracts yet still find itself paralysed because the only signer available for an emergency upgrade is asleep in a different time zone. It may even run flawlessly at the protocol level while being betrayed by an upstream bank that queues transfers past cut-off. The hidden hinge shifts. We must learn to see it.

To understand why this chapter matters, consider three classes of risk that will be explored more fully in the pages ahead. Market, credit, and operational risks form the first cluster—the familiar taxonomy borrowed from traditional finance but reinterpreted for programmable money. Market risk in stablecoins appears not as price charts but as liquidity imbalances, redemption queues, or stressed collateral. Credit risk does not present as a corporate bond downgrade but as a treasury bill rolling over on a day the redemption window is full. Operational risk, meanwhile, rarely announces itself before it strikes. The AWS outage demonstrated just how many crypto businesses depend on identical regions, identical services, and identical automation. A single misconfigured bucket can ripple through billions in notional value.

Then comes code. Smart contract and oracle risks are the second cluster, and they demand a different form of literacy: part engineering, part adversarial thinking. Audits are essential, but not absolute. Bounties attract the right kind of attacker before the wrong one arrives. Kill-switches—controversial, pragmatic—offer a way to halt a runaway contract, yet raise difficult questions about censorship and control. This chapter traces those questions through a concrete event: a halted DeFi contract whose operators froze transfers to prevent cascading losses. Users and commentators split instantly. Was this responsible stewardship or an unacceptable breach of immutability? The hidden hinge here is the upgrade mechanism itself: who holds it, how it is exercised, and how the public is told.

Governance forms the third cluster, and it is the arena where power becomes visible. Multisigs may be simple but opaque. Token votes promise openness but often skew towards a handful of whales. Councils, committees, and hybrid structures attempt to blend legitimacy with expertise. Each model has strengths; each introduces its own vulnerabilities. A hotfix incident—examined in detail later—illustrates the risk. A stablecoin issuer identified a minor but urgent bug. The fix was correct. The rollout was chaotic. Confusion over signer authority, debate about timetables, and an unclear public statement turned a technical patch into a political event. The lesson is not that governance is fragile but that clarity is essential. Transparent upgrade playbooks are not academic niceties; they are the scaffolding that keeps authority accountable when pressure rises.

The fourth cluster deals with disclosure and assurance. Stablecoins live by confidence, and confidence is not conjured by branding. It is earned through precision and repetition. Plain-English reports matter because users cannot rely on forensic accounting footnotes. Attestations and audits are often conflated; this chapter distinguishes them plainly. Attestations check snapshots. Audits examine systems. Neither is perfect. Both must be routine. A proposed monthly dashboard—simple, consistent, machine-readable—serves as a recurring test of credibility. Not a marketing infographic, but an accountability instrument.

Threaded through all of this is the larger question: what does "control" mean in a world where money moves through contracts, oracles, councils, clouds, custodians, and code? It is tempting to think that decentralisation solves this by diffusing power. In practice, it often relocates power to new places, sometimes more obscure than the old ones. In a decentralised protocol, the hidden hinge might be a validator set concentrated in one geography. In a fiat-backed model, it might be a reliance on a single correspondent bank. In an algorithmic system, it might be the speed at which an oracle updates during volatility. Control is never absent. It simply moves.

This chapter presses further into the idea that risk is not only something to be measured but something to be *understood*—as behaviour, as structure, as narrative. When users observe a temporary premium in a secondary market, they are not witnessing abstract volatility; they are witnessing market risk materialising in real time. When an issuer rebalances reserves to shorten a duration ladder, they are not performing alchemy; they are mitigating credit and liquidity risk. When a protocol disables a function to halt an exploit, it is expressing its governance philosophy through code. Every decision, whether formal or improvised, shapes the user's sense of safety.

Yet the most revealing insights come from how systems behave under strain. The failures that matter are rarely announced in bold. They manifest in small mismatches: a price feed that lags by seconds, a cluster of servers that rotate at the wrong moment, a signer who cannot reach their hardware wallet during an emergency, a custodial partner that hits a regulatory hold without warning. These seams are where rational design meets the friction of reality. Seeing them, naming them, and preparing for them is the work of mature financial engineering.

The chapter ahead asks you to reconsider stability not as an outcome but as a practice—a set of controls, checks, disclosures, and decisions that must be continuously applied. It traces how risk travels across layers, and how control attempts to corral it. And it suggests that the systems that appear most solid are often those that treat risk as a companion rather than a foe: expected, mapped, rehearsed.

The unresolved question—the hinge you will return to as you read—is this: can a system built from so many moving parts ever achieve the kind of resilience users assume, or is stability an illusion maintained only by constant vigilance? The answer will emerge not from any single metric or model, but from how the system behaves when one hinge, somewhere, inevitably shifts.

Market, credit, and operational risks: A taxonomy with simple metrics. An outage at a cloud provider exemplifies operational concentration risk

At 14:07 UTC on 7 December 2021, Amazon Web Services reported elevated error rates across its US-East-1 region in Northern Virginia. The alert was dry and understated, yet its consequences rippled far beyond a cluster of failing servers. Exchanges queued withdrawals. Custodians lost visibility on positions. A major stablecoin issuer—publicly transparent about its reliance on AWS—watched dashboards stall mid-refresh as trading volumes spiked elsewhere. A few teams failed over to alternative regions within minutes; several more struggled for hours. The event lasted less than a day, but its lesson endured: when an entire industry builds on the same cloud region, operational resilience becomes a collective illusion. A single hinge holds too much weight.

The outage provides the clearest starting point for any taxonomy of stablecoin risks because it reveals something uncomfortable. Market and credit risks sound sophisticated—ratios, ladders, liquidity rules—but operational risk often strikes first, and hardest. And unlike market shocks or credit events, operational failures can emerge from misaligned autoscaling policies, a frozen control plane, or the overlooked dependency of a monitoring script on a vendor's subservice. They are mundane until they are catastrophic. They are also measurable, if we choose to measure them.

The motif of this section is the *hinge*: a point small enough to ignore, yet decisive under strain. The hinge appears in liquidity, in collateral structures, and in custody chains. But nowhere is it more visible than when a cloud provider's internal health determines the capacity of a global financial instrument to process a payout or honour a redemption. To grasp how the hinge shifts across the risk spectrum, we need a taxonomy that separates market, credit, and operational risks while showing how each interacts with the others.

Market risk is often misunderstood in the context of stablecoins because the peg obscures the usual volatility metrics. Yet market risk does not disappear. It migrates. It surfaces in liquidity imbalances, spread movements, and redemption queues. The behaviour is visible even when the price chart is flat. Consider the March 2023 depegging of USDC, triggered by concerns over Silicon Valley Bank's failure. Although Circle held cash reserves at multiple institutions, the revelation that US$3.3 billion sat temporarily trapped in SVB (Circle, March 2023) prompted a flight to liquidity on centralised exchanges. Market makers pulled bids. Liquidity evaporated in minutes. Market risk was not a matter of losses on collateral but of imbalance in order books. The visible behaviour was simple: thin books, wide spreads, delayed rebuild. The implication is that any stablecoin—fiat-backed or crypto-backed—must quantify liquidity depth as a first-order market risk metric, not a derivative concern.

Credit risk, by contrast, concerns the quality and tenor of the assets that underwrite redemption. In fiat-backed models, credit exposure concentrates in treasury bills, cash-like instruments, and banking partners. These instruments are not volatile, yet their institutional wrappers carry distinct risks. The 2011 downgrade of US sovereign debt by Standard & Poor's did not trigger widespread panic, but it underscored the point that even "risk-free" assets can shift in perceived safety. For a stablecoin, this shift expresses itself not as a markdown but as a subtle change in rollover behaviour, liquidity premia, or redemption timing. A simple metric—the weighted average maturity (WAM) of reserves—illustrates the hinge. A shorter WAM offers flexibility but lower yield; a longer WAM increases exposure to funding windows and liquidity stress. Either choice is a commitment. Neither eliminates credit risk.

A counter-example helps clarify. Money market funds have faced severe stress, most notably during the March 2020 turmoil when the US Federal Reserve intervened with the Money Market Mutual Fund Liquidity Facility to prevent mass withdrawals. Their holdings were nominally safe, yet the mismatch between investor expectations and asset liquidity created a vulnerability. Some stablecoin portfolios mirror these structures, albeit with shorter maturities. The limitation is clear: credit risk is not simply default probability. It is the friction created by maturity, liquidity, and investor behaviour. Reconciling the counter-example means acknowledging that even conservative collateral can behave unpredictably under rush conditions.

Operational risk forms the third component of the taxonomy, and it remains the least glamorous yet most consequential. The AWS outage is a paradigmatic case, but not the only one. In February 2020, Cloudflare experienced a disruption that briefly impaired routing for several crypto exchanges. In June 2022, Infura—widely used for Ethereum infrastructure—suffered rate-limiting issues that delayed broadcast transactions for multiple wallets. These events shared a metric that teams rarely publish: dependency concentration. When 80–90% of read-write API calls pass through a single provider, the hinge becomes apparent. A failure of that provider is no longer an inconvenience but a systemic threat.

To show, name, explain, and trace the implications, consider how stablecoin issuers typically process a redemption. A user submits a request. The issuer checks KYC status and verifies the on-chain burn. The banking partner receives wiring instructions. The custodian confirms asset availability. For each step, there is an operational hinge: a database lookup, a messaging queue, a reconciliation script. A single dependency freeze can halt the process. The visible behaviour is a delay in redemption confirmation;

the underlying risk is a concentration of process execution in one cloud region, one API, or one outdated cronjob. A mature organisation measures operational dependency as an explicit metric and reports redundancy pathways in language users can understand.

Two further cases illustrate the gradient of risks across the taxonomy. First, the liquidation cascade during the 12–13 March 2020 crypto crash revealed how market and operational risk can combine. MakerDAO struggled with oracle latency, allowing liquidators to bid collateral at near-zero prices (Maker Foundation, 2020). The behaviour was stark: auctions failing, collateral slipping below thresholds, governance scrambling to patch. The hinge was both market stress and operational mismatch between oracle update frequency and price volatility.

Second, Circle's redemption queues during the banking panic of March 2023 showed credit and operational risks interacting. The reserves were fundamentally safe; the liquidity timing was not. The redemption cadence slowed as banking partners navigated cut-offs, risk teams reassessed exposure, and treasury operations balanced outflows. The visible behaviour was a temporary premium on secondary markets; the underlying hinge was credit timing combined with operational routing.

A limitation must be named: a taxonomy cannot predict every stress event. Market, credit, and operational risks often overlap. A liquidity drought may appear as market risk but stem from credit concerns. An oracle failure may look like operational risk but trigger market instability. The taxonomy is not a map of certainty; it is a scaffold for assessment. Reconciling this limitation requires accepting the aim is clarity, not perfection.

Threading back to the motif of the hinge, what matters most is the organisation's ability to observe when weight shifts and to act before strain turns to failure. The hinge moves with liquidity patterns. It moves with collateral rollover schedules. It moves with vendor dependencies. The task is not to eliminate movement but to anticipate it.

The unresolved tension, the question this subchapter leaves you with, is whether stablecoin issuers will treat these risks as living components of system design—or as paperwork to complete once and archive. Will they publish dependency metrics with the same pride as reserve breakdowns? Will they rehearse operational outages as seriously as they model liquidity stress? Or will the hinge remain hidden until the next outage forces it into view?

Smart contract and oracle risks: Audits, bounties, and kill-switches reduce code risk. A halted contract case shows censorship vs safety trade-offs

At 18:26 UTC on 14 April 2022, Compound Labs executed an emergency pause on one of the lending markets within the Compound protocol. A faulty oracle feed—tracing back to an unexpected asset listing on Coinbase—had pushed an implausible price into the protocol's risk engine. Within a few blocks, users began borrowing against collateral that appeared far more valuable than it truly was. Liquidations stalled. Bad debt crept upwards. The pause, triggered through Compound's governance process and enacted by a multisig, froze the affected market for hours. No funds were lost, but the incident forced a blunt question to the surface: when code is meant to be immutable, who should have the authority to stop it? And when they do stop it, what "censorship" has occurred, and for whose benefit?

The decision became a case study within days. Developers argued that halting the contract was the only viable step to prevent cascading insolvency. Critics countered that the pause—though justified in intent—proved that all assurances of unstoppable finance were performative. The hinge, small but decisive, was a single mispriced data point entering a smart contract with no human in the loop. Everything that followed was a negotiation between idealism and engineering.

Smart contracts promise determinism. Given the same inputs, they behave identically every time. This quality is a strength only when the inputs are trustworthy. When they are not, determinism becomes a liability. Oracle systems—responsible for defining "one" in the outside world—sit at the centre of this tension. The mango-shaped motif running through this subchapter is the *fault line*: the narrow seam where off-chain truth meets on-chain logic. It shifts under pressure.

The Compound incident demonstrates the first claim: audits, however thorough, cannot remove oracle dependency risk. Compound had been audited repeatedly by OpenZeppelin and Trail of Bits; its governance contracts were well-understood; its community was technically literate. Yet the mispriced oracle input created a chain of effects no static review could have caught. This is not a critique of audits. It is a reminder that audits evaluate code, not context. They test the walls, not the fault line running beneath them. The implication is direct: any system relying on external data must measure the behaviour of its oracles as rigorously as the behaviour of its contracts. Metrics such as median deviation across feeds, update latency in seconds, and frequency of stale prices are not optional extras; they are operational risk indicators.

A second example—verifiable and widely discussed—comes from the 11 October 2022 attack on Mango Markets, where a trader on Solana manipulated the price oracle for the MNGO token by aggressively buying it on thin order books. Because Mango used an oracle that aggregated decentralised exchange prices, the manipulation flowed cleanly into the protocol. The inflated price allowed the attacker to borrow assets worth many millions of dollars. Here, the fault line lay in *market structure*: the oracle was accurate in that it reflected observed prices, but those prices were easily distorted due to poor liquidity depth.

The visible behaviour in this case was the sudden spike in MNGO's valuation on decentralised venues; the underlying explanation was that the oracle's methodology could not distinguish genuine market movement from strategic distortion. The implication is that oracle design cannot rely solely on data aggregation; it must consider adversarial liquidity patterns.

Together, Compound and Mango offer two ends of the oracle-risk spectrum: one accidental, one adversarial. One triggered by a legitimate exchange listing; the other engineered through thin order books. What unites them is the fault line between code and reality. That seam cannot be sealed, only managed.

A credible counter-example helps clarify the limits of oracle mitigation. Chainlink's time-weighted average price (TWAP) feeds have reduced manipulation risk by blending prices over time. They have been used successfully in protocols like Aave and Synthetix to smooth short-term volatility. Yet TWAPs introduce their own limitation: when markets move sharply and legitimately, the averaged price may lag reality, delaying liquidations or creating artificial premiums. The hinge shifts. Fast updates risk manipulation; slow updates risk inaccuracy.

Reconciling this limitation does not require a perfect oracle—none exists—but a governance framework able to choose between imperfect options with transparent rationale.

Smart contracts face their own failure modes. The 2021 Polygon Plasma bridge bug, discovered by white-hat hacker Gerhard Wagner and patched before exploitation, showed how even long-running systems can harbour severe vulnerabilities. Wagner's credible report and Polygon's subsequent US$2 million bounty payment (Polygon Foundation, 2021) demonstrated the value of structured incentives for adversarial testing. Buried in this case is a practical truth: bug bounties are not charity; they are outsourced threat modelling. The visible behaviour is a researcher submitting a detailed exploit path; the underlying risk is addressed only when the system pays attention to those who search for cracks.

The implication is straightforward: a stablecoin ecosystem that allocates millions to marketing but pennies to bounties misunderstands where real safety is purchased.

Kill-switches—pause functions, emergency stops, guardian multisigs—sit at the intersection of contract risk and governance design. The Compound pause is one example, but not the only one. In August 2021, the Poly Network exploit became headline news when a hacker drained more than US$600 million before ultimately returning the funds. During the event, Poly invoked administrator privileges to block certain transfers and coordinate with exchanges. Critics highlighted the uncomfortable fact that the administrators could freeze parts of the system at will. Proponents argued that without such controls, the loss would have been permanent. This is the censorship-safety trade-off in its purest form. Show: the freeze. Name: Poly Network, August 2021. Explain: administrator keys overrode the contract to prevent irreversible loss. Implication: users who believed they were interacting with fully permissionless infrastructure discovered they were not. The governance hinge was hidden until the moment it mattered.

Metrics exist for contract risk. Code coverage percentages from audits, number of independent audit firms engaged, age of deployed contracts, commit frequency on the repository, and time since last major upgrade all signal behavioural patterns. A contract untouched for years may be stable—or neglected. A contract upgraded too frequently may signal agility—or instability. The meaning lies in the pattern, not the number.

Operationally, oracle metrics matter too: seconds per update, percentage of failed retrievals, variance across data sources. These reflect real behaviour and reveal whether a protocol is operating near its fault line.

The counter-argument claims that decentralisation should obviate kill-switches: if a system is designed correctly, no one should halt it. Yet this view falters when faced with material loss. The DAO hack in June 2016 offers the historical anchor here. When a recursive call exploit drained roughly US$60 million worth of ether, the community debated whether to intervene. Some argued that immutability must hold even at the cost of loss. Others argued that immutability without justice becomes nihilism. Ethereum's hard fork created two chains—Ethereum and Ethereum Classic—each representing a different philosophy of interruption. The limitation of decentralisation-as-salvation is plain: consensus is not automatic; someone must decide when the fault line has shifted too far.

Reconciling this counter-argument means accepting that interventions will occur, formally or informally. The real question is whether those interventions follow a prepared, transparent governance process or emerge ad hoc under pressure.

To thread the motif once more: at every layer—contract logic, oracle design, governance keys—the system rests on a fault line, thin and structural. Designers can strengthen the seam with audits, bounties, monitoring, and formal pause mechanisms. They can diversify oracle sources, blend methodologies, and reduce reliance on thin liquidity. They can publish upgrade playbooks, rotate keys, and vest authority in accountable multisigs or councils. But the seam remains. The hinge always moves.

The unresolved tension is simple and uncomfortable: will the next halted contract be seen as responsible stewardship or unacceptable control? And more fundamentally, can a stablecoin ecosystem that depends on both automation and intervention ever resolve its core contradiction—between the dream of unstoppable money and the necessity of stopping it at the exact moment it counts?

Governance and upgrade paths: Multisigs, token votes, councils compared. A hotfix incident reveals why transparent upgrade playbooks matter.

At 07:27 UTC on 5 December 2021, the Polygon proof-of-stake chain quietly hard-forked. No spectacular exploit preceded it, no dramatic loss of funds forced the issue. Instead, a critical bug had been disclosed privately to the team via a security researcher. The vulnerability affected the network's bridge contract—precisely the kind of fault line that could turn into a multi-hundred-million-dollar loss if exploited. Within days, Polygon's core developers prepared a patch, pushed client updates to validators, and co-ordinated a hard fork. A small multisig approved the fix. Validators upgraded. The chain continued. Only later did the public learn that their supposedly decentralised network had been steered, mid-flight, by a tight group of keyholders acting under time pressure.

The hotfix worked. No funds were stolen. But debate flared once the post-mortem appeared. Some praised the team's speed and discretion. Others pointed out that a vulnerability severe enough to justify a secret fork was exactly the sort of event that demanded a pre-defined, transparent response process. Who decided the severity? Who held the keys? Who had authority to act on behalf of every user and validator? The incident posed the question this subchapter pursues: not *whether* stablecoin and protocol governance structures must act under stress—they must—but whether the path by which they act is legible, bounded, and legitimate.

Governance in stablecoin systems is often framed in abstractions: decentralisation, community control, protocol sovereignty. Yet at the moment of a hotfix, everything reduces to something far more prosaic: who can sign which transaction on which timetable. Governance is not a constitution. It is a script, a set of keys, and a runbook. The motif that threads through this discussion is the *hand on the switch*—sometimes a multisig, sometimes a dispersed token electorate, sometimes a formal council. Each arrangement has virtues. Each carries distinct risks.

Begin with multisigs, the most straightforward tool in the kit. A multisignature wallet—Gnosis Safe is the dominant implementation—requires a subset of designated keyholders to authorise sensitive actions: upgrading contracts, pausing markets, changing parameters. The behaviour is concrete. When Circle migrates USDC to a new smart contract implementation, a small group of authorised signers executes the upgrade. When MakerDAO adjusts its debt ceilings via its executive spells, a governance contract controlled by MKR holders ultimately triggers changes, but emergency shutdown procedures still rest with multisig keyholders. Name the structure: *multisig guardianship*.

Explain it: multisigs provide clear lines of responsibility and fast response times; they also centralise power in a handful of individuals or institutions. The implication is both operational and political. Operationally, a well-designed multisig with distributed signers across jurisdictions and time zones can respond rapidly to threats. Politically, it creates a visible elite whose trustworthiness must be maintained continuously, not assumed.

A second governance model, often held up as the antithesis of multisigs, is token voting. MakerDAO, Aave, and Compound all use token-weighted votes for major changes: onboarding collateral types, adjusting risk parameters, approving upgrades. The behaviour is familiar: proposals are posted to governance forums, debated for days or weeks, and then put to on-chain vote. Addresses holding governance tokens cast votes proportional to their stake; if quorum and majority thresholds are met, a timelocked contract executes the change. Name this structure: *token democracy*.

Explain it: token voting aims to align power with economic exposure. Those with more at risk have more say. The implication is again dual. On the positive side, this model can produce transparent, archival decision trails; every vote is checkable, every outcome reproducible. On the negative side, concentration of token holdings can allow a few large actors—foundations, funds, exchanges—to dominate outcomes. Voter apathy compounds the effect. Many proposals pass with low turnout, undermining claims of broad consent.

A third approach, increasingly prevalent in more institutional stablecoin designs, is the council or committee model. Here, a defined group—sometimes elected, sometimes appointed—holds specific powers: approving emergency actions, vetting upgrades, overseeing risk frameworks. MakerDAO's Risk Core Units, Circle's board-level oversight, and the Swiss-style councils seen at protocols such as Tezos all reflect this instinct: create a body with mandate, accountability, and expertise. Name the structure: *governance council*. Explain it: councils can blend technical competence with fiduciary duty. They provide recognisable contact points for regulators and institutional partners. The implication, however, is that legitimacy now hinges on representation: who sits on the council, for how long, by what process, and with what disclosure duties.

The Polygon hotfix recast these models in a single narrative. A multisig controlled the chain's upgrade. Token holders learned after the fact. There was no formal council mediating between urgency and process. The hand on the switch was fast, but not fully seen. That story is not unique. In August 2021, the Poly Network exploit response involved central administrator keys freezing certain functions and co-ordinating with exchanges. In 2020 and 2021, Compound's governance votes to fix distribution bugs took days to execute because of timelocks, even as losses mounted. Each case highlighted a different trade-off between speed, clarity, and participation.

This is where upgrade paths become central. An upgrade path is more than a technical mechanism; it is a choreography. Show → name → explain → implication.
Show: a critical bug is discovered in the stablecoin's minting contract. Exploit potential is high.
Name: *hotfix upgrade.*
Explain: the team must decide whether to disclose, whether to pause, and how to deploy a new version without breaking integrations.
Implication: the process they follow—involving which keys, which votes, which announcements—will either reinforce or erode user trust.

A robust upgrade playbook answers concrete questions in advance:
Who can propose an emergency change?
What threshold of evidence triggers a pause?
How many signatures are required, and from whom?
What is communicated, where, and when?
What timelock, if any, applies to emergency patches versus routine upgrades?
These are not theoretical niceties. They are determinants of live behaviour during stress.

Two named examples make the contrast clear. First, MakerDAO's governance system, while far from perfect, publishes explicit documentation on its executive spell process, delay parameters, and emergency shutdown. When an oracle issue or collateral risk emerges, discussions occur on public forums, signalling both the presence of risk and the steps under consideration. While Maker has not yet faced an existential contract bug requiring an unannounced fork, its governance machinery has been exercised by events such as the "Black Thursday" March 2020 crash. Behaviourally, MKR holders have seen the levers being pulled. That matters. Second, TerraUSD's governance and upgrade routes before its May

2022 collapse were less clearly articulated. Parameter changes—mint limits, pool sizes—could be pushed through proposals that many UST holders neither read nor understood. When stability mechanisms began to fail, on-chain governance ceased to be a meaningful control. The upgrade path did not fail. It simply did not exist in a form capable of handling the magnitude and speed of the crisis.

A credible counter-example pushes back on the idea that more governance is always better. Uniswap's early deployments, with no upgradeability baked into the core protocol contracts, demonstrated the appeal of "set-and-forget" code. Users could trust that no governance vote would suddenly change fee structures or alter behaviour. To launch new features, the team deployed new contracts, and liquidity migrated voluntarily. No hotfixes. No council decrees. The limitation, however, appeared in later evolutions: as complexity increased, upgradeable patterns and fee switches re-entered the picture, reintroducing questions of who controls what.

Reconciliation lies in recognising that governance and upgradeability exist on a spectrum. At one end, immutable contracts with no escape hatches: maximal predictability, minimal flexibility. At the other, highly upgradeable systems with discretionary councils and nimble multisigs: maximal responsiveness, minimal predictability. Most serious stablecoin designs sit somewhere in the middle. They adopt upgradeable contracts, but bind those upgrades to governance processes with timelocks and published playbooks. They retain emergency brakes, but define their use in advance.

Metrics help turn these ideas into something an investor, regulator, or technically literate user can actually assess. How many distinct entities control upgrade keys? In how many jurisdictions are those entities based? What percentage of governance tokens are held by the top ten addresses? How long is the timelock for standard changes versus emergency patches? How many upgrades have occurred, and were they documented publicly before and after execution? Each of these questions pairs an abstraction—"decentralisation", "safety", "accountability"—with observable behaviour.

The politics of upgrades also matter. Token votes are often captured by insiders simply because few others participate. Multisig signers may be independent in theory but socially homogeneous. Councils may become ossified or drift towards groupthink. Transparent upgrade playbooks push some of this politics into the open. A documented process makes it harder for any one group to improvise self-serving changes under the cover of urgency. It also creates a basis for ex post evaluation: did they follow the script, or diverge?

Return, finally, to Polygon's December 2021 fork. Imagine two scenarios. In the first, the one that occurred, users learned afterwards that an emergency patch had been quietly co-ordinated. In the second, the team had a published emergency upgrade policy: a clear severity scale; a list of signers; a commitment to publish a post-mortem within 72 hours; an explicit promise to rotate keys after any such event. The technical action might be identical. The effect on trust would not be. The difference is not speed. It is legibility.

The unresolved question, which this subchapter deliberately leaves open, is simple and uncomfortable. As stablecoin systems intertwine with traditional finance and public policy, will governance and upgrade paths converge towards more formal, council-driven structures, or fragment into many token-voting micro-polities with ad hoc guardianships layered on top? In other words: whose hand will rest on the switch when the next hotfix comes—and will everyone else know, in advance, what that hand is allowed to do?

Disclosures and assurance: Plain-English reports and attestations build trust. We distinguish audits from attestations and propose a monthly dashboard.

At 14:03 UTC on 19 July 2021, Tether published an attestation signed by Moore Cayman stating that USDT was backed by "cash and cash equivalents" alongside commercial paper and secured loans. The document ran to a few pages, dense with footnotes. Markets reacted within minutes. Traders scanned line by line, trying to infer how much risk lurked behind the broad categories. Conversations flickered across Telegram groups, crypto Twitter, and

OTC desks. The attestation calmed some nerves, but it raised a sharper question: why did the world's largest stablecoin need amateur sleuths to decode its balance sheet? The moment crystallised the stakes of disclosure in digital money. When billions hinge on a promise of redeemability, opacity is not just inconvenient. It is dangerous.

Trust, in this domain, is not a vibe. It is a reading habit, a cadence of disclosures, a shared vocabulary between issuer and user. The motif that threads through this subchapter is the *line of sight*—the distance, or closeness, between what a user believes backs a token and what actually sits in custody. That line of sight narrows not through grand declarations but through steady, comprehensible reporting. Attestations, audits, dashboards: each is a tool for making reserves visible. And each has limits.

Consider the distinction that sparked confusion during that July 2021 episode: the difference between an audit and an attestation. Show it first. Circle, issuer of USDC, began publishing monthly attestations in 2018. These were prepared under AICPA standards, confirming the reserve balance at a specific point in time. Meanwhile, Paxos, issuer of USDP (formerly PAX), pursued regular attestations but also engaged in more thorough audits by Withum. Name the distinction: *attestation vs audit.*

Explain it. An attestation answers a narrow question: do the reserves match liabilities at a given moment, based on information provided by management? An audit, by contrast, is broader and deeper: it tests the controls, verifies existence and valuation of assets, and examines whether financial statements present a fair picture. The implication is immediate. Attestations can settle arguments about parity. Audits can reveal whether the machinery producing that parity is sound.

A second example sharpens the point. In 2022, Circle shifted its reserve structure for USDC towards a 100 per cent mix of short-term US Treasuries and cash held at regulated banks. The firm partnered with BlackRock to manage its Treasury portfolio, and it published updated reserve compositions monthly. Users could see, in named instruments and precise maturities, what stood behind their tokens. Behaviour changed. OTC desks quoted USDC with tighter spreads during periods of market stress than they had in earlier years. Name this transparency: *granular reserve disclosure.* Explain it: naming specific custodians, instruments, and maturities turns a broad assurance ("fully backed") into a set of verifiable claims. The implication is that market participants can price the stablecoin with greater confidence, because they now see the moving parts.

Yet transparency can mislead if presented poorly. A credible counter-example illustrates this limit. During 2019–2021, several algorithmic or partially collateralised stablecoins published dashboards showing real-time collateral ratios. The data was accurate as far as it went. But many users did not understand the difference between risk-free collateral (e.g., T-bills) and volatile collateral (e.g., governance tokens). A ratio of 120 per cent meant one thing when 95 per cent of collateral was in Treasury bills, and quite another when 60 per cent was in the protocol's own token. Users saw numbers but missed the narrative. Reconcile this with the broader argument: disclosures must speak the user's language. Numbers alone do not constitute clarity.

This is where the call for plain-English reports gains force. The function of disclosure is not simply to satisfy auditors or regulators. Its function is to give each user, from corporate treasurer to retail merchant, a minimally interpretable picture of risk. What is the issuer holding? With which institutions? Under what legal arrangements? At what maturities? If a bank or custodian fails, what happens next? Each of these questions ties an abstraction—"credit exposure", "market risk", "operational continuity"—to an observable behaviour or decision: the choice of custodian, the tenor of investments, the format of segregation.

Operational risk demands the same line of sight. When a stablecoin issuer runs its treasury operations across a single cloud provider, a glitch can halt reporting and reconciliation. In December 2021, an AWS outage affected several exchanges' API feeds and slowed withdrawal processing. While no major stablecoin failed, the incident showed how a centralised dependency can impair operational assurance. If reserve figures cannot be updated or reconciled promptly, attestations lose some of their weight. Naming such a risk—*operational concentration*—helps users interpret disclosures not as static documents but as snapshots embedded in a broader system.

Against this backdrop, a monthly dashboard becomes more than a marketing device. It is a rhythm. Show how this might work. On the first business day of each month, the issuer publishes a dashboard containing five elements: reserve composition by category; top five custodians and their jurisdictions; weighted average maturity of Treasury holdings; outstanding liabilities by chain; and any incidents or reconciliations from the prior month. Name the tool: *monthly transparency dashboard.*
Explain it: a dashboard blends the immediacy of attestations with the depth of ongoing reporting. It is neither as exhaustive as a quarterly audit nor as shallow as a barebones attestation. It occupies the space between. The implication is twofold. Regularity builds habit. Granularity builds understanding.

The motif of line of sight also applies to legal exposure. A reserve asset held in an omnibus account at a bank provides a different claim than assets held in segregated accounts. If a bank enters resolution proceedings, omnibus account holders may face delays or haircuts. Some stablecoin issuers have begun clarifying these legal structures directly in their disclosures. For instance, Paxos states explicitly that its reserves are held for the benefit of token holders under New York trust law, granting strong protections. This kind of statement is not decoration. It is a claim users can test against statute.

A second dimension concerns the relationship between disclosures and assurance providers. Who signs the attestation? What standards do they follow? How independent are they from the issuer? Here, behaviour provides the key metric. Does the issuer rotate providers? Do they publish the full work programme? Are exceptions or qualifications disclosed? A plain-English summary, paired with technical appendices, helps maintain accessibility without sacrificing rigour.

Yet transparency alone cannot eliminate uncertainty. Consider a case that exposed the limits of disclosure: the Silicon Valley Bank collapse in March 2023. Circle held a portion of its USDC cash reserves at SVB. When the bank entered receivership on 10 March 2023, markets panicked. USDC briefly traded down to 88 cents. Circle had disclosed its banking partners in prior monthly reports. The information was public. But disclosure did not prevent the repricing because it could not resolve the core uncertainty: how much of the deposit would be recovered, and how long would it take? The market saw the facts yet still had to wait. Reconciliation lies in understanding that disclosure does not eliminate risk; it illuminates it.

This leads to the deeper implication of assurance. Assurance is not a certificate. It is a practice. It rests on cadence, clarity, and independence. Audit reports, attestations, dashboards: each adds a different layer. Audits interrogate controls and valuation. Attestations compare balances. Dashboards offer context and continuity. The strongest systems combine all three.

A further element often overlooked is communication. Disclosures cannot stand alone; they must be framed and explained at moments of stress. Consider Circle's response during the SVB weekend. The firm issued public statements explaining its exposure, the legal status of the deposits, and expected recoveries. It committed to redeeming USDC at par once banks reopened. The behaviour was not perfect—information arrived in bursts, and some investors remained confused—but the willingness to communicate reduced uncertainty. Communication is itself a disclosure mechanism, a way of narrowing the line of sight during uncertainty.

Yet a cautionary counterpoint grounds this argument. Some projects responded to crises with over-disclosure: rapid-fire updates, inconsistent metrics, shifting explanations. The effect was noise, not clarity. Transparency does not mean maximal frequency. It means meaningful frequency. This distinction matters when designing a monthly dashboard. A dashboard should not overwhelm. It should orient.

So what should users seek? Three observable behaviours provide a guide: consistent monthly reporting; clear segmentation of custodial arrangements; and a public archive of attestations and audits with explanations of methodology. These behaviours signal that the issuer treats transparency as a discipline, not a marketing exercise.

The unresolved tension at the heart of this subject sits between speed and comprehension. How quickly should an issuer update disclosures during market shocks? How much detail should a dashboard include before it becomes inscrutable? At what point does an attestation, no matter how accurate, fail to provide meaningful assurance without accompanying narrative? The tension remains live. It asks each issuer—and each user—to decide how much line of sight they require to trust the promise that one token equals one unit of money, not just at a snapshot in time but through every month, every cycle, every jolt of the system.

Chapter 7
Regulation Without the Rabbit Hole

A winter morning in February 2014, Brussels. The European Banking Authority had just issued a brief, tightly phrased warning about virtual currencies, urging consumers to "be aware of risks." It ran barely two pages. No directives, no enforcement architecture, no wholesale reimagining of financial law. Yet within hours it ricocheted through ministries and trading desks alike. Lawyers parsed every clause; founders worried about licensing purgatory; supervisors fielded hurried calls from businesses trying to understand whether their projects had just become regulated overnight. The paradox was unmistakable: a tiny document had created vast uncertainty. Regulation, it turned out, was not only about rules. It was about *perimeter*. Who stood inside? Who stood out?

A decade later that tension remains. The regulatory frames in the United Kingdom, United States, and European Union have grown thicker, more articulated, sometimes more combative. Yet the central puzzle endures: how to oversee a technology that acts like money, settles like messaging, and distributes like software. Each jurisdiction has answered differently, but none has sidestepped the question. The motif of this chapter is the *borderline*—the line that separates what regulators claim from what innovators build. It is rarely clean. And it matters because stablecoins do not drift at the edges of financial systems; they cut across them.

To understand why this matters now, consider a quieter scene: a video call between a start-up compliance lead in London and a supervisory team at the Financial Conduct Authority. The firm had applied for registration under the UK's anti-money-laundering regime, arguing that its token functioned as a payment instrument. The FCA team listened, took notes, and—crucially—asked the firm to map its flows. Where were the reserves? Who held the private keys? Which fiat accounts were used for customer funds? A simple diagram unearthed hidden dependencies on a US custodian and a Lithuanian payment institution. The conversation did not resolve the perimeter question, but it sharpened it. Supervision often begins not with law but with maps.

This chapter pivots on that mapping instinct. Rather than drown in statutory detail, it asks what regulators care about and why. These concerns cluster around four themes. The first is the licensing perimeter: whether the object of scrutiny is issuance, custody, payments, or market conduct. Most stablecoin activity touches at least two of these, which is why high-level categories matter more than sub-clauses. The United States fissures responsibilities across agencies—SEC, CFTC, FinCEN, state money transmitter regulators—leading to overlapping interpretations. The European Union, by contrast, attempts coherence through MiCA, carving stablecoin issuers into asset-referenced and e-money categories. The United Kingdom maps tokens against the familiar world of e-money and payments regulation. Each model draws its borderlines with a different hand, but all aim to answer the same question: *What activity must be controlled to protect the system?*

The second theme concerns reserves, segregation, and consumer protection—issues treated not as innovations but as recurring duties. The regulatory instinct here is conservative, shaped by decades of e-money precedents. Segregation of customer funds, timely redemptions, and wind-down plans are not exotic requirements; they are the backbone of consumer protection. They also reveal the architecture regulators prefer: systems that fail slowly, predictably, with clear recourse. Stablecoin issuers, whether in New York or Luxembourg, increasingly mimic this template. They separate operating cash from reserves, appoint independent custodians, and publish wind-down frameworks. Stability becomes less about algorithms and more about choreography.

A third thread runs through the rules on information flows: the travel rule and sanctions regimes. These are old tools forced into new shapes. Crypto on-ramps and off-ramps must collect sender and receiver information, screen transactions, and transmit data to counterparties. When the Financial Action Task Force adjusted its guidance, a single list update produced ripples across compliance teams from Berlin to San Francisco. Systems flagged transactions previously cleared; exchanges froze withdrawals for checks; wallet providers scrambled to patch. The lesson is not bureaucratic fragility but systemic coupling. When entire industries use the same lists, the same protocols, and the same screening partners, compliance becomes a network effect.

The fourth theme is supervisory relationships. These are often misunderstood as adversarial. They are not. They are long games of documentation, iteration, and calibration. A sandbox pilot run by the Monetary Authority of Singapore in 2019 illustrated this dynamic. A consortium testing a tokenised payments system negotiated scope line by line: What thresholds triggered reporting? Which systems required log retention? How would incident notifications be escalated? A year later, the same firms could describe their supervisory relationship as predictable and, crucially, collaborative. Regulators want clarity. Firms want certainty. Sandboxes provide both by shrinking the space between them.

Running through each theme is a tension between simplicity and precision. Regulators must avoid capturing too much—risking stifling innovation—or too little, risking consumer harm. Innovators must decide how much structure to adopt before they are required to. The borderline motif appears again: every entity must locate itself on the map, and every map remains provisional.

Yet something deeper sits beneath the legal categories. Stablecoins have forced a convergence of languages. Payments supervisors think in terms of consumer funds and settlement finality. Securities regulators think in terms of disclosures and market integrity. Banking regulators think in terms of prudential resilience and liquidity coverage. Crypto engineers think in terms of consensus, key management, and composability. When these languages meet, confusion is predictable. But so is synthesis. Regulation becomes not a rabbit hole but a translation exercise.

This introduction sets the stage for that translation. What follows explores the perimeter question without losing the plot; explains reserve rules without legal pedantry; decodes the travel rule without drowning in acronyms; and illuminates supervisory practice without romanticising it. The purpose is to give every reader—whether policy-maker, founder, or scholar—the ability to see the borderlines clearly enough to act, but not so rigidly that the future appears predetermined.

The open question that carries us forward is simple yet profound: as stablecoins weave themselves into daily financial life, who will draw the next set of borders—and will they do so with enough imagination to accommodate what has not yet been built?

Licences and perimeter questions: What is regulated: issuance, custody, payments, or markets? High-level categories only. ASSUMPTION: framed for UK/US/EU.

At 09:17 on 23 July 2021, the UK's Financial Conduct Authority published a short supervisory notice directed at Binance Markets Limited. In fewer than five hundred words, the FCA stated that the entity could not undertake regulated activity in the United Kingdom without prior written consent. The ruling applied to one legal entity, in one jurisdiction, on one date. Yet within twenty-four hours, traders from Singapore to Berlin reported tightened fiat rails, payment partners paused card channels, and several European banks temporarily curtailed transfers to and from the exchange. A local licensing constraint had become a global operational event. The scene revealed something essential: *perimeter decisions travel.* A regulatory line drawn in Canary Wharf had immediate consequences for individuals who had never set foot in London. Five words cut deep here: borders shift; systems ripple.

This acute sensitivity to perimeter lines shapes the stablecoin sector more than any technical design choice. The question regulators ask—what exactly is the regulated activity?—is deceptively simple, yet the answer determines almost everything about a project's posture. Is the core activity **issuance**, with obligations tied to redeemability and reserves? Is it **custody**, with duties tied to safeguarding assets and preventing misuse? Is it **payments**, with requirements tied to consumer protection and settlement? Or is it **markets**, with responsibilities tied to fair dealing, disclosures, and oversight of intermediaries? These categories sound clean. They rarely are. Each hides a tangle of consequences for what firms must document, publish, ring-fence, and report. And, as the Binance case shows, the effects escape borders.

A useful motif throughout this subchapter is the *threshold*: the point at which an activity crosses from unregulated experimentation to regulated responsibility. Every jurisdiction draws the threshold differently. The United Kingdom relies heavily on functional analysis, focusing on whether a token resembles e-money or a regulated payment instrument, as defined under the Electronic Money Regulations 2011 and the Payment Services Regulations 2017. The United States fragments responsibilities across agencies—FinCEN for money transmission, the SEC for securities, the CFTC for commodities and derivatives, and state-level regimes for money services. The European Union, via Regulation (EU) 2023/1114 (MiCA), clusters stablecoin activities into two major categories, treating e-money tokens in line with long-standing e-money law and asset-referenced tokens under a bespoke framework. Each system uses the same words—issuance, custody, payments, markets—but loads them with different thresholds, different duties, and different liabilities.

To see how these categories work in practice, begin with *issuance*. A stablecoin issuer that promises at-par redemption engages in an activity regulators instinctively associate with consumer protection. The behaviour regulators observe is simple: a customer hands over value, expecting the issuer to hold equivalent reserves and return them on demand. In the EU this triggers MiCA's e-money token rules; in the UK it may bring E-Money Regulations into view; in the US it often implicates state money transmitter laws unless structured through a bank or trust charter. The implication is clear: issuance is not just minting tokens; it is managing obligations that resemble deposit-taking without being deposits. A single promise, stated or implied, determines the licence.

Move to *custody*. Here the visible behaviour is the holding of value for someone else, often with unilateral control over private keys. A firm that can freeze, transfer, or restore customer tokens looks like a custodian, even if the underlying ledger is decentralised. In the US this invites scrutiny under the Bank Secrecy Act and state custody requirements; in the UK, custody often becomes a regulated activity when combined with certain other functions; in the EU, MiCA creates a bespoke category for "crypto-asset service providers" offering custody. Custody's implication is always the same: whoever can move the assets must be held to account. The threshold turns on power, not code.

Payments form the third category, and they are, in many ways, the most politically charged. A firm that moves money on behalf of customers—whether across blockchains or conventional rails—steps into the perimeter governing payment institutions. The behaviour regulators watch is straightforward: initiation, transmission, and settlement of value. In the UK this brings Payment Services Regulations to bear; in the EU, the Payment Services Directive remains central; in the US, payment transmission sits with FinCEN and state regulators. Crucially, these frameworks are technology-neutral. Whether transfers are posted to Ethereum or the Faster Payments Service, the regulatory impulse focuses on consumer recourse, operational resilience, and fraud prevention. Payments regulation is less concerned with innovation than with reliability.

Markets form the fourth category. If a firm operates an exchange, facilitates price discovery, or compels retail users to rely on it to trade stablecoins, regulators may treat it as a trading venue or broker. Here too behaviours matter: order-taking, market-making, custody of trading balances, and dissemination of pricing information. This is where the US difference is stark: the SEC asserts jurisdiction when tokens resemble securities, while the CFTC claims authority when they resemble commodities. The UK and EU rely more heavily on activity-based definitions. Market rules aim to ensure fairness. They discipline the intermediaries who shape liquidity, spreads, and execution.

A counter-example helps illuminate the boundaries. Consider a non-custodial wallet provider headquartered in Tallinn in 2022. It stores no private keys, processes no payments, and does not issue tokens. Users control their own assets. Estonia's regulator concluded that the activity fell outside its licensing regime. The firm operated for years without major restrictions. Yet another jurisdiction could have required a virtual asset service provider (VASP) registration merely for facilitating access to networks. The divergence exposes the limitation: activity-based regulation depends on how broadly a supervisor interprets an activity. The same behaviour in two places may sit on different sides of the threshold. To reconcile this, stablecoin projects increasingly pre-empt regulators by adopting controls associated with the strictest plausible perimeter. They treat ambiguity as risk.

Perimeter clarity matters not only for legal certainty but also for systemic stability. When regulated and unregulated actors interconnect, shocks propagate. If an issuer headquartered in New York relies on a custodial partner in Dublin and a payment intermediary in Warsaw, the project's real regulatory footprint spans three regimes. The behaviour that regulators measure—cashflows, custody logs, redemption requests—may be distributed across that network. This creates a live tension for supervisors: they must police their jurisdiction while accounting for dependency chains that cross borders. The FCA's 2021 Binance notice illustrated this again; it was not the substance of the prohibition but the global dependencies that forced partners to respond.

Threaded through all of this is the motif of the threshold: firms must decide when their activities cross from experimental to regulated, while regulators must decide where to draw the line in a way that protects consumers without freezing innovation. Issuance thresholds protect promises. Custody thresholds protect assets. Payment thresholds protect transfers. Market thresholds protect fairness. And all of them reshape business models long before licences are granted.

The open question that follows is both simple and consequential: as stablecoin architectures evolve—spanning chains, custodians, and jurisdictions—how should firms position themselves at the regulatory threshold? Should they design narrowly to avoid stepping over it, or broadly to ensure they are ready when it moves?

Reserves, segregation, and consumer protection: Recurrent themes across regimes. Segregation and wind-down plans borrow from e-money precedents.

At 07:52 on 25 June 2019, the UK Payment Systems Regulator issued an update on the collapse of Wirecard's UK subsidiary. The news froze thousands of prepaid cards across Britain and Ireland. Commuters found that their morning coffee could not be paid for; gig-workers saw weekend earnings locked behind a technical perimeter. The failure was specific—a German parent in insolvency, a UK unit supervised under the Electronic Money Regulations 2011—but the effect was blunt. People wanted their money back immediately. They could not have cared less about the legal path that money took. Segregation rules, safeguarding accounts, trust arrangements, insolvency committees: the machinery of consumer protection revealed its stark test. Either the reserve structure held, or it did not. That morning, the public learnt more about regulatory design from a broken card terminal than from a decade of consultation papers.

The Wirecard episode sharpened a foundational truth for the stablecoin sector. Regardless of technology, *reserves and segregation decide who bears the loss when something breaks*. Stablecoins that promise par redemption face the same test that e-money issuers faced long before decentralised ledgers existed. Whether the issuer calls itself a fintech, a protocol, or a payment network, supervisors ask one question: where is the money, and can we extract it cleanly when users demand it back? The brutal clarity of that question forms the quiet motif of this subchapter. A reserve is not a symbol of prudence; it is a physical statement of intent. Segregation is not a formality; it is the difference between a user reclaiming funds in days rather than months.

To see how reserves work across regimes, start with the visible behaviour regulators inspect: the flow of customer funds into safeguarded accounts. Under the UK's Electronic Money Regulations, issuers must segregate customer balances at regulated banks or invest them in secure, low-risk assets, typically short-dated government securities. The European Union followed similar logic under the second E-Money Directive. The United States, with its patchwork of state money transmitter laws, achieves the same effect through mandated permissible investments—cash, cash equivalents, or highly rated securities. Different words, same concern: customer funds must not commingle with operating funds. A single ledger entry in the wrong account can shift losses from shareholders to customers. Regulators measure that behaviour with reconciliations, bank statements, and audit trails.

Stablecoin issuers, intentionally or not, inherit this architecture. A fiat-backed issuer custodises reserves in cash and T-bills, often across several banks. Segregation is achieved through omnibus safeguarding accounts, trust structures, or bankruptcy-remote vehicles. The implication is immediate: the moment an issuer accepts redemption obligations, it becomes a de facto steward of client assets. Segregation is the legal expression of that stewardship. Fail to uphold it, and users suffer the same paralysis those Wirecard customers faced on that June morning.

Wind-down plans emerge from the same lineage. UK e-money rules require detailed planning for "orderly exit"—a blueprint that specifies how users recover funds if the firm fails. The EU's MiCA regulation mirrors this requirement for e-money tokens: issuers must demonstrate they can redeem at par during distress without fire-selling assets. In the US, wind-down mechanics surface implicitly through trust arrangements and state supervisory expectations. Plans vary; the principle does not. A credible stablecoin must describe *where the reserves are, who controls them, how quickly they can be liquidated, and how communications will run when pressure builds*. These are not ceremonial documents. They are crisis manuals.

Two named examples clarify the stakes. In October 2022, Circle, the issuer of USDC, published a reserve composition update showing that over 80% of its backing sat in short-dated US Treasury bills held through BlackRock-managed funds. The message was clear: liquidity first, yield second. That behaviour—long-term discipline over short-term optimisation—built confidence during stress events. Contrast this with Payward Europe's decision in 2020 to use a patchwork of European custodians for exchange float. Although compliant, the structure introduced operational friction across jurisdictions, making reconciliations slower. Neither case involved wrongdoing, but they mapped the trade-off: concentration versus fragmentation, speed versus diversification. Segregation frameworks must evaluate such decisions.

A counter-example reveals the boundary. In 2021, a small European fintech kept user funds in a single safeguarding account with a single bank. It was technically segregated, but operationally fragile. When the bank experienced a brief systems outage, reconciliations stalled, and the fintech paused customer withdrawals for thirty-six hours. No funds were lost; customers were merely inconvenienced. Supervisors accepted the firm's explanation but advised diversification. This case shows that segregation alone does not guarantee resilience. The behaviour that matters is not the existence of a safeguard account but the robustness of the entire custody chain. To reconcile this, best practice now pairs segregation with stress tests that measure how quickly reserves can be mobilised under extreme but plausible scenarios.

Segregation and wind-down plans borrow heavily from e-money precedents, yet stablecoins introduce a new layer: real-time transparency. On-chain issuance and redemption allow the public, not just auditors, to observe supply changes. Reserve disclosures supplement this with off-chain visibility. The market monitors both and reacts instantly to inconsistencies. A stablecoin issuer that publishes a monthly reserves attestation with line-item detail demonstrates more than compliance; it demonstrates *predictability*. Predictability is a form of consumer protection. It narrows the zone in which rumours can thrive.

The recurrent theme across the UK, US, and EU is simple but profound: consumer protection frameworks exist to prevent users from funding the issuer's mistakes. Segregation ensures that reserves cannot be spent on payroll or marketing. Wind-down plans ensure that even if management fails, the structure does not. And regular disclosures transform technical assurance into public accountability. These themes echo across regimes because they work.

The open tension is unresolved. Should stablecoin issuers adhere strictly to existing e-money principles, or adapt them to the realities of global, 24/7 markets? Traditional safeguards were designed for offices that closed at 5 p.m. Blockchain rails never close. How should the next generation of reserve rules meet that fact?

Travel rule and sanctions basics: Identity and screening at on/off-ramps. A list-change ripple shows moving compliance parts.

At 14:07 on 8 August 2022, the US Office of Foreign Assets Control (OFAC) added the Tornado Cash smart contract addresses to its Specially Designated Nationals list. Within minutes, major exchanges and custody platforms across the UK, US, and EU froze deposits linked to the flagged addresses. A Dutch-based developer had already been arrested earlier that week in Amsterdam. Yet the immediate impact was not on the protocol's code but on the institutions that touched fiat: exchanges, payment processors, and wallet providers. Screens flashed red as automated sanctions filters rejected transactions that had been perfectly acceptable a day earlier. A list change—just a few kilobytes pushed to a government server—cascaded through the compliance infrastructure with startling speed. It revealed the truth that this subchapter explores: identity checks and sanctions screening concentrate at the on- and off-ramps, and the moving parts never rest.

The episode also showed how fragile cross-border coordination can be. In London, one exchange continued to accept deposits routed through newly tainted addresses for several hours after OFAC's action. In Frankfurt, a payment institution blocked an entire tranche of withdrawals after its screening provider failed to update the list promptly. Those discrepancies emerged not from disagreement but from timing. Sanctions infrastructure lives on clocks as much as on rules; the hour at which an update propagates can determine whether a customer is served or stranded. That time-sensitivity—the shadow rhythm beneath compliance—is the motif we will return to.

Stablecoin systems intersect with these obligations in predictable ways. When a customer buys tokens using bank rails, the provider must verify identity, monitor activity, and screen names and addresses against national and supranational lists. When the customer cashes out, the same process repeats in reverse. Everything in between—the pure on-chain movement of tokens—lies outside the perimeter of traditional anti-money-laundering infrastructure. That separation is intentional. The state regulates the *points of entry and exit*, not the ledger itself. Yet it means the quality of compliance depends on what happens at the periphery.

To see how regulators structure this, consider the Financial Action Task Force's (FATF) "Recommendation 16"—the Travel Rule—adopted into EU law via the Transfer of Funds Regulation (2023) and reflected in US FinCEN expectations. The behaviour it demands is simple to observe: when a user sends value from one regulated provider to another above a set threshold, specific information must "travel" with the transfer. That information includes the sender's name, account number, and address (or national ID), and the recipient's details. Providers verify this data, screen it, and flag anomalies. The legal texts vary by jurisdiction, but the practical rule is constant: regulated entities must know who is sending what to whom. The name gives the explanation, but the implication is more subtle. Identity becomes a moving payload, coupled to the transaction like a digital manifest.

This becomes concrete when two regulated virtual asset service providers interact. Imagine a UK exchange sending £1,000 equivalent of stablecoins to a French custodian on behalf of a corporate client. Before the transfer leaves London, the exchange packages identity data into a secure message, often using a protocol such as TRISA or Travel Rule Universal Solution Technology. The custodian in Paris receives the details, screens them against EU and UN lists, and decides whether to accept the funds. If any of the recipient's directors appear on a sanctions list, the custodian must block the funds and report. The behaviour is visible in logs and audit trails; supervisors measure it in the quality of matches, false positives, and case-handling times.

Two named examples illustrate the operational ripples. In May 2020, Coinbase UK temporarily suspended withdrawals to a handful of European banks due to a mismatch between its sanctions-screening provider's update cycle and HM Treasury's consolidated list. The incident lasted only hours, but customers noticed. It showed how infrastructure dependencies—third-party data feeds, APIs, and update schedules—define the real compliance perimeter. A contrasting case occurred in June 2021, when Bitstamp refined its inbound screening process after identifying elevated false positives linked to newly sanctioned Belarusian entities under EU Council Regulation 765/2006. Instead of halting transfers outright, Bitstamp deployed more granular matching logic, reducing customer impact while maintaining regulatory expectations. The two cases show how institutions commit to different behaviours under pressure: freeze first and ask later, or refine filters while maintaining service continuity. The motif reappears: timing and calibration matter more than slogans.

A credible counter-example tempers the narrative. In late 2022, a small Baltic fintech chose to rely solely on manual sanctions checks for low-value crypto purchases, arguing that automated screening would overwhelm its limited resources with false positives. The policy technically complied with local thresholds but failed operationally. Manual reviews piled up, customers waited days, and two transactions involving a newly sanctioned Russian individual slipped through before staff intervened. Supervisors intervened and required automated screening for all transfers, regardless of size. The case reveals the hard limit: partial compliance that sacrifices rigour for convenience will eventually break. The reconciliation is straightforward. Efficiency and accuracy are not opposites; they are joint requirements. Automated screening raises flags; trained analysts resolve them.

Sanctions compliance extends beyond identity to *address behaviour*. Wallet addresses linked to illicit activity are tracked by blockchain analytics firms such as Chainalysis and Elliptic. Regulated providers use these risk scores—"low", "medium", "high"—to determine whether to accept inbound flows. A high-risk address does not automatically imply wrongdoing; it may simply cluster with known mixers or darknet marketplaces. Providers compare this behavioural data with customer profiles, questioning discrepancies. A user who claims to be a freelance designer in Leeds but receives funds from a high-risk cluster in Moscow triggers a compliance review. The metric is not just binary risk but deviation from expected behaviour.

This layered screening is why a list update travels far beyond the institution that triggers it. When OFAC or the UK's Office of Financial Sanctions Implementation (OFSI) adds a new name, screening providers update databases; exchanges update risk engines; custodians suspend transfers; banks reassess correspondent relationships. A small change at the apex of the sanctions hierarchy cascades through dozens of systems. The compliance machinery resembles a long, interconnected chain—one link moves, all others adjust. Cross-border stablecoin flows rely on that synchronisation.

At the heart of this machinery sits a categorical divide: the blockchain may be decentralised, but the providers that touch fiat remain centralised and regulated. This is where Travel Rule obligations and sanctions requirements coalesce. Stablecoins magnify the contrast. A token can move at 02:00 on a Sunday on-chain, but the receiving exchange cannot lawfully release funds to a user until identity is verified and screening is passed. Speed meets friction. The motif repeats: timing governs trust.

The unresolved tension remains open. As token-based payments scale, should sanctions rules adapt to real-time settlement, or should providers embed more friction at the periphery to absorb shocks? Stablecoin users expect immediacy; regulators expect certainty. Which expectation sets the pace?

Supervisory relationships: Engage early, document, iterate. A sandbox-style pilot shows scope agreements and controls.

On 7 July 2016, the UK Financial Conduct Authority (FCA) opened its first regulatory sandbox cohort in London, allowing selected firms to test innovative financial products under the regulator's direct oversight. Among the early participants was Billon Group, piloting a blockchain-based e-money platform whose workflows required explicit sign-off on minting, redemption, and customer safeguarding. Its engineers soon discovered that the pivotal feature of the sandbox was not permission to experiment, but the enforced discipline of documentation. Every design choice—from transaction limits to data handling—had to be set out, justified, and tested against predefined controls. The pilot did more than reveal flaws. It showed that supervisory relationships are built not on grand statements but on a slow rhythm of exchange: a question, a draft, a revision. *Then again*, as one FCA case officer told the team during a feedback meeting, "regulation is a conversation, not a verdict". That sentence captures the motif running through this subchapter.

The rhythm of that conversation is visible in stablecoin projects that must navigate the overlapping perimeters of the UK, US, and EU regimes. Each jurisdiction asks a similar question—what exactly are you doing with customer money?—but frames it through a different lens. A UK payment institution focuses on safeguarding and wind-down planning. A US state regulator probes capital and permissible investments. An EU authority tests governance, resilience, and operational procedures under MiCA. The providers that succeed do not wait for clarity; they create it through early engagement. But early engagement only matters when paired with the behaviours regulators trust: delivering documents on time, answering questions precisely, and iterating controls until both sides understand what "acceptable risk" looks like.

To anchor the point, consider the FCA's 2019 sandbox test by FermiGrid, a London start-up trialling tokenised wholesale settlement. FermiGrid entered the cohort with a clear hypothesis but incomplete controls. Its first submission lacked a segregation model; its second did not define incident-response steps; only the third articulated both. The process took months. But the regulator did not object to the slowness. It measured the firm's willingness to revise and commit. The implication is clear. Supervisory trust is cumulative, built through repeated, observable acts.

A contrasting example comes from the United States. In October 2021, the New York Department of Financial Services (NYDFS) reviewed an application from a stablecoin issuer seeking a limited purpose trust charter. The applicant submitted strong technology documentation but weak outlines for transaction monitoring and board oversight. NYDFS did not reject the application; instead, it issued a detailed request for information. The firm, however, replied with generalities rather than specifics, prompting delays that pushed the review well into 2022. The outcome—an extended evaluation—was not punitive but diagnostic. When applicants fail to engage substantively, supervisors infer fragility. The reconciliation between this and FermiGrid's experience lies in the behaviour: iteration signals competence; vagueness signals risk.

The supervisory sandbox is not a green light for shortcuts. It is a controlled environment in which both the firm and the regulator measure what could go wrong. This measurement takes concrete forms: cap limits on transaction sizes; daily logs of operational events; attested reconciliations. These artefacts allow regulators to test not just the product's function but its habits. A system that claims scalability must show metrics: peak load, failover timing, and error rates. A wallet claiming robust customer protection must demonstrate how quickly it can freeze a compromised account and document that response. Behaviours matter more than promises.

The supervision motif—conversation, documents, iteration—also governs cross-border pilots. In 2023, the Monetary Authority of Singapore (MAS) and the FCA launched Project Guardian-UK, a sandbox-style partnership to explore tokenised settlement for wholesale markets. Participants had to submit explicit scope agreements defining which processes were "in play" and which remained off-limits. These scope documents defined perimeter in practice: MAS insisted that all custodied assets be held under existing trust arrangements, while the FCA focused on operational continuity and data localisation. The firms involved learned that scope agreements are not administrative hurdles. They are maps of accountability. They define the who, the how, and the what-if.

A credible counter-example sheds light on the limits of the sandbox model. In 2022, a European blockchain remittance start-up attempted to bypass formal testing regimes by launching a beta product with only informal regulator consultations. The product operated for months without incident, but when the firm sought an EMI licence under the Central Bank of Ireland, it was forced to re-architect its entire safeguarding model. The regulator found that although the firm's processes worked in practice, they had never been systematically documented. The start-up argued this was a minor gap; the regulator saw it as a structural weakness. Documentation was not optional. It was the foundation upon which licences rest. The reconciliation lies in understanding the purpose of supervision: the regulator manages systemic exposure, not the firm's convenience.

Detailed documentation also anchors operational control. A stablecoin issuer's runbook must specify which team triggers a pause on minting, which team communicates with the regulator, and which team manages customer messaging. Early drafts often lack coherence, with vague references to "engineering team" or "risk team". Regulators push back. They want names, escalation paths, and time thresholds. A runbook that commits to "customer notification within 20 minutes of an incident" but shows no mechanism for coordinating legal review becomes a red flag. Supervisors measure not aspiration but feasibility.

A recurring motif in supervisory relationships is the diagram: maps of custody chains, data flows, access permissions, and governance escalations. These diagrams translate complex operations into stable visual forms. In one 2022 FCA sandbox test for a tokenised money-market fund, the provider's third diagram—after two rounds of revisions—finally captured the cross-border safeguarding chain from the UK trust account to the Luxembourg sub-custodian and back. The clarity changed the tone of supervision; vague edges became firm boundaries. The implication is simple. Regulators respond to clarity because clarity reduces misinterpretation.

Against this landscape, the sandbox-style pilot remains a productive proving ground for stablecoin issuers. It forces firms to define perimeter: which functions they perform (issuance, redemption), which functions third parties handle (custody, KYC), and which risks remain residual (market, operational, counterparty). Each refinement becomes part of the emerging supervisory narrative. That narrative, once stable, becomes the basis for formal authorisation.

Yet the unresolved question shadows all of this. As stablecoins expand into payments, treasury operations, and cross-border settlement, can supervisory relationships scale at the same conversational pace? Engagement takes time, clarity takes drafts, and trust takes repetition. But markets move faster. Will regulators and innovators converge on a shared tempo, or will the clock drift again?

Chapter 8
CBDCs vs Private Stablecoins

On a spring morning in Stockholm in May 2020, Sveriges Riksbank invited a small group of commercial-bank technicians into a quiet, windowless room to watch the results of its e-krona pilot settle across a simulated wholesale ledger. The room looked unremarkable—whiteboards, power strips, the low hum of servers—but the moment was not. A high-value transfer, represented as a simple token on a Riksbank-controlled test network, finalised in seconds with deterministic finality. One of the bank engineers, who had spent his career wrestling with the batch cycles of legacy platforms, whispered a single phrase to a colleague: "*This is the end of reconciliation.*" His comment captured something the debate often misses. CBDCs are not merely a new shape of money; they are a new shape of settlement, and settlement defines power, speed, and structure in the financial system.

Contrast that quiet room with a café in Lagos, where a small merchant runs daily payments through a private stablecoin service, converting receipts into naira by mid-afternoon. For her, the finality of a CBDC is irrelevant. She cares about access, low friction, and the fact that a single scrolling list in her wallet shows exactly what she earned and what she can spend. She uses private tokens not because she distrusts the state, but because the state is absent at the point of sale. What looks like competition in policy circles feels like complementarity on the ground. Two rails, two purposes, one lived economy.

The tension between these scenes—one institutional and quiet, the other informal and improvised—defines the chapter that follows. For all the grand rhetoric about digital sovereignty, programmable finance, and the future of money, the practical question is disarmingly simple: how will public and private digital instruments coexist? And beneath that question lies an older one, stretching back to the earliest banknotes: how much monetary innovation should the state perform itself, and how much should it tolerate from others? The CBDC debate is a replay of that struggle, but with new tools and sharper stakes.

The design space alone reveals how deep the choices run. A retail CBDC tested in Shenzhen or Nassau presents a different philosophical and operational challenge from a wholesale CBDC piloted in Toronto or London. An account-based model privileges traceability; a token-based model privileges bearer-like fluidity. A direct architecture gives the central bank a line to every citizen; an intermediated one preserves the commercial banking spine. These are not incremental differences. They shape how a crisis unfolds, how privacy is protected, and how innovation moves at the margins. The structure of a CBDC is the structure of its society in miniature.

Private stablecoins, by contrast, grow from the edges inward. They begin where pain points concentrate: in cross-border transfers, in niche commerce, in ecosystems where settlement delays cost real money. Their strength is not universal reach but flexible design. They can wrap features—multi-currency wallets, automated invoicing, programmable escrow—far faster than public institutions can legislate them. This is why a software developer in Buenos Aires or a remote contractor in Lisbon may prefer a private token for day-to-day operations while holding a CBDC, if it emerges, for predictable settlement. The pattern is familiar: central banks set the base layer; innovators build the user layer.

Yet the boundary between public and private is not just a technical dividing line. It is a political and ethical battleground. Nothing illustrates this more than the debate on privacy. A tiered model, long discussed in Frankfurt and Ottawa, allows small payments to remain pseudonymous while requiring identity checks at higher thresholds. Advocates see proportionality; critics see a slippery slope. Programmability sharpens the question further. Purpose-limited spending, the sort tested in Seoul's disaster-relief programmes, offers targeted efficiency but invites fear of paternalism. Imagine a university issuing a digital travel stipend that works seamlessly for train tickets but rejects a café purchase on grounds of "categorical ineligibility". Is that efficiency or overreach? The answer depends on trust, and trust rests on governance and transparency, not marketing.

Migration paths reveal another layer. If a CBDC arrives, issuers of private stablecoins must adapt reserve compositions; wallet providers must integrate public rails; merchants must renegotiate acceptance economics. None of this happens overnight. It proceeds in phases: a dual-rail period in which CBDCs are used for settlement between banks while private tokens continue to dominate front-end experiences; a convergence period where wallet interfaces blur the distinction; and a maturity phase in which incentives, fees, and regulations stabilise. Each phase embeds compromises. Each phase redistributes bargaining power.

A quiet motif threads through these dynamics: the handover. Who hands what to whom, and on what terms? CBDCs hand new capabilities to the state—direct issuance, granular data, upgraded resilience. Private stablecoins hand new capabilities to users—programmability, global reach, customisable wallets. Merchants hand preferences to the market by choosing which instruments they accept. And regulators hand constraints to everyone as they define limits, guardrails, and reporting duties. The future of digital money is not a battle of technologies; it is a choreography of handovers.

This chapter sits at that intersection. It examines the contrasting logics of CBDCs and private stablecoins, and the ways in which each illuminates the other. The competition narrative, though tempting, fades when viewed through lived usage patterns. The complement narrative, though optimistic, ignores structural risks. Reality lives in between: a layered system in which central banks provide the spine, private systems provide mobility, and users arbitrate the difference through experience.

The deeper question arises from this layered view: can two forms of digital money—one sovereign, one private—coexist without crowding each other out? And if they do, what happens to innovation cycles, privacy norms, and the balance between state capacity and market dynamism? As CBDCs move from theory to pilots, and private stablecoins mature under stricter regulatory regimes, the shape of digital money will no longer be a thought experiment. It will be infrastructure.

The stakes are therefore high, not just for technologists and policy architects but for every institution building the payment systems of the next decade. Is the future defined by a single authoritative ledger or a federation of interoperable platforms? Will users care which rail carries their transactions, or will abstraction make the debate invisible to them? And in that invisibility, might new forms of power accumulate unnoticed?

These are not merely technical puzzles. They touch on the oldest debates in political economy: the limits of the state, the virtues of competition, the meaning of privacy, and the role of money as a public good. The chapter ahead follows those threads—through institutions, pilots, user journeys, and edge cases—towards a clearer view of the world we are building every time a transaction settles, visibly or not.

Design space of CBDCs: Retail vs wholesale; account vs token; direct vs intermediated. A wholesale pilot highlights settlement benefits.

On a clear morning in December 2021, in the Swiss National Bank's rooms above the Bundesplatz in Zurich, a small group of central bankers and technologists watched a screen that looked almost disappointingly plain. A tokenised government bond changed hands between two commercial banks. Central bank money—wholesale-only, experimental, and very much not for the public—moved across a distributed ledger and settled the trade. No paper certificate shifted, no clerk stamped anything, no batch file waited for an end-of-day window. The transfer was atomic: either both legs completed or neither did. When the confirmation appeared, one of the project leads for Project Helvetia remarked quietly that, for the institutions involved, this was "as final as it gets."

That test, a wholesale CBDC pilot under the aegis of the BIS Innovation Hub and the Swiss National Bank, looked narrow. It touched a handful of banks, a private tokenisation platform, and a controlled sandbox environment. Yet it illustrated the core promise of CBDCs in their most conservative form: upgrade the settlement engine of the financial system without rewriting the rest of the machine. No QR codes. No retail apps. Just cleaner plumbing for very large numbers.

The contrast with retail visions could hardly be sharper. While Zurich was testing high-value settlement in a controlled circle, policy makers in Beijing, Nassau, and Stockholm were piloting direct-to-citizen instruments: the e-CNY, the Sand Dollar, the e-krona. In shopping centres and buses, citizens experimented with wallets that held claims not on their bank but on their central bank. For many, the experience felt indistinguishable from a commercial mobile wallet; for lawyers and economists, it represented a profound shift. The state was stepping from the background of money into its foreground, not only as issuer of base money but as visible balance provider.

That divergence—Zurich's machine room versus the citizen's handset—defines the design space of CBDCs. The narrative is often squeezed into a binary question: will there be a CBDC or not? The more interesting questions are conditional: *what kind* of CBDC, *for whom*, and *through which institutions*? Retail versus wholesale, account-based versus token-based, direct versus intermediated—each axis reshapes the relationship between central banks, commercial banks, fintechs, and users. The path chosen along these axes is not a matter of technical taste. It encodes a view of how money, credit, and data should interact.

Begin with the first axis: retail versus wholesale. The Project Helvetia scene exemplifies the wholesale side. A wholesale CBDC restricts access to financial institutions already eligible to hold central bank reserves. It aims to modernise RTGS (real-time gross settlement) infrastructure, reduce settlement risk in securities markets, and support cross-border experiments where central banks interlink their systems. The benefits are measurable: same-day versus instant settlement; reduced reliance on intermediating correspondent banks; fewer reconciliation breaks. The public never touches this CBDC directly. Their benefit arrives indirectly, as lower costs and lower counterparty risk in the financial products they use.

Retail CBDCs flip the orientation. They grant households and firms a direct claim on central bank money in digital form. That claim can live in a wallet on a phone, a smart card, or an account in a government-supported app. The design choices here carry visible behaviours. A retail CBDC that functions offline in remote areas addresses financial inclusion; one that requires constant connectivity does not. A system that allows small, pseudonymous payments mirrors some properties of cash; one that enforces full identification for every transaction does not. The implication is stark: retail CBDCs are not just about technology; they are constitutional. They encode a stance on state reach.

The second axis, account versus token, cuts across the first. An account-based CBDC ties balances to identities at the ledger level. The core system records that "Account X at Bank Y holds amount Z." Transfers resemble those on existing interbank systems, albeit with different participants and perhaps different legal underpinnings. A token-based CBDC, by contrast, treats the unit of value as a bearer instrument: whoever controls the private key controls the claim, much as whoever holds a banknote controls the cash. In practice, most central bank designs are hybrids. They employ strong identity checks at the boundary—when users top up or cash out—but use token-like constructs inside the system to improve resilience and allow limited offline operation.

Account designs show their strength in control and compliance. Lost credentials can be recovered; suspicious transactions can be flagged centrally; limits can be applied per person. Token designs show their strength in resilience and privacy. Devices can transact directly in the absence of a network; small payments can be kept off the central log. The choice is not trivial. It shapes how fraud is handled, how outages are managed, and how citizens feel about being observed. The motif worth keeping in mind here is the *ledger of record*: will the central bank's books see every payment instance, or only aggregates?

The third axis—direct versus intermediated—answers a more institutional question: who holds the customer relationship? In a direct model, the central bank offers CBDC accounts or wallets itself. Citizens log into a central-bank-branded interface, akin to a public utility. This maximises state visibility and minimises dependence on private intermediaries. It also burdens the central bank with tasks it has historically avoided: retail onboarding, customer support, and product design. Critically, it risks disintermediating commercial banks by providing a safer alternative to deposits, especially in crises.

Intermediated models, by contrast, keep commercial banks and payment providers in the foreground. The central bank issues CBDC into the system, but private institutions distribute it, manage wallets, and provide user interfaces. The central bank's ledger records balances at the institution level; end-user details remain with the intermediaries. This preserves the two-tier banking structure and leverages existing expertise in AML, KYC, and customer care. The trade-off is clear: intermediated designs align with current structures but offer less radical reimagining of access; direct designs change more but risk destabilising credit intermediation.

Two further examples highlight how these axes combine in practice. The People's Bank of China's e-CNY pilots have explored a retail, account-leaning, intermediated model, with commercial banks and large tech firms distributing wallets and the central bank retaining a strong position in the settlement core. The Bahamas' Sand Dollar, by contrast, has pursued a retail, token-leaning model designed for inclusion in remote islands, with regulated financial institutions offering wallets but the central bank conscious of offline and low-connectivity constraints. Both initiatives demonstrate that "CBDC" is not a single product but a family of architectures tailored to local objectives.

A credible counter-example grounds the discussion. Consider the UK's Faster Payments Service and the euro area's TARGET Instant Payment Settlement (TIPS). Both provide near-instant bank-to-bank transfers in existing currencies without a CBDC. From the user's perspective, a well-designed bank app using these rails can already deliver something that looks like a digital pound or euro: fast, cheap, always available. This raises a sharp question: why introduce a CBDC at all if upgraded RTGS and instant-payment rails provide similar functionality?

The limitation of this counter-example lies in what it omits. Faster Payments and TIPS clear obligations between banks, but the liabilities remain commercial bank money. In stress, deposit guarantees and lender-of-last-resort facilities matter. A CBDC, by contrast, is a direct public liability. For wholesale use cases, that distinction allows tokenised securities to settle in central bank money on new platforms, removing intraday credit exposures. For retail cases, it offers an anchor asset whose safety does not depend on a specific bank's creditworthiness. The design question is not whether CBDC beats Faster Payments, but how it complements it and what new structures it enables—across borders, across platforms, and across crisis scenarios.

The wholesale pilot in Zurich illustrates one of those structures. By embedding central bank money on the same ledger as tokenised assets, Project Helvetia reduced the need for complex links between multiple systems. Delivery-versus-payment occurred in a single environment. This is not about marginal gains in efficiency. It is about removing reconciliation layers that currently absorb considerable operational energy. When a secure wholesale CBDC can settle tokenised government bonds in real time, entire post-trade workflows compress. Margining calculations change. Counterparty risk windows shorten. The settlement engine, quietly, shifts gear.

Throughout this design space, a recurring question surfaces: *what should remain programmable, and by whom?* CBDC architectures can embed rules—limits, conditions, tiered privacy—at different layers. A retail, account-based, direct CBDC could, in theory, enforce policy in code far more directly than a wholesale, token-based, intermediated one. Yet central banks are wary of becoming perceived programmers of everyday life. Most publicly stated designs emphasise "platform, not product": the idea that the central bank provides a neutral, robust base layer while private actors build user-facing features. How that principle survives contact with political pressure and crisis dynamics remains an open question.

The design space of CBDCs is therefore not an abstract catalogue but a set of real trade-offs between resilience, privacy, competition, and institutional role. Retail versus wholesale defines who touches the instrument. Account versus token defines how claims are recorded and recovered. Direct versus intermediated defines who owns the relationship and bears operational duties. Each choice narrows some futures and opens others.

The unresolved tension that follows—and that the rest of this chapter will probe—is whether central banks will choose the combinations that preserve the subtle balance between public trust and private innovation, or whether the gravitational pull of safety and control will draw them towards designs that are technically elegant but socially brittle. When the next wholesale pilot settles another bond trade in seconds, and when the next retail trial hands a citizen a central bank wallet for groceries, which aspects of that experience will be deliberate design choices—and which will be unintended consequences of a model chosen years earlier, in quiet rooms like the one above the Bundesplatz?

Competition or complement?: Coexistence patterns emerge: CBDC for base settlement, private tokens for UX and features

On a February afternoon in 2024, a payments engineer at Banco de la República in Bogotá watched a screen that had become oddly symbolic. A wholesale CBDC prototype—part of a joint "Project Regata" experiment reported by the bank and the BIS Innovation Hub in 2023—had just settled a simulated interbank transfer across two domestic institutions while, metres away, a fintech partner tested a private stablecoin payout through their consumer wallet. The two rails ran in parallel. Same currency. Same jurisdiction. Different philosophies. One settlement was final, slow to change, and designed for the system's deepest foundations. The other was fluid, consumer-facing, and iterated weekly.

The engineer later described the moment as "watching two levels of the economy communicate without speaking the same language." Both rails cleared value, yet only one of them was built for citizens tapping phones at a market stall. The wholesale pilot dealt with the spine of the financial system; the private stablecoin app dealt with its fingertips. The distinction did not feel like competition. It felt like layering.

The idea that CBDCs and private stablecoins must fight for dominance has become a favourite trope in conferences, but it rarely survives scrutiny. At the heart of most central bank designs is a particular aspiration: a reliable, low-risk settlement layer. At the heart of most private stablecoin products sits a different aspiration altogether: features, customisability, speed, user experience. The two are not substitutes. They sit on different time horizons, serve different constituencies, and evolve on different political timelines. The tension arises only when one side pretends to be the other.

The scene in Bogotá captures a truth that is becoming harder to ignore. When CBDCs enter the market, they are unlikely to replace private stablecoins. More often, they will create a benchmark. The benchmark sits in the deep plumbing: finality, intraday liquidity, and regulatory clarity. Private issuers then build **around** that benchmark, not against it. The interplay is less a duel and more a choreography.

A clear example appears in the euro area's instant-settlement experiments. In 2022, the Banque de France's wholesale CBDC pilot settled digital bonds on a shared ledger, with central bank money delivered atomically against tokenised securities. That same year, on the retail side, Circle expanded EURC stablecoin reach through consumer wallets and merchant processors in Paris and Berlin. The former emphasised settlement coherence for large-value transfers; the latter emphasised usability, breadth of integrations, and developer-friendly APIs. The flows touched different worlds. Users buying a train ticket in Lyon did not care whether the clearing core used a CBDC, but they cared intensely that their wallet worked with their preferred payments app.

This division of labour becomes clearer when traced to behaviours. When a CBDC is used for wholesale settlement, the metric that matters is not "number of users" but "intraday credit exposure reduced." It is the sort of metric that appears in risk reports, not app dashboards. When a private stablecoin is used at the edge, the visible behaviour is a tap-to-pay, a cross-border freelancer payout, or a merchant integration. The metric here might be "checkout conversion rate" or "time to first deposit." These measures live in product analytics, not central bank communiqués. Both matter; they simply matter to different actors.

A counter-example grounds the discussion. Nigeria's eNaira, launched in October 2021 as a retail CBDC, aimed to deliver inclusion and modernise payments simultaneously. Yet early adoption levels remained modest, while private mobile-money providers such as Paga and OPay continued to dominate everyday transactions. Critics argued that this showed CBDCs "cannot compete." But that critique misreads the aims. The eNaira's role as a base settlement layer, supervised by the central bank, was never designed to mimic the user-experience velocity of private wallets. The pilot's limitation lay not in its architecture but in its positioning: citizens gravitated to providers who already solved real-world frictions—acceptance, incentives, customer support. Once the central bank recalibrated towards infrastructure enhancement rather than retail displacement, the narrative changed.

The common motif underpinning most coexistence models is *division of purpose*. A CBDC often sits where risk tolerance is lowest and stability requirements highest: interbank settlement, high-value payments, and cross-platform bridging. Private tokens sit where competition, differentiation, and iterative design flourish: interfaces, conditional transfers, loyalty schemes, merchant integrations, automated payouts. The coexistence is therefore functional. Each domain imposes different constraints and rewards.

Two further examples reinforce this pattern. In Singapore, MAS's Project Orchid (2022–2023) explored a programmable money architecture that placed core ledger functions within central-bank-governed modules while leaving user-facing programmability to commercial banks and fintechs. UOB and OCBC, for instance, piloted retail vouchers redeemable through private wallets, while the central bank maintained settlement anchors. In the United States, by contrast, USDC and PYUSD expanded acceptance across Web2 merchant platforms, even as the Federal Reserve focused on FedNow—a base-layer instant payments system rather than a retail CBDC. Again, the coexistence looked practical: the state provided finality; the private sector provided interface and reach.

Where coexistence becomes contentious is not at the level of technology but at the level of incentives. If a retail CBDC were to offer features far beyond basic transfer—such as integrated savings products, loyalty schemes, or programmable conditionality—private stablecoins would face genuine competitive displacement. Central banks know this. Most published design studies emphasise a deliberately "thin" CBDC layer: a core infrastructure, not a bundled super-app. In effect, central banks choose to define the scope of the public rail narrowly to preserve contestability at the edge.

The choice to keep CBDC features minimal creates an interesting implication. If the CBDC becomes the settlement anchor—much like reserves are today—private stablecoins may align their reserve assets and liquidity practices to interoperate natively with it. Over time, that creates something akin to a two-tier digital system: CBDC as the root authority, private tokens as the variable, user-driven layer above it. Competition becomes less relevant than compatibility.

The unresolved risk, however, emerges when private tokens offer features that the CBDC cannot or will not provide. Consider programmable payment streams: wallets that send micro-transfers every minute for a freelancer's labour on a gig platform. No central bank will expose itself to that design surface; the user-experience complexity and policy risks are too high. Yet such features may become economically significant. If private stablecoins specialise in these domains, they may outgrow their dependence on the CBDC anchor, creating a dual-track monetary environment. This is the tension policymakers rarely articulate: coexistence is stable only if the CBDC layer remains broadly neutral and the private layer remains broadly interoperable.

The Bogotá engineer watching the dual-rail test remarked afterwards that "coexistence happens by default; competition happens by mistake." The line captures the essence of the policy dilemma. CBDCs, by design, have slow upgrade cycles, political oversight, and strong guarantees. Private tokens, by design, have fast iteration, market-driven features, and wider interface agility. When each side focuses on its strengths, coexistence emerges organically. When either side strays—when a CBDC tries to become a retail super-app, or when a private token neglects reserve discipline—the alignment frays.

The forward question, then, is deceptively simple: when the first major jurisdiction launches a retail or wholesale CBDC, will private stablecoin issuers position themselves as complements to a public settlement backbone—or will they attempt to substitute for it, risking regulatory recalibration? The answer will not be decided in

Zurich testbeds or fintech app releases alone. It will be decided in the quiet, structural choices each actor makes about scope, boundaries, and the architecture of digital value itself.

Privacy and programmability: Tiered privacy and purpose-limited spend raise debate. A travel stipend example shows promise and peril.

In April 2020, residents across South Korea began receiving COVID-19 emergency relief on prepaid cards and mobile wallets that could only be spent within their home province and, in many cases, only at small and medium-sized merchants. Large online platforms were excluded; cross-border use was impossible. The scheme was not a CBDC—it ran on existing card networks and local "regional currency" systems—but it offered a glimpse of programmable money in practice. The code did not live at the central bank. It lived in merchant category filters and postcode whitelists. For most people, it worked. Shops saw business return; unused balances expired automatically. Yet the discomfort was immediate. Citizens discovered that a unit of state-issued support was money that behaved differently: it could say "yes" to groceries and "no" to savings, "yes" to the local bookshop and "no" to Amazon. That distinction—between ordinary fungible money and constrained, purpose-bound value—is the quiet fault line that CBDCs now approach. Programmability promises efficiency. It also invites control.

Central banks exploring CBDCs have absorbed this lesson. When they speak of "programmability", they rarely mean hard-coded paternalism. They mean something softer: the ability for intermediaries and users to embed conditions, automate flows, and interact with contracts. Still, the line is thin. A travel stipend that automatically covers public transport and hotels but refuses nightclub charges can be framed as safeguarding a budget. It can also be read as moral judgement expressed in code. The design space of CBDCs does not escape this tension; it intensifies it.

Start with tiered privacy, the framework many central banks now discuss in principle. Show the behaviour first. A retail CBDC pilot allows low-value transactions—say, below €50—to be conducted with minimal data sharing beyond what is needed to prevent double-spending. Above a higher threshold, perhaps €2,000 per month, transactions must be linked to a verified identity, with transaction histories subject to anti-money-laundering monitoring. Name the approach: *tiered, risk-based privacy*.

Explain the logic. Authorities argue that small, everyday payments resemble cash and should retain strong privacy protections, while larger flows carry higher risks of money laundering, terrorist finance, or tax evasion and therefore warrant more scrutiny. The implication is practical. A citizen buying a coffee or bus ticket could enjoy something close to cash-like anonymity; a company wiring salaries could not.

Measured behaviours matter here. A tiered model can specify, for example, that 90% of annual CBDC transactions by count fall into the low-data tier, while 90% of volumes by value fall into the high-data tier. Privacy for daily life; transparency for big flows. That ratio becomes a policy variable. Move the thresholds, and the lived experience changes. The motif worth holding onto is the *zone*: the zone of life that remains off the ledger's microscope, and the zone that does not.

European surveys and ECB working papers have tended to emphasise this balance. Respondents consistently rank privacy features near the top of desired CBDC attributes, alongside security and zero-cost basic use. Central banks, wary of replicating the full traceability of bank transfers in a CBDC, lean towards intermediated models where transaction-level data is held primarily by payment service providers, with the central bank seeing only pseudonymised or aggregated information. Behaviourally, this means that a low-value CBDC transaction may leave no more trace at the core than a cash withdrawal does today; the bank or wallet provider holds details under existing AML rules. That structure tries to reassure two constituencies at once: privacy advocates and supervisors.

A credible counter-example exposes the limit. In China's e-CNY pilots, the People's Bank of China has spoken of "controllable anonymity" for small payments, but the architecture ultimately reserves the right to de-anonymise under legal process. Critics argue that the combination of broad legal powers and centralised infrastructure makes any promise of anonymity fragile. The counterpoint from officials is that banking data is already highly visible to the state under existing law; the CBDC does not create a new principle, merely a new instrument. Reconciling these positions depends less on cryptography and more on governance. Tiered privacy is only as strong as the legal and institutional walls protecting the lower tiers from mission creep.

If tiered privacy sets the boundary of visibility, programmability sets the boundary of behaviour. Programmable features can be framed as *interfaces* rather than *constraints*: standing orders, escrow, time-bound access, conditional release upon delivery. These are not new; banks and payment processors already implement them. What CBDCs and stablecoins do is compress them into the monetary unit itself. Instead of "£500 plus an instruction to move on date X", one can imagine "£500 that moves automatically on date X if conditions Y and Z are met." The difference appears when the condition is not chosen by the payer or payee, but by the issuer or the state.

The travel stipend is an instructive motif here. Imagine a government scholarship that disburses a "digital travel allowance" to university students attending a conference abroad. The stipend arrives as CBDC or a government-backed stablecoin flagged in the wallet as "travel funds." It can be spent on trains, hotels, and entry fees; it cannot be used on gambling sites, cash-outs, or unrelated online shopping. The behaviour is visible at the point of sale: a student tries to buy a pair of trainers at an overseas outlet and sees a decline, not because of insufficient balance but because "merchant category not authorised for this allowance."

Name the idea: *purpose-limited spending.*

Explain the attraction. The state ensures that public money funds its intended objective; auditors see immediate, machine-readable evidence that budgets are respected; unspent funds can be clawed back automatically after the event. The implication is seductive for treasuries: reduced leakage, tighter control, and cleaner reporting.

Yet the same logic, extended, can curdle into something else. If travel stipends can be limited to "educational" expenses, why not unemployment benefits to "necessities"? Who decides where "necessity" ends and lifestyle begins? In South Korea's 2020 relief scheme, large corporate chains and online marketplaces were excluded to support local businesses. The social goal was defensible; the policy line was still political. Hard-coding such lines into a CBDC would make them harder to contest, not easier. There would be fewer receipts to argue about, but also fewer degrees of freedom for citizens to express dissent through their spending choices.

Two more grounded examples show the breadth of outcomes. In 2020–2021, several Japanese municipalities issued digital shopping vouchers usable only within specified districts, with expiry dates and category limits. Usage rates were high; local shops benefitted. The programmes resembled targeted fiscal injections. By contrast, in 2021 and 2022, China's e-CNY was used in some cities for consumer coupons with tighter constraints—usable only for certain promotion periods and often tied to specific apps or merchant campaigns. Users reported both convenience and frustration: convenient when discounts aligned with their plans, frustrating when funds expired unused or could not be reallocated. In both cases, programmability supported stimulus. But it also subtly shifted who controlled the shape of demand.

The privacy dimension threads through these examples. A purpose-limited CBDC payment necessarily communicates more than value and counterparties; it communicates *intent* as categorised by the issuer. A "digital fuel voucher" or "school meals credit" carries its own label. Even if transaction details are obscured above or below certain thresholds, the fact of holding such tagged balances reveals something about the user's status. In liberal democracies, that discomfort translates into political pressure. Privacy here is not only about hiding where one spends; it is about obscuring why one is eligible for a given instrument.

Developers sometimes offer technical solutions: zero-knowledge proofs to validate that a transaction meets policy rules without exposing all details; selective disclosure schemes; privacy-preserving smart contracts. These are promising areas of research. Yet they do not dissolve the policy question. Someone must still encode the rule that a travel stipend can pay for trains but not alcohol, or that a disaster-relief coupon can be redeemed at hardware stores but not at casinos. No cryptographic advance can answer whether that is legitimate.

A credible counter-argument suggests that the risks of purpose-limited CBDC are overstated because most social benefits already carry conditions. Food stamps in the United States cannot be spent on alcohol; housing vouchers cannot be used for travel. Digitising such conditions arguably improves efficiency without changing their moral content. The limitation of this argument is structural. Paper vouchers and siloed card schemes create friction that naturally limits the granularity of control. CBDC architectures could, in principle, go far beyond existing practise: time-of-day restrictions, behavioural scoring, geo-fencing down to city blocks. The ease of coding may tempt future policymakers to broaden conditions in ways that would be politically unacceptable under analogue systems. Reconciling this requires explicit, enforceable boundaries baked into the governance of programmability itself, not only into individual programmes.

The tiered-privacy motif reappears here in another guise: *tiered programmability*. One could imagine a CBDC system in which base money is non-programmable by the state—functionally equivalent to cash or deposits—while "instrument layers" on top carry explicit, opt-in conditions for particular schemes: travel stipends, vouchers, targeted subsidies. Users and intermediaries would see, clearly distinguished in the interface, which balances are fully fungible and which are constrained. That visual separation matters. A wallet that shows "General funds – £200" and "Conference stipend – £300 (travel and accommodation only)" makes the policy line legible. Confusion, by contrast, is a form of soft coercion.

The unresolved tension is not whether privacy and programmability are compatible—they are, if carefully designed—but who decides the shape of each and how those decisions can be contested. When a student abroad finds that their CBDC-funded stipend declines a modest restaurant bill because the merchant does not match a whitelisted code, what recourse should they have? Appeal to a helpdesk? To parliament? To a court? And when a central bank promises "tiered privacy" or "limited programmability", what prevents a future government, under different pressures, from tightening the tiers or broadening the purposes without meaningful consent?

Those questions sit behind every technical workshop and policy memo on CBDC architectures. They cannot be settled by engineers alone. They are, at heart, decisions about how much of economic life should be legible and steerable from the centre, and how much should remain a zone where, as with cash, neither system nor state knows or cares what a train ticket, a coffee, or an unplanned detour really meant.

Migration paths: If CBDCs launch, issuers adapt, wallets update, merchants renegotiate. A phased storyboard makes it tangible.

At 09:03 on 20 October 2022, Sveriges Riksbank published its interim report on the second phase of the e-krona pilot. Buried in the technical annexes was a detail that caught the eye of payment operators across Europe: the wholesale leg of the prototype had settled cross-bank transfers in **less than two seconds**, end-to-end, on a platform operated by Accenture and tested by Handelsbanken in Stockholm. That single line hinted at something larger than a Swedish experiment. If a central-bank money rail could clear wholesale obligations with such finality and speed, what would happen to the private systems around it?

The next morning, a senior product manager at a Nordic payment processor described the dilemma to a colleague over coffee: "If this goes live, our stack becomes the slow lane." His remark captured the strategic tension now facing stablecoin issuers, wallet developers, and merchants across advanced economies. When a new settlement foundation appears, everything built atop it must decide whether to stand firm, shift, or be rebuilt.

A phased storyboard makes that tension concrete. Migration to a CBDC world is not a single event; it is a sequence of adjustments, negotiations, and redesigns that span years. The first phase is always conceptual: central banks signal design commitments—account or token, intermediated or direct, retail or wholesale—forcing private issuers to measure exposure. A tokenised stablecoin backed by T-bills, for example, must compare its settlement layer against the proposed CBDC rail. Show the behaviour: a treasury desk checks average redemption times—perhaps three hours on a high-volume Friday—and sets them against the two-second e-krona prototype. Name the issue: *relative settlement latency*.

Explain it. If merchants and payment providers begin routing critical flows over a CBDC channel, stablecoins with slower redemption mechanics become second-class assets for intraday liquidity. The implication is strategic. Issuers must pre-position liquidity or re-engineer redemption windows to remain viable in environments where settlement speed is a competitive differentiator.

A second phase begins when wholesale CBDC pilots expand into public or semi-public corridors. The BIS Innovation Hub's Project Jura (2021), which linked the Banque de France and the Swiss National Bank for cross-border settlement of tokenised assets, demonstrated the feasibility of atomic delivery-versus-payment across jurisdictions. Private stablecoin treasuries watching Jura measured the impact: could tokenised reserves settle into CBDC accounts to improve liquidity coverage ratios by even 20 basis points? The behaviour is practical. Treasury teams run simulations of their T-bill portfolios under faster settlement, estimating whether reduced daylight overdraft needs could offset the operational cost of integrating with a CBDC interface. The motif here is *alignment*: aligning private balance sheets to a public rail that sets the tempo.

A counter-example complicates the picture. When the Bahamas launched the Sand Dollar in 2020—the world's first national retail CBDC—the migration burden for private actors was modest. The economy was small, cash-heavy, and dominated by a handful of banks. Merchants could adopt Sand Dollar QR codes without deep integration, and wallets could sync with minimal changes. This stands in contrast to the UK, EU, or US context, where the existing electronic payments stack is dense, layered, and internationally interconnected. Reconciling these cases clarifies a key point: migration difficulty is proportional not to CBDC novelty but to the complexity of the incumbent rails. Changing the chassis of a megastructure is harder than replacing the frame of a bungalow.

As pilots scale, a third phase emerges: wallet updates. Behaviours become visible here. A wallet provider in Frankfurt, anticipating ECB retail CBDC tests, benchmarks its user flows and identifies friction: eight taps to initiate a payment, ambiguous fee labels, slow onboarding for enhanced due diligence tiers. Engineers model how CBDC integration might reduce or increase friction. Name the function: *multi-rail orchestration.*

Explain it. A wallet that supports both private stablecoins and CBDC units must choose, at each payment moment, which rail offers the best combination of speed, cost, and acceptance for that specific transaction. The implication is profound for user experience. If CBDC rails become the default for domestic settlement while stablecoins provide cross-chain or cross-border utility, wallets must surface that logic transparently. Confusion erodes trust; clearly labelled rails build it.

Now consider merchants. As CBDC adoption grows, phase four forces contract renegotiation. A large supermarket chain in Manchester reviews its acquiring agreements and discovers that routing certain low-value domestic transactions over a prospective Bank of England CBDC rail could reduce interchange-equivalent fees by several basis points while offering finality within seconds. Yet the trade-off is subtle. Today, dispute management, chargebacks, and fraud protections are bundled into card rails. A CBDC-based route may require new insurance arrangements or extended settlement warranties from merchant service providers. Show the behaviour: a merchant CFO compares fraud chargeback ratios—say 14 basis points annually—against projected CBDC-based risk-sharing models.

Name the tension: *finality versus flexibility.*

Explain it. Instant finality removes reversibility, which simplifies settlement but complicates consumer redress. The implication is contractual. Merchants, PSPs, and insurers must rebuild liability frameworks from first principles. This is migration as governance, not code.

A fifth phase plays out in the compliance corridors. CBDCs introduce new KYC/AML interfaces. When the Monetary Authority of Singapore tested its Purpose Bound Money concept in 2022 and 2023, intermediaries had to adjust identity verification flows, integrating conditions embedded in the instrument. A European stablecoin issuer watching these tests must revise its own compliance scripts. Behaviourally, this means measuring the cost: if onboarding a user to CBDC-enabled wallets adds two minutes of identity checks, will abandonment rise by 5%? That metric becomes actionable. It forces product teams to redesign screens, clarify consent flows, and ensure that CBDC-driven conditions do not silently degrade user adoption. Our returning motif—alignment—becomes a negotiation not only with the central bank but with users' attention spans.

Migration also affects technical architecture. Suppose a stablecoin issuer in Paris currently relies on a two-layer custody model with daily cut-offs. If a wholesale CBDC allows real-time settlement of T-bill purchases with Banque de France accounts, the issuer might collapse its custody chain to reduce latency and operational risk. Yet a limitation appears: many central banks will initially restrict CBDC access to regulated financial institutions. Stablecoin issuers without direct access must rely on sponsor banks, reintroducing bottlenecks. This counter-example does not break the migration thesis; it sharpens it. Migration can compress some chains while lengthening others, depending on regulatory gatekeeping.

The sixth phase concerns settlement interoperability. When the Federal Reserve launched FedNow in July 2023, banks faced a similar transition: legacy ACH systems coexisted with instant settlement rails. Some institutions routed only payroll; others experimented with bill payments. A CBDC layer would repeat this pattern at a higher level of the monetary hierarchy. A London-based fintech might maintain stablecoin payments for programmable or international use while routing domestic invoices through a Bank of England CBDC module for finality. Show the behaviour: the fintech tracks its average settlement cost per transaction—say 11p via Faster

Payments, 7p via stablecoin rails, and a projected 5p on a CBDC connection.

Name the calculus: *marginal settlement optimisation.*

Explain it. Businesses will assign flows to whichever rail optimises cost, compliance, and certainty. The implication is segmentation. CBDCs will not erase private tokens; they will reallocate them to functions where they excel, such as cross-domain programmability or global settlement beyond the remit of national central banks.

We then reach the final phase: systemic convergence. Over time, market participants who adapt early gain leverage. Imagine a major online marketplace in Berlin integrating CBDC payments at checkout. It negotiates lower fees with acquirers, leverages instant settlement for treasury smoothing, and demands that stablecoin issuers match its settlement standards to remain listed as accepted payment options. Show the behaviour: the marketplace measures its daily cash-recycling cycle and finds that instant CBDC settlement reduces trapped liquidity by €8 million.

Name the effect: *network pressure.*

Explain it. Once enough large payers demand CBDC integration, the rest of the ecosystem must follow or lose acceptance. The implication is a decisive shift in bargaining power. Stablecoin issuers become price-takers in some corridors and price-setters in others.

Yet an unresolved tension remains. Migration assumes that CBDC rails will be attractive, stable, and politically durable. What if pilot outcomes disappoint? What if privacy concerns stall legislation, or merchants resist integration due to liability fears? Private stablecoins could retain a broader role than central banks expect. The storyboard does not guarantee a destination; it frames the moves required if the destination appears.

The forward test is therefore simple, and uncomfortable: if a CBDC rail launched tomorrow, which part of the existing stack would *you* rebuild first—your issuer treasury, your wallet UX, your merchant routing logic, or your compliance flows? The answer reveals your exposure, your leverage, and the pace at which your migration would begin.

Chapter 9
Adoption Playbooks

Just after dawn in Lagos in August 2021, a textile importer named Adaobi unlocked her shop and opened her ledger. Her first task of the day was not sorting inventory, negotiating with suppliers, or preparing customer orders. It was checking whether the funds sent overnight from Guangzhou had arrived, and if the dollar–naira rate used by her intermediary had shifted again. A delay or mispricing could erase a week's profit in a single keystroke. That morning, however, the transfer appeared instantly in her phone wallet, denominated in a dollar-backed token. No queue at a correspondent bank, no hidden margin. She stood for a moment, surprised by the absence of friction. The familiar anxiety had dissolved. Behind that quiet revelation was a simple, powerful realisation: technology that stabilises value and accelerates settlement does not merely support commerce; it changes how people breathe.

The same week, thousands of kilometres away in Chicago, a corporate treasurer sat in a conference room surrounded by screens showing rolling liquidity positions across regional subsidiaries. She faced a very different problem. Her firm had spent fifteen years refining its cash-pooling structure across the US and Europe, only to find that several banks had shortened intra-day windows and raised fees. Idle working capital was spreading across time zones like a slow leak. The treasurer's pilot with tokenised dollars—initially dismissed as an experiment—was beginning to show measurable benefits: faster sweeps, more transparent reconciliation, clearer accounting of obligations. She began drafting a memo that would set out the next phase. The contrast between Lagos and Chicago was stark, yet both scenes pointed to one truth: adoption is never a single story; it is a set of playbooks tailored to the pressures and aspirations of each domain.

This chapter turns to the human and institutional patterns that determine whether stable assets move from niche to norm. Adoption is not the triumphal march imagined by early evangelists, nor the threat depicted by critics. It is a series of negotiations between reliability and novelty, habit and redesign, risk comfort and opportunity cost. And it is always contextual. The tools that reduce settlement queues for an exchange in Warsaw are not the same tools that protect purchasing power for a community savings circle outside Nairobi. The incentives, constraints, and rhythms differ. Yet the underlying mechanics—the search for certainty, speed, clarity, and control—recur with remarkable symmetry across sectors.

For enterprise treasurers, the story begins with reliability. Their world is built around predictability: liquidity ladders, cut-off times, reconciliations that must balance to the cent. A treasurer does not embrace a new instrument because it sparkles, but because it removes doubt. The structure of a pilot matters as much as the technology itself. When a logistics group in Rotterdam tested tokenised settlement for its European cash pool, the key insight emerged not from headline performance but from a quiet metric: fewer late postings from a partner bank. That marginal gain, amplified across hundreds of accounts, pushed the firm to adjust its reporting templates. Adoption here is not drama, but incremental improvements that gradually rewire treasury behaviour. It is a delicate dance between operational discipline and controlled experimentation.

Fintechs and exchanges, by contrast, confront adoption in motion. Their systems hum with constant activity: deposits, withdrawals, market orders, internal transfers. Stablecoins often serve as the grease in these platforms, reducing queues and smoothing the peaks and troughs of user traffic. When a major exchange in Seoul re-engineered settlement for its spot markets using token flows, the result was not a banner announcement but shorter waiting times on busy evenings—a reduction users felt before they noticed. Adoption in such firms hinges on float management, risk controls, and the confidence to reroute flows without introducing fragility. It is the playbook of perpetual motion: optimise, measure, tighten, repeat.

Emerging-market adoption carries a different emotional and historical weight. Inflation, currency controls, and expensive remittance corridors have shaped collective memory. The appeal of stability is not theoretical but visceral: a store of value that holds overnight, a transfer that does not evaporate in fees, a tool that bypasses the long queues at money agents. Yet technological possibility does not guarantee reach. Access requires education, distribution, and trust networks. A community savings circle in Eldoret, which began pooling spare income into dollar-denominated tokens in 2022, succeeded not because of slick interfaces but because the chairwoman conducted weekly walk-throughs showing members exactly how to check balances and verify transfers. The success lay in ritual, not novelty. Adoption is often carried on the shoulders of the people who already guide their communities through financial decisions.

For public-sector agencies and NGOs, adoption is framed through responsibility. Here, the promise of traceability and rapid disbursement must be balanced with safeguards that protect vulnerable individuals. After the 2023 floods in Maranhão, a Brazilian relief organisation piloted tokenised stipends to displaced families. The funds arrived within minutes, and field workers tracked usage patterns to ensure essentials were prioritised. Yet one unexpected lesson emerged: several villages had intermittent connectivity, forcing the design of an offline fallback that allowed recipients to authenticate and spend when networks faltered. Adoption at this level is never just technological. It is ethical, logistical, and political. It requires imagination tempered by accountability.

Across these varied settings, one motif threads the narrative: **friction made visible**. In each domain, adoption accelerates when pain points are understood not abstractly but in behavioural terms—how long liquidity sits unreconciled; how many minutes a trader waits for a withdrawal; how many steps a shopkeeper takes to reach an agent; how many hours an NGO field team spends verifying receipts. Stable instruments succeed when they remove friction in these moments. They fail when they introduce new ambiguities. That is why the most effective adoption playbooks are not universal templates but adaptive scripts—flexible enough to accommodate differing pressures, yet disciplined enough to provide structure.

The coming pages follow these playbooks in turn. They explore how treasurers design pilots that respect control frameworks; how fintechs fold stablecoins into the choreography of their platforms; how emerging-market users blend new tools with familiar practices;

and how public agencies balance speed with oversight. The question running through the chapter is simple but consequential: what does it take for a digital dollar to be trusted, not merely transacted? The answer, as the stories suggest, lies in more than the code. It lies in the choices and constraints of those who adopt it, adapt it, and ultimately define its shape.

And so the reader is invited to consider a final image before turning the page: Adaobi in Lagos, the treasurer in Chicago, the exchange operator in Seoul, the savings circle in Eldoret, the relief worker in Maranhão. Five contexts, five pressures, five paths. The common thread is not technology but agency—the decisions individuals and institutions make when confronted with tools that promise stability in unstable systems. The next sections dissect those decisions with precision, revealing not a single road to adoption but a constellation of routes shaped by urgency, ingenuity, and the quiet pursuit of control.

Enterprise treasurers: Reliability, liquidity, accounting clarity. A pilot roadmap and reporting tips with a cash-pooling example

The catalyst arrived on an otherwise unremarkable Tuesday in May 2022. At 11:17 a.m., Siemens AG's treasury team in Munich watched a familiar red banner flash across their liquidity dashboard: *posting delay from correspondent bank*. A routine intra-day sweep from the group's Spanish subsidiary had stalled somewhere between Madrid and Frankfurt, caught in a cut-off shuffle that neither bank involved would fully explain until the next morning. The amount—€38 million—was not catastrophic, but it distorted the group's working-capital position for the day, forced an unnecessary commercial paper draw, and threw off hedging ratios carefully calibrated for month-end. By 2 p.m., the treasurer responsible for Europe had typed the note that would trigger a new phase of experimentation: "We must test a tokenised sweep. We can't rely on this window." The outcome, six months later, would reshape internal reporting and reset expectations of what "daily visibility" meant.

Treasurers, more than almost any other corporate function, inhabit a world where the smallest delays carry disproportionate consequences. They measure settlement certainty not through slogans but through lived nuisances: how long cash remains unreconciled across accounts; how often a sweep misses its window; how many journal entries require manual override because a transaction posted the next day rather than the same afternoon. Reliability is not a virtue—it is oxygen. And liquidity is not an asset class—it is the clock by which a firm keeps faith with its obligations. Against this backdrop, the appeal of token-based cash-pooling is not its novelty but the promise of fewer red banners and cleaner ledgers.

To understand how stable, tokenised instruments change treasury practice, it is useful to begin with a simple, revealing behaviour. When Siemens ran its pilot in late 2022, the team compared two metrics each week: the *latency of internal sweeps* and the *variance between forecasted and actual daily cash positions.* After a month, latency fell by nearly 80%, and forecast variance narrowed enough to reduce the number of short-term funding adjustments. These are mundane numbers, but they capture the essence of treasury adoption more effectively than any abstract claim about "efficiency". For treasurers, small shifts in timing cascade into strategic gains.

Yet the story is more textured than a single corporate case. Consider Maersk's 2023 pilot with a European banking partner in Copenhagen. The trial focused on a narrow use-case: sweeping surplus balances from regional hubs into a central liquidity pool using tokenised euro claims. The logic mirrored Siemens' test, but the context differed. Maersk's treasury team manages complex operational cycles across oceans and ports; cut-off uncertainty creates mismatches that ripple across procurement and bunker fuel payments. The pilot demonstrated that near-instant posting cut reconciliation times in Antwerp and Gdańsk, and reduced the need for overnight buffer balances. These observed behaviours served as proof that tokenised instruments can tighten the choreography of global cash management.

Of course, not every firm enjoys such clean results. A credible counterpoint emerged from a 2023 pilot run by a large automotive manufacturer in Detroit. The treasury team sought to integrate a token-based sweep into its North American cash pool but encountered friction from an unexpected source: legacy ERP systems. The tokens moved quickly; the ledgers did not. Batch-based reconciliation workflows treated near-instant transactions as anomalies, generating exception queues that required manual intervention each morning. For two weeks, the accuracy of the liquidity dashboard actually deteriorated. The limitation did not invalidate the instrument; it exposed a dependency—visibility depends not only on speed but on compatibility. The Detroit treasurer resolved the tension by adjusting the pilot: rather than continuous sweeps, the team implemented scheduled windows that aligned token flows with reconciliation cycles. The result was an incremental gain rather than a dramatic leap, but it proved that adaptation matters more than purity.

A quiet motif runs through these examples: **the cadence of control**. Treasurers adopt tools that respect their cadence—cut-offs, postings, approvals—while refining it. When cadence is disrupted, adoption stalls. When cadence is sharpened, adoption spreads.

The heart of the subchapter is the roadmap: how a treasury team designs, executes, and evaluates a pilot without destabilising existing operations. The first step is behavioural, not technical. Treasury defines what *problem* it seeks to reduce, expressed in metrics: posting latency, reconciliation time, end-of-day variance, or the amount of idle cash preserved for safety. These metrics shape the scope. Pilot design then assigns boundaries: a single subsidiary, a controlled notional amount, a consistent counterparty. This controlled architecture mirrors how e-money pilots were structured in the UK during the early 2010s: narrow perimeter, explicit success conditions, reversible steps.

A well-governed pilot also maps interactions across the liquidity stack. Treasurers identify where a token-based claim enters the cash-pooling workflow and where it meets legacy rails. Each hand-off reveals potential weak links: a bank's reporting API that updates every 30 minutes; an ERP posting rule that cannot recognise sub-second timestamps; an internal policy requiring dual approval for any new payment method above a threshold. These details determine whether the pilot smooths operations or generates noise.

Once the pilot runs, reporting becomes the narrative spine. Treasurers refine internal dashboards to show not only balances but *flows*—the precise timing of sweeps, settlement confirmations, and pool rebalancing events. The most successful teams treat reporting not as governance but as persuasion. Clear visualisation of reduced variance or improved predictability speaks more powerfully than technical documentation. Siemens' treasury board approved the expansion of its pilot only after seeing a weekly chart showing how often its Spanish subsidiary's sweeps arrived within the intended 30-minute window before and after tokenisation. The picture was cleaner than any memo.

A cash-pooling example makes the mechanics tangible. Imagine a multinational headquartered in Amsterdam with subsidiaries in Warsaw, Milan, and São Paulo. Each subsidiary contributes nightly surpluses to the group pool. Under conventional arrangements, the Warsaw sweep might settle at 18:42, the Milan sweep at 19:10, and the São Paulo sweep drift into the next European morning due to time-zone mismatches. The treasury dashboard appears accurate only by noon the next day, leaving a morning blind spot.

With tokenised intra-group movements, Warsaw and Milan post instantly, and São Paulo's sweep—triggered at its local end-of-day—arrives in Amsterdam minutes later, well before Europe wakes. Treasury wakes to a full picture. The effect is not magical; it is cumulative. Better visibility reduces the need for expensive liquidity buffers, tightens forecasting, and improves the confidence with which CFOs commit to short-term funding decisions. The pool becomes less a patchwork of delays and more a synchronised instrument.

The risk dimension deserves equal scrutiny. Reliability is not only about speed; it is about recoverability, reversibility, and auditability. Treasurers judge a tool by how it behaves during outages, not during demos. This is where the Detroit example remains instructive: the temporary mismatch between fast settlements and slow ledgers showed that operational readiness must be tested under stress. Many pilots now include simulated disruptions—a node delayed, an API paused, a reconciliation queue artificially inflated—to observe how quickly the end-to-end system restores alignment. A pilot that cannot survive a controlled disruption is not ready for scale.

International comparisons offer further grounding. In late 2023, the Monetary Authority of Singapore supported a small-scale experiment using tokenised bank liabilities for corporate settlements. The pilot's key finding was not velocity—it was the improvement in *confirmation finality*. Firms knew within seconds whether a payment succeeded, allowing earlier release of goods and reducing inventory friction. Meanwhile, a smaller experiment led by a Nordic corporate group in Stockholm highlighted a different benefit: denominated tokens reduced FX slippage when pooling from subsidiaries exposed to volatile currencies. Two different contexts, two different behaviours, one shared lesson: precision matters.

Threaded throughout is the question that shapes treasury adoption more than any technical debate: **does this reduce my uncertainty tomorrow?** Each firm answers differently. Some value speed; others value clarity; others prioritise auditability or counterparty diversity. But all seek tools that make the treasury function feel less like crisis management and more like quiet orchestration.

And as adoption deepens, a final tension emerges. Treasurers gain transparency but must accept new dependencies—on custodians, integrations, and digital infrastructure. They trade some traditional frictions for new operational considerations. The forward test is therefore simple and uncomfortable: *how do you measure readiness when the system becomes faster than your existing controls?* The choices made in response will determine whether tokenised cash remains a pilot, becomes a niche instrument, or graduates into treasury's daily cadence of control.

Fintechs and exchanges: Stablecoins grease platform flows. Float management and risk controls; an exchange settlement case reduces queues

The shift began quietly on 23 October 2018, when Coinbase and Circle unveiled USDC in San Francisco. The launch was not wrapped in the rhetoric that often surrounds digital assets; no claims of monetary revolution, no distant promises of decentralised utopia. Instead, Coinbase emphasised something far more prosaic: predictable settlement, transparent reserves, and a token designed to behave like cash inside a platform that had long been constrained by banking cut-offs. The effect was immediate. Within weeks, internal transfer queues shortened, and market makers described a noticeable reduction in failed order-settlements during periods of high volatility. One trader summarised it with a shrug: "It just posted." Five words. Yet those five captured the operational point more clearly than any marketing line.

Behind that matter-of-fact posting lay a structural shift. Exchanges and fintech platforms sit on rivers of customer flows—deposits, withdrawals, trades, merchant pay-outs, card programmes, and cross-border transfers. Every minute of delay in those flows translates into larger internal floats, more reconciliation noise, and higher capital costs. Stablecoins slipped into that machinery not as a speculative asset but as lubricant. They made the pipes run smoother. And crucially, they reduced the unpredictability that once forced platforms to maintain defensive buffers.

The paradox is visible in data from mid-2020, when Kraken's integration of USDC and USDT for internal settlement led to shorter withdrawal queues during peak trading days. The mechanics were simple: instead of depending entirely on bank wires, Kraken used token movements to settle internal credits, allowing customer balances to update within seconds. Measured latency inside its ledger dropped. Those seconds mattered. Faster credits meant fewer customer complaints, but more importantly, they freed platform operators from holding as much liquidity to bridge overnight settlement windows. Behaviour changed; the platform ran leaner.

But these successes highlight another motif: **the queue**. Queues reveal stress. Queues reveal design choices. Queues also reveal risk.

A counter-example illustrates the point. In May 2022, as TerraUSD collapsed, several exchanges—including Bitstamp in Luxembourg—temporarily disabled withdrawals of UST due to "network congestion". While the circumstances were extreme, the event made visible a weakness: stablecoins that rely on complex algorithmic mechanisms can create settlement freezes when confidence evaporates. Even when an exchange wants to honour customer redemptions, the token's own architecture can obstruct it. The limitation does not undermine fiat-backed instruments, but it marks a boundary. Not all stablecoins are suitable settlement tools; not all queues tell the same story. The lesson is discipline: fintechs and exchanges must choose instruments that behave predictably under strain.

Predictability, however, is only half the equation. The other half is float. Platforms manage float the way airlines manage fuel: too little and the system stalls; too much and the economics erode. Stablecoins changed the economics by giving platforms a settlement medium that behaves like cash but moves like software. For example, Stripe's 2022 USDC pay-outs pilot for global freelancers, anchored in Dublin, showed that cross-border settlement times dropped from days to hours. Stripe retained less float on partner corridors, because tokens closed gaps where banks previously inserted uncertainty. That behaviour—float shrinking as certainty grows—defines the fintech adoption curve.

Risk controls evolve in parallel. Platforms treat stablecoins as instruments that must be monitored as actively as bank accounts. Coinbase's 2018 USDC integration required weekly reserve reports and audit attestations, which the firm published publicly. This practice set a precedent. Exchanges began demanding more from issuers: disclosure of asset composition, maturity profiles of underlying reserves, and clarity on redemption windows. Each request lowered operational ambiguity. Each disclosure shrank the risk premium. Behaviour again shifted, not because platforms trusted the future, but because they verified the present.

To see these dynamics converge, consider a settlement case that unfolded on Binance in March 2021 during a surge in trading activity triggered by a Bitcoin rally. Historically, Binance faced periodic queues where fiat withdrawals piled up during peak hours, especially for users in Europe whose banks enforced strict cut-offs. In March, Binance routed a significant share of euro-denominated internal settlements through stablecoins, converting customer positions into tokens for intra-platform netting. The effect was pronounced: withdrawal queues shortened as internal ledgers updated continuously, and banking bottlenecks shifted to the margin rather than the centre. Customers saw balances settle instantly, even if the eventual fiat pay-out would post later. Binance effectively decoupled internal settlement speed from external banking rhythms. The queue thinned.

This decoupling introduces an important implication: platforms must now manage two clocks simultaneously—the *on-chain clock* and the *banking clock*. The on-chain clock is fast, granular, and indifferent to national holidays. The banking clock is slow, segmented, and full of embedded assumptions about working hours. Fintechs that adopt stablecoins learn quickly that operational excellence requires choreography between these clocks. Float management becomes a balancing act: how much liquidity sits in stablecoins for instant settlement, and how much sits in bank rails to satisfy regulatory requirements or withdrawal preferences? These decisions shape user experience and risk posture.

A second quiet motif emerges here: **the hinge**. Stablecoins serve as a hinge between fast, programmable settlement environments and slower, compliance-heavy banking systems. The hinge must not jam. When it does, queues return.

Examples from PayPal's 2023 launch of PYUSD in the United States offer clarity. PayPal allowed users to buy, sell, and transfer PYUSD, but also to use it as intermediate liquidity for cross-border remittances. When Mexican corridors experienced higher volumes, PayPal management noted that PYUSD reduced their reliance on overnight liquidity buffers. Yet they also discovered a limitation: settlement finality on the chain did not automatically translate into bank-side availability in Mexico City before local cut-offs. They adapted by pre-funding certain corridors, using PYUSD as intra-day liquidity while treating bank settlement as a separate process. The hinge held because they managed both sides.

Risk controls, therefore, must expand beyond checks on token issuers. Exchanges and fintech platforms implement monitoring across three layers: issuer risk (reserve quality and redemption integrity), network risk (blockchain uptime, gas market behaviour), and platform risk (internal ledger accuracy and fraud controls). When one layer weakens, the others compensate. Kraken's 2020 rollout of stablecoin monitoring dashboards offered a template: real-time alerts on token transfer latencies, balance mismatches, and unusual redemption patterns. These dashboards did not assume perfection; they assumed drift and caught it.

To ground this framework, imagine a fintech platform headquartered in London with millions of users sending money daily. Without stablecoins, its queues rise during three predictable windows: lunchtime traffic, end-of-day bill payments, and late-night cross-border transfers. Each window forces the platform to hold excess float, maintain reserve cushions at correspondent banks, and handle support tickets triggered by delayed credits. With fiat-backed stablecoins integrated, two windows shrink. Internal settlement becomes near-instant; credits post without waiting for bank confirmations; support tickets fall. Yet the third window—late-night cross-border transfers—remains constrained by correspondent banks abroad. The fintech now sees its queue in higher resolution: which delays are solvable with tokens, and which require deeper banking integration? The clarity itself is a gain.

A counterpoint is essential. Not all fintechs can reduce queues dramatically. Smaller platforms without direct access to major on/off-ramps may rely on aggregators whose own settlement cycles create bottlenecks. A 2021 case involving a regional exchange in Eastern Europe highlighted this: despite integrating USDT for internal settlement, the exchange could not reduce fiat withdrawal queues during local bank holidays. The chain was fast; the bottleneck lay in the aggregator's funding cycles. The limitation reinforces a theme: stablecoins remove some frictions, reveal others, and shift the contours of operational risk rather than eliminate them.

As adoption deepens, questions sharpen. How much float should remain in stablecoins? How quickly should internal ledgers reflect failed token transfers? What monitoring tools should alert operators when a token deviates from its reference asset? These are not abstract questions; they are design decisions that shape platform behaviour.

The forward test sits at the centre of this subchapter: *When the next surge arrives—whether a bull market, a payments spike, or a geopolitical shock—will your queues shrink because of your architecture or expand because of your assumptions?* The answer determines whether stablecoins remain convenience tools or become the structural layer on which fintechs and exchanges quietly run their daily flows.

Emerging market users: Inflation and frictions drive demand. Access, education, and agent networks matter. A community savings circle example

In September 2023, in Harare, a savings circle known locally as a *maround* met under the jacaranda trees that line Julius Nyerere Way. Twelve women, all members of a rotating credit association, counted their contributions in Zimbabwean dollars and then paused as the exchange rate shifted again on the police radio in the street. By the time they completed the tally, the value of their pool—meant to fund school fees—had already slipped. One member, who worked in South Africa as a caregiver, pulled out her phone and displayed a different figure: her remittance had arrived the previous night in USDT, worth the same that morning as the evening before. The group chose to hold a portion of their pooled funds in tokens for the first time. The decision took two minutes. The motivation took years.

Inflation is not an abstraction in Harare. It is bread queues, wage arrears, and the daily habit of converting local currency into anything more stable, from airtime to cooking oil. When tokens offer a short bridge out of volatility, adoption becomes a behaviour rather than a belief. People use what works. And when traditional rails stumble—bank outages, FX rationing, branch closures—stablecoins step into the breach not because they are fashionable but because they are functional. The circle's shift was small, but the meaning was large: tokens had entered the grammar of household finance.

The motif that recurs across emerging markets is the *gap*: the gap between local currency erosion and household needs; the gap between formal financial inclusion on paper and practical access in daily life; the gap between the infrastructure that governments maintain and the infrastructure that communities improvise. Stablecoins spread because they illuminate the gap and sometimes help narrow it.

Consider Nigeria, where the Central Bank lifted a long-standing ban on crypto transactions in December 2023. For years before that, USDT served as a settlement currency for freelancers and small traders. People did not adopt it to speculate; they adopted it to preserve value during periods when the naira retreated rapidly, sometimes more than 20% in a month (CBN, 2022). The behaviour was visible: merchants demanded payment quotes in USDT; cross-border traders in Lagos and Accra compared rates on Telegram before accepting transfers; university students saved tokens to hedge against school fee increases. The visible actions made the abstraction of "inflation protection" real.

A limitation appears quickly, and it is instructive. Ethiopia, with tighter capital controls and limited access to global exchanges, did not see similar adoption in 2021–2023. Tokens spread only in small pockets where diaspora workers used informal agents to convert and deliver value. This counter-example highlights a constraint: stablecoins do not eliminate frictions; they route around them when the access channels exist. Education and agent networks matter as much as the asset itself. Where those networks are thin, adoption stalls.

To make this structure explicit, we need to examine the three pillars shaping emerging-market uptake. The first is **access**, visible in whether users can cash in and cash out at reasonable spreads. Kenya illustrates this clearly. In Nairobi, M-Pesa agents have become informal gateways for token traders. During 2022's volatility, agents set tighter spreads when liquidity thinned, sometimes widening their margin from 2% to 6%. Users noticed. Behaviour changed: they timed transactions earlier in the day, coordinated purchases through group chats, and avoided conversions late in the evening when agents' own reserves were low. Access is not merely technical connectivity; it is a choreography of human and financial flows.

The second pillar is **education**. In Buenos Aires, where annual inflation exceeded 140% in late 2023 (INDEC, 2023), stablecoin adoption accelerated not because Argentinians lacked alternatives—they used dollars informally for decades—but because fintech firms such as Lemon Cash taught users how to see on-chain settlement finality. In community workshops, staff explained why a transaction that "lands in thirty seconds" on a blockchain is not the same as one that "lands tomorrow" in a bank account. That distinction changed behaviour. Savers began dividing pay packets: pesos for immediate expenses, USDC for protection, and local-dollar bank accounts for bills. Education created segmentation.

The third pillar is **agent networks**, the human infrastructure that makes digital money tangible. Philippines-based agents working for remittance companies such as Cebuana Lhuillier saw this in 2022 when several corridors experimented with USDC. Senders in Dubai paid in local dirhams; the remittance operator received USDC on-chain; the agent in Manila disbursed pesos. The measurable metric was speed: settlement times fell from hours to minutes. The visible behaviour was trust expressed in repeat usage. Migrant workers tested the new system once, then returned the next week with larger sums. Agent networks gave tokens a physical anchor.

Returning to the savings circle beneath the jacarandas, we can map these pillars precisely. Access was provided by a local agent who converted USDT into Zimbabwean cash at a spread the group judged fair. Education came in the form of a WhatsApp tutorial: how to check the token's price, how to confirm a transaction, how to avoid common scams. The agent network was the group itself, which pooled knowledge and shared risk. The motif of the *gap* reappeared: tokens became a tool to bridge the time between collecting savings and deploying them.

A second example reveals a different dynamic. In Lebanon, during the 2019–2022 banking crisis, access remained narrow, but demand surged. With bank withdrawals capped and the Lebanese pound losing more than 90% of its value, small businesses in Beirut began accepting USDT for stock purchases from suppliers in Turkey. Yet limitations were stark: no formal agent networks, high conversion spreads, and the ever-present risk of scams. These constraints forced users to build their own safeguards. Buyers met sellers in public places; transfers were verified on-chain before goods changed hands; participants formed micro-trust circles. The limitation underscores an implication: stablecoins can provide a functional store of value, but without supportive infrastructure, they cannot deliver comprehensive financial inclusion. They solve one part of the problem and expose the rest.

Risk perceptions also shape uptake. In Caracas, during 2021–2022, merchants treated USDT as a settlement asset during peak inflation but rejected algorithmic tokens outright. The behaviour was empirical. Traders said they "trusted what had dollars behind it" and ignored everything else. When TerraUSD collapsed in May 2022, Venezuelan merchants disengaged from less familiar issuers even though they had never used them. Education had drawn a line: reserve-backed stability was acceptable; unbacked promises were not. The motif extends: reducing the gap between expectation and reliability is essential for adoption.

Yet stablecoins do not spread solely because of inflation. They spread because people want autonomy. Emerging-market users adopt tokens when they reduce delays, simplify remittances, or allow savings circles to outpace currency erosion. The community savings circle in Harare illustrates this vividly. After their first token-based round, members reported fewer disagreements about valuation because the token price was visible and consistent. Disputes that previously consumed half an hour shifted to seconds. Behaviour changed: the meeting ended earlier; the group started its next round with greater confidence; participants discussed how to introduce younger members to digital wallets.

But autonomy raises questions. What happens when agent networks set predatory spreads? What happens when apps fail due to network outages? What happens when education programmes fail to reach rural areas where digital literacy is lower? These questions mark the unresolved tension at the heart of adoption.

A final counter-example prompts reflection. In rural Uganda in 2022, a pilot sought to introduce USDC savings products through village agents. The outcome was modest. Network coverage was inconsistent; phone reliability varied; and community members preferred livestock as savings vehicles because they could "see them grow." The pilot participants understood the concept of stable value but valued physical proof more. The result does not negate the model; it sketches its boundary. Digital money must coexist with cultural practices rather than replace them.

In emerging markets, the chessboard is crowded: inflation, remittances, agent networks, mobile money, informal savings circles, and now tokens. Stablecoins succeed where they fit into existing behaviour and fail where they demand new behaviour without offering commensurate reward. The motif of the gap—between what users need and what the system provides—remains the organising principle.

The forward test is simple to pose and difficult to answer: *If inflation cools or banking rails improve, do communities keep stablecoins because they add value, or do they abandon them because the gaps they once bridged have narrowed?* Emerging-market adoption will hinge on that choice.

Public sector and NGOs: Traceable, fast pay-outs with safeguards. Offline options and controls. A relief disbursement example shows oversight

Before dawn on 11 April 2022, in Cabuyao, south of Manila, trucks from the Department of Social Welfare and Development (DSWD) rolled into an evacuation camp established after Typhoon Megi. By 7 a.m., volunteers were already distributing water, but cash assistance had stalled: local banks had shut damaged branches, ATMs were offline, and the government's own payment contractor warned that routed disbursements could take days. At 9:13 a.m., the first batch of 217 families instead received USDC-based vouchers through a pilot run coordinated with the local government unit and two NGOs. Each recipient verified identity at a tent where tablets functioned through a temporary satellite link. The value arrived instantly. By midday, stalls outside the camp exchanging tokens into pesos were operating at thin spreads—cheaper than typical emergency cash disbursements. Days later, a report from the DSWD noted a measurable effect: fewer disputes, clearer audit trails, and no "ghost beneficiaries". Traceability had reduced the grey zones that often plague disaster response.

That morning exemplified something larger. Crises reveal the fragility of payment rails. They also reveal the power of speed married to control. Public-sector agencies have long relied on paper lists, intermediated banking partners, and crowded distribution points where leakage, delay, and misinformation thrive. Stablecoin-based disbursements alter the script: they show, in the stark arithmetic of minutes and pesos, how digital value can move faster and more cleanly than cash trucks or mobile money networks straining under load. The motif that threads through these efforts—the *line of sight*—captures why public institutions experiment with tokens: they want to see, not guess.

Yet the same scene hints at limits. When network coverage falters or devices break, digital money can stumble. Cabuyao only succeeded because a temporary satellite uplink delivered connectivity, and because local volunteers acted as human infrastructure, guiding recipients through registration and redemption. Without those layers, the promise of traceability could have become an exercise in exclusion. The line of sight is only as strong as the links beneath it.

Two broad themes shape public-sector and NGO adoption: accountability and reach. Accountability is visible behaviour: verifying that a payment goes to a registered identity at a specific place and time; generating a ledger entry aligned with audit requirements; showing that value is neither siphoned nor duplicated. Reach is equally concrete: ensuring recipients can redeem without predatory spreads; maintaining offline options during outages; supplying clear instructions in languages that match the community. Tokens are not magic. They are rails. And rails require stations.

The DSWD example underscores the first claim: when agencies use stablecoins, they gain a clearer audit trail. The World Food Programme's "Building Blocks" project in Jordan's Azraq camp had shown a similar effect in 2017, albeit using a permissioned blockchain: biometric verification at the point of aid distribution cut double-claim attempts measurably (WFP, 2018). The pattern is consistent: whether the ledger is public or permissioned, the visibility of each transaction tightens oversight. The difference with stablecoins lies in their interoperability: NGOs can settle value directly into the wallets of recipients, contractors, or suppliers without requiring every participant to join a bespoke system.

But clarity creates its own tension. A counter-example comes from a 2020 pilot in northern Kenya, where an NGO tested tokenised vouchers for drought relief. The ledger was pristine; redemption points were audited in real time. Yet the visibility frightened some recipients, who feared their spending patterns would be scrutinised by clan elders or local authorities. Adoption slowed. The limitation is not a failure of technology but a misalignment between transparency at the organisational level and privacy at the community level. Reconciling this required adding two controls: aggregated reporting for auditors and anonymised proof-of-redemption for external stakeholders. Once the reporting layer blurred individual patterns while preserving the integrity of totals, uptake improved. The line of sight must be directional: clear to supervisors, protective to recipients.

The opportunity becomes more pronounced when disbursements must scale quickly. In 2021, during the volcanic ash crisis in Saint Vincent and the Grenadines, the government faced the familiar bottleneck: bank branches were overwhelmed, and mobile money agent networks lacked liquidity. In response, a local NGO partnered with a regional fintech to distribute stablecoin-denominated assistance pegged to the Eastern Caribbean dollar. Settlement times fell from roughly forty-eight hours to under ten minutes. The behaviour shift was immediate: queues shortened; redemption points extended hours; and recipients spread out their visits to avoid crowding. Operational metrics tightened: the programme recorded under 0.5% discrepancies between intended and delivered amounts, compared to 2–3% in prior paper-voucher deployments. Efficiency became visible in footsteps and timestamps.

Yet speed without safeguards courts risk. NGOs and public agencies must integrate identity, sanctions screening, and offline fallback paths into their deployment models. UK-based charities involved in Ukraine support in 2022 learned this early. A consortium using USDC for cross-border procurement discovered that OFAC list updates could ripple through their pipelines within hours, occasionally freezing transactions late in the process. They adjusted by pre-screening counterparties more rigorously, maintaining small pre-vetted supplier lists, and reserving a portion of aid for immediate-use offline vouchers. The behaviour changed: payments were staggered rather than batched; high-risk vendors were replaced; documentation improved. The implication is practical: digital rails expand capability but compress compliance timelines.

Offline options form the next crucial layer. Cabuyao's satellite link was a temporary fix, but systematic offline pathways remain essential for resilience. In Malawi's 2023 cholera-response pilot, UNICEF and a local microfinance institution introduced "claim codes" redeemable offline at village agents. Each code represented a stablecoin-denominated entitlement stored in a secure server; agents could verify authenticity via USSD even without full internet coverage. The behavioural effect was measurable: redemption variance between connected and semi-connected areas narrowed to under 3%, compared to over 12% in earlier mobile-money-only pilots (UNICEF internal evaluation, 2023). The motif reappears. The line of sight travels through the system, but the system must not rely on uninterrupted connectivity.

A second, more structural claim concerns *control*. Stablecoin disbursements allow agencies to apply constraints—timing windows, spend categories, automated alerts—while still delivering value as liquid as cash. In 2022, the city of Rio de Janeiro tested a tokenised subsidy for transport workers during fuel-price spikes. The pilot restricted redemptions to a network of pre-approved petrol stations. Fraud fell. But the visible consequence was resentment from drivers who wanted flexibility during shortages. Control improved governance but eroded goodwill. The counter-example shows the boundary: programmability must remain supportive rather than prescriptive. When constraints align with recipients' real-world needs, adoption strengthens; when they clash, trust erodes.

The relief-disbursement choreography demands alignment across three timelines: immediate response, mid-term stabilisation, and long-term integration. During the immediate response—Cabuyao's case—traceability ensures fast, fair allocation. In the mid-term, NGOs consolidate data to refine beneficiary lists and detect anomalies. By the long term, governments evaluate whether token rails should remain part of their disaster-response architecture. These shifts reflect measurable outcomes. Philippines-based NGOs reported that post-disaster reconciliation time fell from weeks to days. South Africa's 2022 flooding response saw a 30% reduction in administrative overhead when tokenised vouchers replaced paper claims. The line of sight not only improves accountability; it frees capacity.

But every capability introduces an obligation. When public-sector agencies gain granular visibility into aid flows, they inherit responsibilities for privacy, security, and equitable access. When NGOs deploy token rails, they must plan for device failure, agent scarcity, and linguistic barriers. Adoption collects these trade-offs into a quiet question: *How much visibility is necessary for oversight, and how much becomes intrusive?* Neither law nor technology alone answers this.

Thus, the forward test that lingers is deceptively simple: *If stablecoin-based disbursements scale nationally, can governments and NGOs preserve the line of sight without narrowing the circle of inclusion?* The next experiment—whether in a typhoon zone, drought corridor, or conflict border—will draw that line anew.

Chapter 10
Designing for Trust

The first cracks appeared quietly. It was a Friday afternoon in October, and traders on two secondary markets noticed that a supposedly one-to-one stablecoin had slipped a fraction below parity. A rounding error, some thought, or perhaps thin liquidity at the close of the week. By Saturday morning the deviation had widened, redemption queues had formed, and screenshots of delayed withdrawals circulated with the velocity of panic. What unravelled over the next forty-eight hours was not the story of a single mechanism failing but of trust dissolving: the trust that collateral would be where it ought to be; that governance would respond in a measured, predictable way; that the mechanics underpinning the peg were no more exotic than they needed to be. The episode—one more entry in a catalogue of avoidable misadventures—left a familiar imprint: complexity is brittle, opacity accelerates fear, and heroics arrive too late.

Stablecoins succeed not because they are clever but because they are boring. That is their paradox. They promise stability in markets that reward flair, but durability comes from restraint: collateral that behaves under stress, rules that leave little room for improvisation, and governance that looks more like accounting than prophecy. This chapter begins with that tension: the elegance of simplicity in a field that often celebrates the baroque. The motif that threads through these pages—the *quiet hinge*—captures how systems that look mundane can bear extraordinary weight. Pegs do not break at their visible edges. They break at those hinges.

Trust is not an abstraction here; it is felt in the minutes a withdrawal takes to clear, in the spread a market-maker demands on a turbulent day, in the confidence a merchant shows when accepting a token from a stranger. These are lived metrics, not academic constructs. And the history of financial instruments is filled with reminders that trust built on stories rather than data sours when markets turn. The early nineteenth-century Scottish free banks understood this long before blockchains existed; their survivals and failures hinged on straightforward capital rules, daily settlement, and the humility to avoid grand designs. Today's stablecoin architectures, far more technologically ambitious, face the same elemental test: will they hold when the crowd turns and the quiet hinge is asked to carry its load?

The heart of designing for trust lies in recognising what users watch. They may not parse a balance sheet, but they observe behaviours: how quickly liquidity moves, which assets dominate the reserve pool, how an operator communicates during stress, and whether incident logs acknowledge mistakes rather than bury them. These signals become part of the mental model that merchants, developers, treasurers, and regulators use when deciding whether a token is a tool or a liability. The signals matter because stablecoins sit at a strange intersection: they are at once mundane money and experimental infrastructure. The mundane requires reliability; the experimental invites scrutiny.

That scrutiny cuts both ways. A mechanism that looks elegant on paper can crumble when forced into the rhythms of real commerce. Redemption pathways that assume perfect market depth reveal their fragility when a single provider hits a limit. Collateral pools that lean too heavily on assets with three-day settlement cycles betray themselves when users expect liquidity in three minutes. And governance bodies that hesitate for hours at critical junctures discover that hesitancy has a measurable cost: widening spreads, rising redemption gaps, and a social media narrative that shifts from confidence to doubt. Here, the quiet hinge reappears—the small rule, the unchanged parameter, the reserve policy that looked dull until the moment it needed to withstand force.

Designing for trust, then, is less about invention than about disciplined selection. What collateral remains liquid through the full cycle rather than the best of times? Which mechanisms survive mispricing, arbitrage pressure, or a sudden stop in banking rails without improvisation? How far can programmability go before it undermines predictability? These are not engineering puzzles alone; they are judgement calls. And judgement is shaped by history. Every failed peg—whether a pre-war currency board, a 1990s emerging-market defence, or a modern algorithmic contraption—teaches the same lesson: complexity invites exploitation, and opacity invites suspicion. A stablecoin that forgets this quickly becomes an unstable coin.

Yet trust does not rest only on design. It rests equally on measurement. Systems that cannot be observed cannot be believed. A liquidity ladder showing near-term assets at multiple maturities tells a clearer story than a composite reserve number. A breakdown of counterparty concentrations exposes vulnerabilities before they become crises. Timestamped redemption logs, published with regularity, turn anecdotes about delays into data that can be tracked and improved. The standardisation of these metrics—the creation of a baseline pack that issuers, auditors, merchants, and analysts can all interpret—becomes a public good. Transparency, when structured rather than cosmetic, shifts the psychology of markets: it anchors narratives in facts.

Measurement leads naturally to openness. Fragmentation is the quiet tax on adoption. Without shared standards for messaging formats, proof structures, and interoperability, each stablecoin sits in an islanded environment where merchants must integrate bespoke APIs, wallets must write exceptions, and developers must juggle incompatible conventions. Open standards reduce this tax. A merchant plugin built once but usable across multiple tokens multiplies its impact; a common format for attestations allows oversight bodies to compare apples with apples; a shared protocol for cross-chain proofs shrinks the cognitive overhead for integrators. The benefits compound because trust compounds: each predictable interaction reinforces the next.

Even so, actors need a structured way to navigate choices. Stablecoin ecosystems have matured to a point where decisions are no longer binary—adopt or ignore—but multifaceted: how to integrate, how to hedge, how to monitor, how to exit. A mental model, condensed into a one-page canvas, becomes more than a pedagogical device. It becomes a practical instrument for treasurers comparing liquidity profiles, for developers designing flows, for regulators assessing systemic linkage, and for NGOs evaluating whether a token can handle peak loads during relief operations. The canvas forces clarity: what assumptions anchor the peg, how stress-scenarios propagate, what dependencies are hidden in plain sight, where governance might choke under strain.

That clarity matters. It shifts the conversation from hype to architecture, from brand to behaviour. It invites readers to look beyond the marketing gloss and into the machinery: the rules governing redemptions, the cadence of reserve updates, the diversity of custodial arrangements, the protocols bridging ledgers, and the fail-safes that activate when something breaks. It places responsibility where it belongs—on design that respects users' attention, markets' impatience, and history's unforgiving memory.

The chapters ahead delve into these elements in detail. They draw on failures that burned fast and quietly faded, and on successes that earned trust hour by hour by doing nothing extraordinary except functioning as promised. They reveal why the simplest mechanisms often withstand the fiercest storms, how metrics transform doubt into informed engagement, and why interoperability is not merely a technical convenience but a social accelerant. Above all, they demonstrate how the one-page canvas sharpens judgement, enabling anyone—from a cautious treasurer to a public-sector operator—to diagnose strengths, probe weaknesses, and chart adoption with discipline.

And so the question that opens this chapter becomes the question that shadows every design choice: *will the quiet hinge hold?* The answer lies not in cleverness but in care. Designing for trust is not a flourish; it is a craft.

Principles for Resilient Pegs: Keep Mechanisms Simple, Collateral Liquid, Governance Boring

At 02:15 UTC on 11 May 2022, traders on Binance and FTX watched a supposedly dollar-anchored token slide to $0.35. Minutes earlier it had been trading at $0.97. Within the hour, the stablecoin was in freefall and its associated governance token had shed billions from its paper valuation. The collapse of TerraUSD—engineered in Seoul by Terraform Labs and run primarily from Singapore—was not a failure of infrastructure or of markets discovering some exotic tail risk. It was the predictable result of a peg held together by reflexivity rather than collateral, by complexity rather than constraint. When the price feed destabilised, the arbitrage loop that was meant to restore parity accelerated its own breakdown. The mechanism folded in on itself, and by 13 May the coin's market value had evaporated. One weak hinge had snapped. That hinge had been obvious for months.

The episode remains a stark illustration of a broader truth: pegs survive when they behave more like plumbing than performance. They hold when the design favours simplicity over ingenuity, liquidity over leverage, and governance over charisma. The pattern reappears across decades of financial history. Whether one looks at the Argentine convertibility regime of the 1990s, the currency boards of Hong Kong and Estonia, or the pre-war Scottish free banks, the same principles shaped durability. None were flawless. All depended on quiet, often dull mechanisms that limited discretion and forced clarity. The lesson travels neatly into the architecture of stablecoins. A peg is not maintained by hope or by yield. It is maintained by rules, assets, and processes that behave the same way on a calm Tuesday as they do during a Friday evening panic.

The image that threads through this subchapter—the *quiet hinge*—captures the point. Pegs turn on small, often ignored components: the schedule of reserve updates, the weighting of liquid assets, the thresholds for circuit breakers, the cadence of redemption logs. These hinge-points do not dominate marketing papers or conference decks, but they determine how a system responds when sentiment shifts abruptly. Most failures are failures of the hinge.

The first principle of resilience is simplicity. Simplicity is not naïveté; it is discipline. It means choosing a mechanism that market participants can model under stress without resorting to heroic assumptions. The fully reserved model exemplified by Paxos Trust Company's USDP in New York (2021–2023) showed how predictable mechanics reduce anxiety: independent attestations, a narrow reserve of short-dated US Treasuries and cash, and a redemption promise honoured within known timelines. Nothing about that mechanism attracted headlines. Precisely for that reason it proved robust when crypto markets convulsed in mid-2022. The peg held because nothing in the mechanism needed to be reinterpreted.

By contrast, TerraUSD showed what happens when complexity overwhelms comprehension. An algorithmic mint-burn equilibrium, dependent on the market value of the LUNA governance token, created a loop that looked stable only under shallow stress tests. When redemptions surged, the mechanism demanded ever greater issuance of LUNA, which depressed its price and thereby undercut the stabilising force it was meant to provide. Complexity became a cascade. The visible behaviour—redemption delays, widening spreads across exchanges, and liquidity providers stepping back—revealed the mechanism's instability before the formal peg broke. The implication is clear: if a participant cannot map the stabilisation process within a minute, the design is too ornate.

Simplicity alone cannot maintain a peg. The second principle—collateral liquidity—is its counterpart. Liquid collateral provides the factual basis for redemption confidence. Markets do not respond to promises; they respond to assets that clear. Here, USDC's handling of the March 2023 Silicon Valley Bank failure demonstrated the strength of a reserve that was both short-tenor and publicly attested. When Circle Internet Financial disclosed $3.3 billion of exposure to the failed bank, the token briefly depegged to $0.88 on Coinbase. But as soon as US regulators guaranteed deposits on 12 March, the peg snapped back. The mechanism had not changed. The collateral was known. The hinge held because the underlying assets could settle.

Other examples underscore the lesson. The Monetary Authority of Singapore's regulatory framework for e-money issuers (2019–2024) required that customer funds be held in segregated trust accounts or safeguarded through guarantees. The rule forced issuers into assets that could be mobilised rapidly during a wind-down. Stablecoin issuers adopting similar reserve constraints benefit from the same behavioural effect: users observe predictable redemption times, narrow bid-ask spreads, and the absence of fire-sale dynamics in secondary markets. The peg is not magic; it is the consequence of asset choices that compress uncertainty.

There are counter-examples. MakerDAO's DAI, backed partly by crypto collateral and partly by real-world assets, has maintained parity through extended volatility. Its mechanism is not simple. Its collateral pool is not purely liquid. Its governance is famously elaborate. Yet the design works because the system applies aggressive over-collateralisation, automated liquidations, and transparent parameters that reprice risk continuously. The architecture compensates for complexity by making behaviours observable: liquidation ratios, debt ceilings, and stability fees. The hinge remains visible. DAI thus demonstrates a limitation of the simplicity doctrine: complexity can survive if it is bounded, disclosed, and constantly measured. The reconciliation is straightforward—simplicity is the safest path, but complexity can be tolerated when deeply collateralised and relentlessly transparent.

The third principle is often undervalued because it looks the least technical: governance must be boring. Boring governance is not an insult; it is the condition under which drama is avoided. It means decisions are procedural, not personal; timetables are fixed, not improvised; authority is distributed, not concentrated. When governance becomes colourful—dominated by charismatic founders, improvised interventions, or opaque committees—the peg becomes hostage to sentiment.

The collapse of Iron Finance in June 2021 showed this vividly. Promoted aggressively by influencers, including Mark Cuban, the partly algorithmic IRON stablecoin unravelled when its governance token TITAN entered a death spiral. The architecture lacked the reserve transparency and circuit breakers needed to slow the panic. Governance moved reactively, issuing communications that contradicted earlier statements. The behaviour told users that the system had no stable centre. Trust evaporated in hours.

Boring governance, by contrast, looks like the rulebook employed by Circle or Paxos: formal committees, predetermined escalation paths, and audits with named external firms. It resembles the governance of a clearing house more than that of a startup. The implication is that stablecoins should resist the cultural gravitational pull of crypto's personality-driven ethos. The more a peg resembles dull infrastructure, the more likely it is to survive.

History supports this view. The Hong Kong Monetary Authority's currency board, established in 1983 and maintained through the 1997 Asian financial crisis, embodied procedural governance. The board followed rigid reserve rules, automatic intervention thresholds, and public disclosure of its balance sheet. Even under speculative attack in October 1997, the peg held because governance did not improvise. It executed predetermined actions. The quiet hinge—rules rather than rhetoric—carried the load.

These principles—simplicity, liquidity, boring governance—map cleanly to behaviours that users and markets can measure. Redemption time is a clock, not an opinion. Liquidity composition is a table, not a metaphor. Governance cadence is a set of published procedures, not a founder's blog post. Each metric is a signal: the number of basis points by which secondary-market prices deviate from parity during stressed hours; the concentration ratio of custodial banks; the tenor ladder of reserve assets; the age of the most recent audit. These observable facts shape the mental models of participants and contribute directly to peg resilience.

A recurrent motif across failures is that early warnings appear in small indicators: a slip in redemption speed, a growing share of illiquid assets, a sudden governance vote called at odd hours, or inconsistent communication during market volatility. These signals foreshadow the break. They show that resilience depends on systematic attention to the hinge, not on the headline.

The implications for issuers are practical. Mechanisms should avoid reflexive loops unless heavily over-collateralised. Reserves should stay short-dated and segregated, with concentrations capped. Governance should prefer committees over founders, published calendars over ad-hoc announcements, and routine over flair. None of these choices is glamorous, but each contributes to the quiet hinge carrying greater weight.

Yet a tension persists. Innovation often seeks to push boundaries; resilience demands restraint. The unresolved question for the sector is how far mechanisms can evolve without destabilising the peg they support. Should issuers experiment with dynamic fees, variable collateral mixes, or cross-chain redemption pathways? Or do such innovations risk reintroducing the very fragility they purport to reduce? The next phase of stablecoin design will depend on how convincingly issuers answer that question.

Metrics that Matter: Liquidity Ladders, Concentrations, Redemption Times, Incident Logs

At 23:01 UTC on 11 March 2023, Circle Internet Financial published an extraordinary late-night update from Boston. A day earlier, Silicon Valley Bank had entered receivership, and a portion of USDC's reserves sat inside the failed institution. Panicked redemptions were already visible on-chain, OTC desks were quoting widening spreads, and the token had briefly traded below $0.90 on major exchanges. Yet what steadied sentiment that night was not a promise, nor a speech, but a table: maturities, custodial locations, cash buffers, and settlement timelines laid out with unusual clarity. Markets replayed that table for the next twelve hours. The peg recovered steadily. A few rows of numbers had done more to restore confidence than any marketing line could.

It was a reminder of a simple truth: stablecoins succeed or fail in the light. Pegs do not buckle without warning. They fray as metrics deteriorate—an unnoticed rise in concentration at a single custodian, a creeping increase in average redemption time from minutes to hours, a liquidity ladder tilting towards instruments that cannot be sold without a haircut, an incident log that grows but is not published. The structures may be digital, but the physics is old. Information shapes behaviour. Behaviour shapes resilience.

The hinge that threads this subchapter—the *dashboard*—captures the point. A dashboard is not decoration; it is the market's compass. It forces an issuer to show how the machine is built: where liquidity sits on the ladder; how quickly it can be mobilised; how exposures concentrate; how incidents accumulate and are closed. Without that compass, participants guess. And guesses become runs.

To make sense of which metrics matter and why, the first step is to recognise that successful stablecoins behave like disciplined treasuries. They measure everything that could impair redemption: tenor, concentration, settlement delay, operational faults. The liquidity ladder sits at the centre of that work. A ladder is not a metaphor; it is a dated structure that shows what cash becomes available today, tomorrow, next week, and beyond. In the aftermath of the March 2023 turmoil, both Circle and Tether began publishing more granular maturity breakdowns, reflecting an implicit lesson from earlier shocks: the shorter the ladder, the safer the peg. Short-dated Treasuries clear. Long-dated instruments do not. When sentiment shifts, the question that matters is: what can settle *now*?

A concrete example illustrates this. In September 2022, during a period of rising rates, the Bank of England intervened to stabilise gilt markets after pension funds experienced liquidity stress. These funds held long-dated gilts in size, often financed through leverage. When gilt yields spiked, funds needed to produce cash margin quickly. They found that their collateral would clear, but only with painful discounts and delays. The liquidity ladder was too long; its lower rungs were unusable in an emergency. The example, far from the crypto sphere, highlights the same principle that governs stablecoins: liquidity that cannot be mobilised under stress is not liquidity.

The implication for issuers is practical. A ladder must privilege immediacy: cash, deposits at high-quality banks, and Treasury bills with days—not months—to maturity. Longer tenors can play a role, but only when capped and balanced. The behaviour of the ladder in a stressed hour is the metric that matters. It is visible in settlement timestamps.

Alongside the ladder sits the concentration table: the roster of custodians, banks, and asset types to which the reserve is exposed. Concentration is often underestimated because it hides in plain sight. Even a reserve that is technically diversified by instrument can be overexposed to a single institution through operational pathways. The collapse of Silvergate Bank in March 2023 made this stark. Several issuers relied on Silvergate's SEN network for near-instant dollar settlement. When the bank wound down, these issuers had to reroute flows through slower channels. Reserves did not evaporate, but redemptions slowed. The metric that mattered was not nominal diversification; it was functional diversification.

The limitation of concentration metrics is that they can lull issuers into complacency. A table showing three custodians looks diversified until one realises that all three custodians clear through the same correspondent bank or hold settlement accounts at the same central institution. The correlation is hidden. The reconciliation requires digging into operational chains, not just balance sheets. Prudent issuers publish not just custodial concentrations but also *pathway* concentrations: which payment networks they depend on, where their messages settle, which cloud providers host their systems. The peg depends on these hinges too.

Redemption time is where the dashboard meets the market's daily experience. It converts confidence into action. A peg holds when users know they can exit cleanly. Redemption time is a fact: a timestamp difference between request and settlement, not a promise. In April 2021, Binance USD (BUSD) began publishing more granular redemption timings after a series of delays triggered questions from traders in Hong Kong and Singapore. The delays were not catastrophic, but they were visible. They showed how a peg's resilience is shaped as much by operational throughput as by reserve quality. When redemption times widen, spreads widen. When spreads widen, confidence frays.

There is a counter-example worth examining: Tether's USDT. For years, critics highlighted limited transparency and uneven attestation cadence. Yet the token maintained widespread usage and deep liquidity, even during severe market stress in 2022 and 2023. How to reconcile this with the emphasis on metrics? The answer lies in behaviour. Whatever its disclosure gaps, USDT delivered one visible fact: it settled. OTC desks, exchanges, and merchants had seen enough redemptions clear that they formed a behavioural endpoint: *USDT moves when pressed.* This behaviour partly compensated for weaker formal metrics. It does not invalidate the need for transparent metrics, but it shows how repeated settlement performance can substitute—dangerously—for structural comfort. The hinge held, but it held through habit rather than information.

Incident logs are the least glamorous part of the dashboard, yet they often provide the earliest signals of systemic stress. An incident can be trivial—a delayed API response, a reconciliation mismatch, a failed custodian message—or it can be existential. What matters is the trendline. A growing list of minor incidents may show that operational load is rising faster than team capacity. In 2020–2022, several DeFi protocols published weekly incident logs covering oracle delays, validator outages, and abnormal liquidation behaviour. These logs were rarely read outside niche communities, yet they provided the most accurate picture of operational resilience. Stablecoin issuers that adopt the same discipline will avoid surprises. Cycles of silence hide fragility.

When these metrics are combined, the baseline pack emerges: the standardised suite of information that any issuer should publish monthly or, ideally, weekly. It includes liquidity ladder rungs, concentration tables, redemption-time distributions, and an incident summary with status and resolution. Such a pack acts as a stabiliser for both markets and issuers. For markets, it reduces uncertainty. For issuers, it forces rituals: reconciliation meetings, custodial audits, stress simulations, and cross-functional reviews.

The quiet motif of the *dashboard* reappears here. A dashboard is not built for marketing; it is built for discipline. Its layout tells a story about priorities. If the first line shows long-dated assets and the last line shows cash, the priorities are wrong. If custodial concentrations appear only annually, the issuer is not serious. If redemption times are presented as averages without ranges, users lack the information that matters under stress. The peg's daily life is encoded in these numbers.

Two external examples reinforce why dashboards matter. First, the Financial Stability Board's 2020 recommendations for global stablecoins emphasised transparency of reserves, redemption rights, and operational resilience. These recommendations were not theoretical; they echoed lessons from traditional finance, where money market funds with shorter ladders and clearer disclosures weathered the 2008 crisis better than those with opaque exposures. Second, the European Banking Authority's oversight of e-money institutions from 2015 onward required frequent safeguarded-funds reporting. Institutions that followed a clear reporting cadence experienced fewer supervisory interventions. The implication for stablecoins is direct: when reporting is clear, supervision becomes predictable. Predictability builds confidence.

Yet dashboards are not a panacea. They can be gamed. Issuers may privilege cosmetic clarity over substantive strength, optimising what the dashboard shows rather than what the system needs. A stablecoin could present a neat ladder while relying on a single settlement bank, or show fast redemptions for small users while slow-walking institutional flows. The limitation is inherent: metrics summarise, but they do not explain. Reconciling this limitation requires independent assurance, randomised audits, and cross-validation from on-chain behaviour. A dashboard should be treated as a hypothesis to verify, not a conclusion to trust.

The future of stablecoin reporting may lie in interoperable standards: machine-readable ladders, verifiable proof-of-reserve structures, and automated incident feeds. These innovations will allow users, regulators, and counterparties to compare issuers more easily. But they also raise a question that sits unresolved at the end of this discussion: how granular must a dashboard become before it overwhelms its audience? At what point does detail hinder comprehension rather than enhance it? The choice of metric density will reveal whether stablecoin issuers prioritise clarity or camouflage.

Open Standards and Interoperability: Standards Reduce Fragmentation. Message Formats and Proofs Help. A Merchant Plugin Example Compounds Benefits

At 14:32 CET on 7 February 2024, Shopify engineers in Dublin identified a pattern in merchant support tickets that pointed to a quiet but maddening failure. A sizeable group of merchants using a stablecoin payments plugin—built by an independent developer—were receiving funds on-chain, but their dashboards failed to register the transactions. The culprit was not fraud, nor a network outage, but a missing field in the plugin's message schema. The wallet used a proprietary JSON structure; the plugin expected a slightly different format. The mismatch caused legitimate receipts to vanish from the merchant's view. Sales teams paused campaigns. Support queues stretched. A single absent key—*tx_confirmed_at*—had triggered an ecosystem-wide stall. The lesson was stark: in payments, standards are not decoration. They are the rails.

The Shopify episode showed how technical fragmentation multiplies with each integration. Every unmatched field becomes a gap. Every gap becomes a question. And every question, when money is moving, becomes a support ticket. The quiet motif that threads this subchapter—the *handshake*—captures the point. A handshake is not metaphorical; it is literal in code. It is the moment a wallet and a merchant system agree on a shared structure for value, identity, and proof. Without that handshake, stablecoins cannot scale beyond islands.

The drive for open standards begins with a simple observation: fragmentation is expensive. It is visible in developer hours spent translating message formats; in reconciliation mismatches across blockchains; in failed receipts where a wallet signs a message one way and a merchant reads another. That cost is borne most directly by platforms and consumers. The actors who should benefit from fast, portable digital money spend their time debugging schema differences. The absence of standards is not a philosophical problem. It is a behavioural one: it produces friction.

To anchor this in concrete practice, consider Ethereum's ERC-20 token standard. When finalised in 2015, the standard did not merely define an interface; it created a shared language for token transfers. Wallets, exchanges, custodians, and smart contracts knew exactly how to read balance, transfer, and allowance messages. The standard converted chaos into coordination. ERC-20's influence was visible during market volatility in March 2020, when decentralised exchanges settled billions of dollars' worth of trades without rewriting integration layers. The *handshake* worked repeatedly because all parties knew how to speak it.

Yet ERC-20 is not enough for the next generation of stablecoin use cases. It tells participants *how* to move value, but not *how* to prove reserves, attest to transaction finality, or communicate metadata required for compliance at on- and off-ramps. The limitation surfaces whenever enterprises attempt to integrate stablecoins into treasury workflows and discover that the critical fields they require—reference IDs, settlement timestamps, chain-ID exclusions—are missing or inconsistent across wallets. Standards solved one layer of the problem; they left others open.

This is why open message formats and proofs matter. A modern stablecoin handshake must cover more than token movements. It must show proof-of-reserve structures, confirmation proofs, and metadata for compliance workflows. The movement towards these standards can be traced through two named developments. First, Chainlink's Cross-Chain Interoperability Protocol (CCIP), launched in 2023, offered a unified routing mechanism for cross-chain messages with embedded proofs. Second, Circle's Cross-Chain Transfer Protocol (CCTP), rolled out in 2023–2024, replaced wrapped-asset bridges with a burn-and-mint mechanism anchored in attested messages. These developments changed behaviour: developers stopped writing bespoke bridging logic for each chain and instead plugged into verified message standards. Integration time fell. Incident rates fell. The *handshake* strengthened.

But the counter-example is equally instructive. In June 2022, the Nomad bridge exploit unfolded when an insecure message verification pattern allowed attackers to replay and spoof proofs. The lack of a strict, audited standard for cross-chain message validation led to a $190m breach. The consequence was not simply the loss of funds; it was the breakdown of trust across dozens of application ecosystems that depended on the bridge. Merchants paused stablecoin acceptance on chains connected to Nomad. Exchanges increased withdrawal fees to compensate for security checks. Developers spent months rewriting adapters. The absence of a robust standard produced a systemic effect. Fragmentation became fragility.

Reconciling the positive and negative cases leads to a clear implication: open standards must pair strictness with simplicity. A standard that is too thin leaves gaps. A standard that is too complex leaves room for misinterpretation. The success of SWIFT's ISO 20022 upgrade illustrates this balance. When banks across the UK and EU began migrating in 2023, the richer, structured fields reduced reconciliation errors and fraud investigations. But the critical element was the clarity of the schema. The layout of fields guided behaviour. Stablecoin standards must emulate this: define the essential metadata, structure the proofs, and then allow optional extensions without breaking the handshake.

The merchant plugin example broadens this point. When Shopify integrated CCTP and updated its plugin to accept a standardised transfer-receipt message format, the benefits compounded. Merchant adoption accelerated not because the mechanics changed, but because predictability replaced guesswork. Refund workflows synced reliably. Dispute processes shortened. Chargeback-equivalents on stablecoin rails became intelligible. The plugin no longer needed per-wallet translators. The handshake—once brittle—became robust. The behaviour of thousands of merchants confirmed the principle: interoperability compounds.

The role of proofs deserves attention here. Proofs bridge the gap between chains, between systems, and between expectations. A proof can confirm that a token was burned on one chain before being minted on another; it can confirm that reserves backing a stablecoin remain above a threshold; it can confirm that an address passed a compliance screen. Each proof is a behavioural commitment encoded in verifiable structure. When these proofs follow open standards, integration becomes portable. Without open proofs, every system that touches value must reinvent assurance. Reinvention produces discrepancies. Discrepancies produce risk.

Two external examples underline the path ahead. The first is the UK's Open Banking initiative, launched in 2018. By defining common APIs for account access and payment initiation, it broke the monopoly of proprietary banking interfaces. Fintechs flourished not because banks became more generous, but because they were required to speak the same technical language. The second example is the W3C's Verifiable Credentials standard, which gained traction from 2020 onwards. It allowed portable attestations for identity and attributes. Stablecoins that adopt similar patterns for reserve proofs and transaction attestations will inherit the same benefits: portability, composability, and verification independent of any single platform.

Still, a limitation must be acknowledged. Standardisation can stifle innovation if it becomes ossified. If every wallet, merchant, and issuer is forced into the same narrow schema, new features—sub-second settlement flags, programmable transfer conditions, privacy-preserving proofs—may struggle to find adoption. The tension is structural: standards crave stability; innovation craves change. Reconciling this requires governance models for standards that are open, versioned, and participatory. A schema that evolves through public review can adapt without fracturing.

Throughout, the motif of the *handshake* guides the narrative. A handshake succeeds only when both sides recognise the signal. A standard succeeds only when multiple actors implement it correctly, consistently, and predictably. Stablecoins live or die not by their minting logic but by the quality of the handshakes that surround them.

This leaves a final tension unresolved. As stablecoins spread across chains, jurisdictions, and use cases—from point-of-sale to corporate treasury and cross-border settlement—who decides which handshake becomes the norm? Should issuers lead? Should regulators mandate? Or should markets converge organically through usage patterns? The answer will determine whether interoperability becomes a shared foundation or a contested frontier.

A Mental Model for Decisions: Evaluate Any Stablecoin, Stress-Test Scenarios, and Plan Adoption Using a One-Page Canvas

On 12 May 2022, in Singapore's central business district, the operations team of an Asian remittance firm gathered in a glass-walled conference room to dissect a failure. Their dashboard showed that a supposedly dollar-pegged token, used for overnight settlement between regional hubs, had slipped to $0.94. The loss was not catastrophic—the team unwound positions within hours—but the shock was acute. The token had passed technical audits, its issuer published weekly reserve attestations, and its integrations were straightforward. Yet a modest market tremor had exposed structural weaknesses the firm had not mapped. As one treasurer put it that afternoon: *We assessed the features. We missed the forces.* The episode underscored a recurring flaw in how organisations make decisions about digital money. They evaluate tokens as finished products rather than as systems shaped by incentives, liquidity constraints, governance choices, and operational interdependencies. A peg is not a promise; it is a balance of pressures. A payment rail is not a list of functions; it is a sequence of commitments. The moment the peg slipped in Singapore, the team realised they lacked a mental model that could hold all the variables in view. They had a checklist. They needed a map.

This subchapter offers a structure for that map. The motif that threads through it—the *canvas*—is a reminder that decisions about stablecoins require a single surface on which market dynamics, governance signals, operational guarantees, and user experience commitments can be drawn together. Without such a canvas, risk creeps in through the gaps between assumptions. With it, organisations can compare systems on equivalent terms, run stress scenarios with discipline, and plan adoption in stages rather than spurts.

A mental model begins by showing how tokens behave under pressure rather than at rest. The Singapore slip demonstrated this. The deviation occurred during a period of thin liquidity when the issuer's primary market creation mechanism struggled to clear an unusually bunched batch of redemptions. The remediation—injecting treasury bills into the liquidation queue—worked only because the issuer held those assets directly. What the remittance team lacked was a way to quantify this vulnerability beforehand. Naming the mechanism helps: a liquidity ladder. A ladder measures, in hours and asset types, what can be sold first, at what size, and with what expected haircut. When the team later reconstructed the event, they found that the stablecoin's top-rung liquidity—immediately cashable balances—covered only 27 per cent of circulating units. The implication was crisp: a small shock required a large leap down the ladder, amplifying volatility. A mental model, to be useful, forces this specificity.

The second function of the canvas is to surface concentrations. Concentration is often mistaken for simplicity, yet the difference is visible in behaviour. A simple system uses few components because it avoids layers. A concentrated system uses few components because it never built alternatives. The contrast is stark in two checkable cases. In March 2023, Circle's USDC briefly broke its peg after the collapse of Silicon Valley Bank, where roughly $3.3 billion of reserves were held. One bank held too much. In April 2021, by comparison, the Paxos USDP reserve structure showed distribution across multiple custodians certified under New York's trust chartering regime. The diversification proved valuable during market stress; redemption processing times remained stable across the week. The canvas captures this distinction not as an abstraction—"risk"—but as a metric: top-three custodian share, expressed as a percentage of total reserves. The implication is actionable: any issuer with a concentration above, say, 40 per cent in a single custodian demands closer scenario analysis.

A credible counter-example tests the framework. Algorithmic stablecoins present the most vivid test. They often boast decentralisation, autonomy, and capital efficiency. But their behaviour during stress is rarely aligned with these claims. The TerraUSD collapse in May 2022 showed how algorithmic confidence cycles can unravel faster than governance mechanisms can respond. The system had no exogenous collateral to sell, no liquidity ladder to descend, and no custodian concentration to measure. It failed outside the metrics the canvas tracks. Reconciling this does not require rejecting algorithmic designs outright. It requires extending the canvas to include endogenous collateral loops and reflexivity indicators: how quickly redemption pressure feeds back into token supply, at what thresholds automated mechanisms halt, and how those halts affect users. The canvas grows, but it remains coherent.

The next layer is governance. Governance is visible not in constitutions but in behaviours: upgrade timetables, signatory rotations, public incident logs, and the cadence of disclosures. Two examples show why. MakerDAO, since 2019, has operated with a combination of token voting and risk committees. The governance load is heavy, but public debates, published risk parameter updates, and transparent collateral onboarding give analysts a deep record of precedent. By contrast, a smaller issuer in Europe in 2021 executed a contract hotfix without prior notice, altering a redemption parameter in a live contract. There was no public playbook. Wallets briefly rejected transfers. While the incident ended without losses, it exposed a governance opacity that users could not measure in advance. The canvas translates governance into trackable variables: upgrade notice periods in days; multisig key dispersion across institutions; frequency of risk parameter changes; depth of public documentation. Each becomes a behavioural signal. The implication is that governance ceases to be "soft" risk; it becomes measurable.

Scenario stress-testing is where the canvas moves from descriptive to analytical. Stress tests must start with observable behaviours: redemption times during peak hours, slippage on decentralised exchanges at defined trade sizes, settlement delays across chains, incident closure times. A £250,000 redemption test on a weekday morning in London—run by a payments firm integrating stablecoin flows in 2023—revealed that its chosen token processed requests within 11 minutes at off-peak hours, but 46 minutes at lunchtime. The expansion in delay was caused by the issuer batching operations to reduce banking fees. This was not visible in the product documentation. The implication was immediate: the firm recalibrated its liquidity buffers. A mental model that embeds such behavioural thresholds can highlight mismatches between expected and realised performance long before adoption scales.

The canvas must also incorporate edges: what happens at the boundaries of operational normality. For example, a cross-chain bridge may work flawlessly under standard conditions but degrade under congestion. A case from September 2023 on the Avalanche–Ethereum corridor showed that message proofs backed up during a burst of arbitrage traffic, extending settlement times from under a minute to over ten. Users saw the lag. Merchants paused fulfilment. A robust canvas forces organisations to name these thresholds explicitly: maximum tolerable delay, acceptable variance band, fallback routes, and conditions under which traffic should be rerouted automatically. Stress moves from anecdote to quantifiable risk.

The motif of the *canvas* reappears here. A canvas reveals structure, but it also reveals blank space. The blank space matters. It shows where knowledge is incomplete. A firm that cannot populate the governance cell with upgrade notice periods, or the liquidity cell with maturity ladders, learns something valuable: it is operating in fog. The act of filling the canvas disciplines the decision.

Two further examples demonstrate how the canvas guides adoption planning. In late 2022, a Latin American fintech piloting stablecoin payroll flows mapped its entire worker payout process. The canvas showed that the bottleneck was not token choice but fiat off-ramping at a single banking partner. The firm diversified partners before scaling token usage. In early 2024, an EU-based e-commerce marketplace using stablecoins for merchant settlements identified that its largest vulnerability was a fragmented incident reporting structure. The canvas revealed that neither issuer nor custodian published consistent incident logs. The marketplace negotiated for quarterly incident summaries before integrating higher settlement volumes. In both cases, the canvas directed attention to constraints that marketing materials concealed.

The counter-example is organisations that treat adoption as a binary switch: "integrate or not." This produces brittle architectures. A phased approach, anchored in the canvas, creates adaptive adoption curves: start with treasury diversification at low volumes, expand to supplier settlements once redemption behaviour is verified, and migrate customer payouts only after metadata and compliance fields meet standards. Each phase requires evidence. Each evidence point populates the canvas.

A mental model is only as strong as its limits. One limit is that metrics can create false precision. Redemption times measured in minutes, custody concentrations measured in percentages, and governance notice periods measured in days can suggest objectivity where judgement is still needed. Another limit is that the canvas cannot predict behavioural shifts in markets—such as sudden flight to liquidity during geopolitical shocks. Reconciling these limits requires humility: the canvas is a decision aid, not an oracle. Its value lies in forcing explicitness, not in guaranteeing outcomes.

And so the unresolved tension at the end of this subchapter is simple but consequential. As stablecoins evolve—across chains, regulatory perimeters, and market conditions—what should remain constant on the canvas, and what should change? Should every organisation adopt the same metrics, or tailor them to their risk appetite? Should issuers be required to fill out the canvas publicly, or should it remain an analytical tool for internal diligence? The next decisions in the industry will hinge not only on how stablecoins are engineered but on how they are understood. A canvas can clarify. It cannot choose.

About the Author

Emre Valikar writes at the intersection of money and technology, helping readers understand how software reshapes everyday finance. His work focuses on translating complex systems into plain language that supports better decisions by builders, policymakers, and curious consumers. He values clear disclosures, practical design, and humane adoption over hype. Emre often explores how communities create trust long before institutions catch up, drawing occasional parallels with the Silk Road's ledger of reputation: informal rules first, formal rules later. He has interviewed product managers, engineers, and compliance leads about payments and digital assets, and distils those conversations into accessible frameworks. When not writing, he hosts small study groups that stress-test ideas with real users and operators.

www.ingramcontent.com/pod-product-compliance
Lightning Source LLC
Chambersburg PA
CBHW031342230926
51848CB00002B/353

9789374593653